# To Catch
# a King

Charles II's Great Escape

CHARLES SPENCER

WILLIAM
COLLINS

William Collins
An imprint of HarperCollins*Publishers*
1 London Bridge Street
London SE1 9GF

www.WilliamCollinsBooks.com

HarperCollins*Publishers*
1st Floor, Watemarque Building, Ringsend Road
Dublin 4, Ireland

First published in Great Britain by William Collins in 2017
This William Collins paperback edition published in 2018

3

A catalogue record for this book is
available from the British Library

ISBN 978-0-00-815366-3

Map by John Gilkes

Printed and bound in the UK using 100% renewable
electricity at CPI Group (UK) Ltd

CHARLES SPENCER was educated at Eton College and obtained his degree in Modern History at Magdalen College, Oxford. He was a reporter on NBC's *Today* show from 1986 until 1995, and is the author of six books, including the *Sunday Times* bestseller *Blenheim: Battle for Europe* (shortlisted for History Book of the Year, National Book Awards) and *Killers of the King: The Men Who Dared to Execute Charles I*.

'*To Catch a King* is an exhilarating read'    *Daily Telegraph*

'*To Catch a King* does for us exactly what Charles II intended when he asked Pepys to commit his story to paper: ensure that this most extraordinary episode is never forgotten. One of the joys of this book is ... just how close the reader gets to the action ... Charles Spencer is the perfect person to pass the story on to a new generation. His pacey, readable prose steers deftly clear of jarring modern idioms and coasts elegantly through [this] great tale'
ANNA KEAY, *Literary Review*

'A book of quite extraordinary period atmosphere, the most diligent research and an appropriately cracking pace'
*Sunday Express*

'Accessible and pacey, Spencer's retelling of Charles's escape vividly depicts the numerous false starts, close shaves and covert communications that bedevilled events'    *BBC History Magazine*

'This fine book would be an exciting and patriotic addition to the history curriculum'    ALLISON PEARSON, *Sunday Telegraph*

'Charles Spencer's pacey accessible account is an evocative look at a dynamic story'    *History Revealed*

'[A] pacey account of the bizarre episode in 1651 when the future Charles II spent six weeks on the run from Cromwell's men'
*Mail on Sunday*

'Excellent descriptions of Charles's transformation from monarch into humble wood-cutter ... the author does justice to the most famous episodes of the King's flight'
*Country Life*

*Also by Charles Spencer*

ALTHORP: THE STORY OF AN ENGLISH HOUSE

THE SPENCER FAMILY

BLENHEIM: BATTLE FOR EUROPE

PRINCE RUPERT: THE LAST CAVALIER

KILLERS OF THE KING: THE MEN WHO DARED
TO EXECUTE CHARLES I

For Karen

# *Contents*

## PART THREE: A LEAGUE OF GENTLEMEN

## PART FOUR: REACTION, REWARDS AND REDEMPTION

# Illustrations

Charles during his European exile, by Philippe de Champaigne, c.1653. (*Art Collection 3/Alamy Stock Photo*)

Charles I and Queen Henrietta Maria, by van Dyck. (*Photo by Fine Art Images/Heritage Images/Getty Images*)

Lucy Walter, engraved by H. Van den Berghe from an original by S. Harding, c.1640. (*Photo by Archive Photos/Getty Images*)

Sir Edward Hyde, later 1st Earl of Clarendon, by Jacob van Reesbroeck. (*Paul Fearn/Alamy Stock Photo*)

James Grahame, 1st Marquess of Montrose, by William Dobson. (*Heritage Image Partnership Ltd/Alamy Stock Photo*)

Parliamentary propaganda cartoon mocking Charles's alliance with the Scots. (*Culture Club/Contributor*)

The battle of Worcester. (*BLM Collection/Alamy Stock Photo*)

A view of Boscobel, Whiteladies and the Royal Oak, by Robert Streater. (*Royal Collection Trust/© Her Majesty Queen Elizabeth II 2017*)

James Stanley, 7th Earl of Derby, by van Dyck. (*Bridgeman Images*)

Major General Thomas Harrison, engraved by M.V. Gucht from an original painting. (*Photo by Kean Collection/Getty Images*)

Richard Penderel, after Gilbert Soest. (*National Portrait Gallery, London*)

Father John Huddleston, by Huysmans, 1685. (*Bridgeman Images*)

Henry, Lord Wilmot, later 1st Earl of Rochester. (*National Portrait Gallery, London*)

Charles and Major Careless in the oak tree, by Isaac Fuller. (*ART Collection/Alamy Stock Photo*)

The Royal Oak today. (*Jon Lewis/Alamy Stock Photo*)

Charles and Jane Lane riding to Bristol, by Isaac Fuller. (*ART Collection/Alamy Stock Photo*)

Parliament's proclamation offering a reward of £1,000 for Charles's capture. (*Private collection/Bridgeman Images*)

Colonel George Gunter.

Colonel John Lane. (*National Trust Photographic Library/ Bridgeman Images*)

Thomas Whitgreave. (*Private collection*)

Oliver Cromwell and John Lambert, by Robert Walker. (*Private collection/Photo © Philip Mould Ltd, London/Bridgeman Images*)

Priest hole at Moseley Hall. (*The National Trust Photo Library/ Alamy Stock Photo*)

Bentley Hall, drawn and engraved by Michael Burghers for Robert Plot's *Natural History of Staffordshire*, first published in 1686. (*The Trustees of the William Salt Library, Staffordshire*)

The *Surprise* – later renamed the *Royal Escape* – by Willem van de Velde the Younger. (*Royal Collection Trust/© Her Majesty Queen Elizabeth II 2017*)

The Restoration of Charles II at Whitehall on 29 May 1660. (*Private collection/Bridgeman Images*)

Charles II, by Sir Peter Lely. (*Royal Hospital Chelsea/Bridgeman Images*)

*I know how men in exile feed on dreams.*

Aeschylus

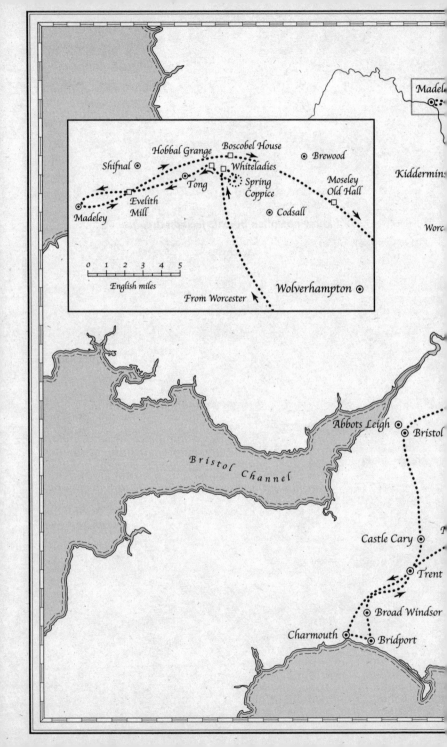

Madele

Kiddermins

Brewood

Moseley
Old Hall

Worc

Hobbal Grange
Boscobel House
Shifnal
Whiteladies
Spring
Coppice
Tong
Madeley
Evelith
Mill
Codsall

Wolverhampton

From Worcester

0  1  2  3  4  5
English miles

Bristol Channel

Abbots Leigh
Bristol

Castle Cary

Trent

Broad Windsor

Charmouth
Bridport

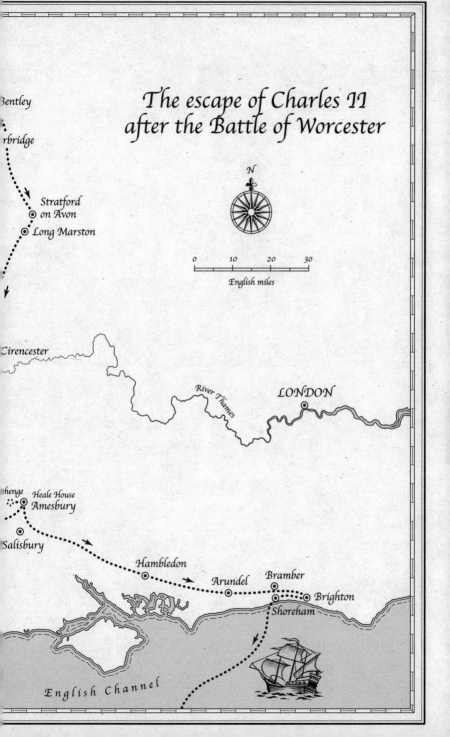

The escape of Charles II
after the Battle of Worcester

N

0    10    20    30
English miles

Bentley

rbridge

Stratford
on Avon
Long Marston

Cirencester

River Thames

LONDON

henge    Heale House
Amesbury

Salisbury

Hambledon

Arundel    Bramber

Brighton

Shoreham

English Channel

# *Introduction*

King Charles II had a favourite story. It was about the six weeks when, aged twenty-one, he had been on the run for his life. Those hunting him down had included the regicides – those responsible for his father's trial and beheading – who feared him as a deadly avenger; the Parliamentary army, who viewed him as the commander of a defeated, foreign, invasion; and ordinary people, because upon his head sat not the English crown of his birthright, but a colossal financial reward.

This brief period of Charles II's life stood alone for many reasons. While there were many other times when the bleak reality of his situation fell well short of any reasonable princely expectations, it marked the low point of his fortunes, both as man and royal dignitary. It was uniquely exhilarating for him, in a way that only a genuine life-or-death tussle could be. And it showed off personal qualities that were not always evident in an individual whose self-indulgence and sense of entitlement could infuriate even his most loyal devotees. In his hour of greatest danger, he was proud to note, had arisen within him a quickness of wit, an adaptability, and a hard instinct for survival, that had saved his neck.

In the spring of 1660 Charles returned to England, to claim his throne, on a ship whose figurehead of Oliver Cromwell had hastily been removed, and whose name had been changed from the *Naseby* (the battle that had been his father's most punishing defeat) to the *Royal Charles*. Samuel Pepys was a fellow passenger, and wrote in his diary for 23 May 1660 of how: 'Upon the quarterdeck he [Charles] fell into discourse of his escape from Worcester, where it made me ready to weep to hear the stories that he told of his difficulties that he had passed through, of his travelling four days and three nights on foot, every step up to his knees in dirt, with nothing but a green coat and a pair of country breeches on, and a pair of country shoes that made him so sore all over his feet, that he could barely stir.'

In the subjects of the kingdom that he had been allowed suddenly and unexpectedly to gain, Charles had found a fresh audience for his pet tale. They would hear repeatedly of their new young king's exploits. Not that Pepys complained, for the retelling of events that had taken place when he had been a young man of eighteen, six months into his first year at Cambridge University, particularly intrigued him. They awoke, in this most famous of English diarists, the tracking instincts of an investigative journalist. He decided to check how much of the king's recollections of the six weeks' adventure were true, and to what extent they had been seasoned by royal fancy, or compromised by forgetfulness.

Two decades later, during one of the royal court's stays in Suffolk for the horse-racing on Newmarket Heath, Pepys managed to obtain an audience with the king. In his scratchy shorthand (his eyesight had been failing for more than a decade) he took down what Charles remembered of the most electrifying time of his life. Riveted by what he had heard, Pepys quickly secured a second session, his manuscript revealing additions where he included fresh details that Charles had forgotten the first time round.

Meanwhile Pepys resolved to trace those still alive from the motley bunch that had helped the king on his journey from shattering defeat to miraculous delivery. An exceptionally busy man, being at different times a Member of Parliament for two constituencies, and Chief Secretary to the Admiralty, Pepys had hoped to piece together the whole, correct, version of the astonishing tale of escape, and present it as the definitive account. It appears that he had completed almost his entire collection of relevant documents by December 1684, two months before Charles's sudden death at the age of fifty-four, for that was when he had it bound. A few additions were kept with this volume, including Colonel George Gunter's report, which arrived at some point during the first seven months of 1685.

There is a paragraph, near the start of Colonel Gunter's offering, which underlines the way in which those intimately involved in Charles's escape attempt felt they had been chosen, for whatever reason, to be participants in an event whose eventual outcome had been determined by God. Gunter wrote:

> *Here, before I proceed in the story, the reader will give me leave to put him in mind, that we write not an ordinary story, where the reader, engaged by no other interest than curiosity, may soon be cloyed with circumstances which signify no more unto him but that the author was at good leisure and was very confident of his reader's patience. In the relation of miracles, every petty circumstance is material and may afford to the judicious reader matter of good speculation: of such a miracle especially, where the restoration of no less than three kingdoms, and his own particular safety and liberty (if a good and faithful subject) was at the stake.*[1]

Pepys was not in awe of royalty to anything like the same degree as Colonel Gunter. He had been in the crowd at the beheading of Charles I on 30 January 1649, and it is clear that he had some sympathy with the ruthless Parliamentary justice meted out that day. During his time as a naval administrator he never shirked from locking horns with Royalists if, in his view, they were holding back the progress of the service. His disagreements with Prince Rupert of the Rhine, the poster boy of the Crown's cause in his youth, and Lord Admiral of England in middle age, show a lack of deference to those of the highest birth if he judged them to be wrongheaded, and therefore dangerous to the nation. Pepys was a loyal patriot, but not a fawning one. He therefore makes for an appealing midwife in the delivery of the king's tale.

There was a great appetite for this unique royal story during the king's lifetime, even amongst his most intimate circle. James, Duke of York, wrote to Pepys in the middle of 1681, saying he wanted to read for himself his elder brother's description of his time on the run after the defeat at Worcester. It was his second time of asking this favour of Pepys. Even though the duke promised not to take a copy of the account, Pepys dared to set out that this was a journalistic project that was still very much in progress, and one that he felt especially protective of: 'My covetousness of rendering it as perfect, as the memory of any of the survivors (interested in any part of that memorable story) can enable me to make it,' he wrote, 'has led me into so many and distant enquiries relating thereto, as have kept me out of a capacity of putting it together as I would, and it ought, and shall be, so soon as ever I possess myself of all the memorials I am in expectation of concerning it. Which I shall also (for your Royal Highness's satisfaction) use my utmost industry in the hastening.'[2]

He eventually sent the transcript to the duke, while mentioning that he was still awaiting the key testimony of Father John Huddleston, a Roman Catholic priest who had taken a prominent role in the tale of royal derring-do. Pepys received this in March 1682 from Lady Mary Tuke, a lady-in-waiting to the queen, who forwarded it to him on Huddleston's behalf.

Pepys died in 1703, never having completed his task of stitching together the threads that he had gathered together so painstakingly. Perhaps the death of the central figure in the tale made the undertaking one that seemed less pressing.

Whatever the reason, the testimonies he had assembled, and which he left behind in one place, are invaluable to those that have followed. Indeed, the accounts of Charles II himself, as well as those of Father Huddleston, Thomas Whitgreave and Colonel Phillips, are priceless testimonies to a factual tale that reads like fiction. All four have long been recognised as the key first-hand records of one of the greatest escapes in history.

Thomas Blount provided another sparkling contemporary account of the getaway. Blount was a Roman Catholic, and a Royalist, who gloried in the miracle of the tale, and so might have been tempted by his predispositions to stray from the truth. But he was also a lexicographer and an antiquarian, who studied law. His intellectual discipline, when compiling dictionaries of obscure words or studying the distant past, set a standard for his painstaking research in this field of recent royal history. In his introduction to *Boscobel* Blount assured his readers: 'I am so far from that foul crime of publishing what's false, that I can safely say I know not one line unauthentic; such has been my care to be sure of the truth, that I have diligently collected the particulars from most of their mouths, who were the very actors in this scene of miracles.'

Nearly all of Blount's sources were still alive at the time of *Boscobel*'s completion. Far from disputing his version of events, they were happy to contribute further recollections, which he included in his next edition. It seems that he accurately assembled the memories of his interviewees, many of whom had little or no literacy. They were relying on Blount to disperse their experiences to his readers.

How best to use such remarkable sources? Unlike the king's version of what had happened during the six weeks, the other contributors, of course, concentrated on what they remembered from their own few days or so in the core of the narrative. It is obvious that nothing else in their lives came close to the excitement of being involved in their king's survival. As a result, extraordinary details are remembered – the opening of a bottle of sherry releasing two hornets from its neck; the way the king cooked his collops of lamb; the sight of his battered and bloody feet.

Equally understandable would be the embellishment of tales over time, and the exaggeration of services rendered. I have weighed up the likelihood of things happening as recalled, the closeness of the witness to the action, and the inevitability of human foibles clouding the picture, as best I can. There remains one imponderable, which I try to deal with even-handedly: the competing accounts of Captain Alford and William Ellesdon as to what upended the escape attempt at Charmouth. At least one of them has to be lying, but both had supporting witnesses, so it is hard to draw a conclusion either way.

Charles II himself's memory of events seems to have been accurate, the day-to-day order of events apparently seared into his mind. For a man of hearty appetites, the recall of when and if he was fed, and what with, seems to have been a perpetual concern: when he first spoke to Pepys, he was feasting on pease-pudding, and two different types of roast meat. On the other hand, Charles chose not to deal with fears, or other emotions, in his account. This is a great shame for the modern reader. Perhaps admitting to what might, in the late seventeenth century, have been perceived as weaknesses, was considered a little much.

Those mistakes that Charles makes in his recollections seem to me to be understandably human: he was, for instance, wrong to think that one of his collaborators, Thomas Whitgreave, had the surname of 'Pitchcross', or 'Pitchcroft'. That was, in fact, the name of the field to the north of Worcester where the Royalist troops had mustered before the dismal defeat that brought about his need to run. If anything, such an error simply suggests that Charles's recollections came direct from his memory, rather than from written notes.

Intriguingly rich sources aside, I have also sought, more than many others who have written on this subject before me, to set the narrative in its wider context. The battle of Worcester is pretty much forgotten, even in England. This is something that two future American presidents, Thomas Jefferson and John Adams, condemned when they insisted on visiting the battlefield in 1786. Adams wrote:

> *Worcester were curious and interesting to us, as scenes where freemen had fought for their rights. The people in the neighbourhood, appeared so ignorant and careless at Worcester that I was provoked and asked, 'And do Englishmen so soon forget the ground where Liberty was fought for? Tell your neighbours and your children that this is holy ground, much holier than that on which your churches stand. All England should come in Pilgrimage to this Hill, once a Year.'*

Adams had, I believe, a point.

In England we may pass one of the more than 400 pubs called the Royal Oak, and be briefly reminded of the most lyrical part of this tale. But my conclusion at the end of writing this book is that Charles's escape attempt was not some jolly adventure, but a deadly serious race against an enemy eager to spill fresh Stuart blood on an executioner's block.

In the final analysis, this is a tale of grit, of loyalty, and of luck.

# PART ONE

# KING OF SCOTLAND

# 1

## Civil Warrior

*Now all such calamities as may be avoided by human*
*industry arise from war, but chiefly from civil war,*
*for from this proceed slaughter, solitude, and the*
*want of all things.*

Thomas Hobbes, 'De Corpore', 1655

Charles, Prince of Wales, witnessed the English Civil War up close from its outbreak till its end. He was present at the battle of Edgehill, in October 1642. This was the first major engagement of a conflict that erupted over differences between the Crown and Parliament, concerning the limits of the king's power, and clashing religious beliefs. Nine years later he would command an army at Worcester, the final action in the most bloodstained chapter in British history. By that time the Civil Wars in England, Ireland and Scotland had claimed hundreds of thousands of lives in the three kingdoms.

At Edgehill Prince Charles, then a twelve-year-old honorary captain in the King's Horse Guards, had proved to be a handful. It had been hard to stop him from leading a charge against the rebel cavalry. At another point he and his younger brother James, Duke of York, were nearly captured, and had to take cover in a barn packed with wounded soldiers.

The boys had spent part of that clear autumn afternoon at Edgehill in the care of their father's elderly physician, Dr William Harvey, the English authority on anatomy. It was Harvey who had, in 1628, been the first to write about the circulation of blood in the body. The distinguished doctor took the pair of princes to shelter under a hedge, where he hoped to divert them from the violent bloodshed taking place all around them by reading a book. This distraction did not go to plan, Harvey telling his biographer John Aubrey that 'he had not read very long before a bullet of a great gun grazed on the ground near him, which made him remove his station'.[1]

Despite the dangers, King Charles I remained keen to keep his eldest son by his side during the first two and a half years of the conflict. Towards the end of 1644 he gave the fourteen-year-old prince the title 'first Captain-General of all our Forces', although such duties were in reality performed by the king's nephew, Prince Rupert of the Rhine.

In early 1645, as Parliament began to gain a decisive upper hand in the war, Charles I decided to prevent the possibility of his being caught or killed at the same time as his heir. Keen 'to unboy' his son, 'by putting him into some action, and acquaintance [him] with business out of his own sight',[2] he sent him away to his own, separate, command. The prince was created general of the Royalist forces in the west of England, with real responsibilities. On 5 March 1645 he parted from his father for what would prove to be the last time, riding out of Oxford into a ferocious rainstorm.

With the prince went an escort of 300 cavalrymen. He was safely delivered to Bristol, but it could easily have ended otherwise. On their return journey a large force of Charles's guards were ambushed near Devizes, in Wiltshire. Forty of them were killed, while twenty officers were among the many captured Cavaliers.

A handful of advisers, hand-picked by the king, rode with Charles to Bristol. Prominent among them was Sir Edward Hyde, who had long been involved in the prince's life. In early 1642 he had looked after Charles while his French mother, Queen Henrietta Maria, had sailed to the Continent to raise funds and forces for her husband. It was the start of a relationship that would run the gamut of service, trust, disappointment, triumph, rejection and disgrace.

Twenty-one years older than the prince, Hyde was at heart a traditional patriot who believed in political stability. He had hoped for a peaceful resolution to the tensions between Crown and Parliament, believing a compromise was both possible and desirable. But there was too much fear and suspicion on both sides for reason and sense to prevail.

As civil war became increasingly likely, Hyde's hopes for order gradually turned him from being a critic of Charles I into a Royalist. When the king finally declared war, raising the royal standard at Nottingham in August 1642, Hyde was by his side. After that he lent his fine brain and brilliant oratory to Charles I's cause. Hyde was made Chancellor of the Exchequer, the king justifying the promotion with a rather downbeat endorsement: 'The truth is, I can trust nobody else.'[3]

Hyde found court life complicated. It was hard for him to negotiate a landscape that was pitted with factions, and where insincerity and self-interest were the perpetual themes. Meanwhile a supreme confidence in his own views made it challenging for him to accommodate those of others when they differed.

He brought this inflexible mindset on campaign, when he accompanied Prince Charles as he took up his command in the west. Hyde hoped to bring order to the Crown's resistance there, but his prickly attitude, perhaps fired up by the raging gout that often dogged him, instead diminished what remained of morale in this corner of England. It was a sphere of the war that was going as poorly for the Crown as any other, not helped by the king's leading generals in the region being at odds with one another. One, Sir Ralph Hopton, was a man of sobriety and religion, who once refused to join battle until his men had finished hearing divine service. Another, Lord Goring, was remembered even by his fellow Royalists as the epitome of the hard-drinking, roistering Cavalier. A third, Sir Richard Grenville, had been condemned as 'traitor, rogue, villain' by Parliament after switching allegiance to the Crown. Grenville, grandson of a great Elizabethan naval hero of the same name, had a violent temper and a reputation for ruthlessness in the field. He refused to serve under Goring or Hopton, and would be imprisoned for his disobedience.

Prince Charles arrived in Bristol in early April to find apathy among the area's leading Royalists, and plague erupting in the city. He decided to move thirty-two miles south-west to Bridgwater, a town whose castle was believed to be impregnable, and whose governor, Sir Edmund Wyndham, he knew. Sir Edmund's wife, Christabella, had been Charles's wet-nurse and assistant governess from when he was one until he turned five.

Christabella Wyndham was noted for her great beauty, and for her bossiness. Samuel Pepys noted in his diary that she 'governed' Charles 'and everything else … as [if she were] a minister of state'.[4] Sir Edward Hyde dismissed her as 'a woman of great rudeness and a country pride'.[5] But she had her charms. Christabella, in her late thirties, and Charles, yet to turn fifteen, became lovers during his stay in Bridgwater Castle in 1645. Afterwards, far from exercising discretion, Christabella appalled the prince's advisers by being shamelessly familiar with him, showering him with kisses in public. When Charles proved unable to concentrate on matters of state, thanks to Christabella's distracting influence, his advisers moved him on from Bridgwater as quickly as they could.

That summer Parliament's New Model Army arrived outside Bridgwater in huge numbers, to test its impregnability. Hearing that Oliver Cromwell, the rebel force's second-in-command, was examining the town's defences from the far side of its imposing moat, Christabella Wyndham decided to act. As an insult to the enemy, and as a reminder of her previous role as royal wet-nurse, she is reported as having exposed one of her breasts, picked up a loaded musket, and fired. The shot missed Cromwell, but killed his sergeant-at-arms.

The Roundheads, outnumbering the garrison by eight to one, attacked Bridgwater soon afterwards. With victory rapidly assured, the Parliamentary commander Sir Thomas Fairfax invited Sir Edmund Wyndham to recognise the hopelessness of his position and surrender. Lady Wyndham scoffed at the suggestion: 'Tell your masters,' she told the Parliamentary herald, 'that the breast which gave suck to Prince Charles shall never be at their mercy. We will hold the town to the last!' But Bridgwater was soon ablaze, strong winds whipping flames along as the enemy pushed forward, and Wyndham was forced to capitulate.

The fall of Bridgwater was part of a summer of heavy Royalist losses. After the worst of these, at Naseby, the king wrote a letter to his eldest son from Hereford. It contained a handful of strict instructions that were to remain secret unless the prince's closest advisers absolutely needed to know them. Until that moment, the letter's contents must remain between father and son.

The defeats continued into the autumn of 1645 and beyond. After the surrender of Bristol in September, the young prince was forced to move ever westwards, the demoralised Royalist forces in Devon no match for the rampant New Model Army. Bad luck played a small part in bringing forward the Crown's inevitable downfall in the county. At the siege of Tiverton in October, a cannonball struck and severed the chain holding up the garrison's drawbridge, sending it thudding to the ground in slack-jawed surrender. At the battle of Torrington, in February 1646, a spark found its way into a church where the king's men had stored eighty barrels of gunpowder. The huge explosion that followed brought an end to the engagement, as well as to the lives of the Parliamentary prisoners being held in the church. Now the remaining Royalists withdrew from Devon to Cornwall, the most westerly county on the English mainland.

Lord Colepeper, one of Charles I's leading advisers, warned that, with nowhere else to go, the prince had now entered 'a very Cornish mousetrap'.[6] The king sent instructions for his son to be taken to France for safety. Hyde and the prince's other advisers questioned the call, though, claiming that abandoning England for another country would become 'an argument against his Majesty's sincere intentions'.[7] They put forward the alternatives of the Scilly Isles or Jersey, both Crown dominions.

After continued pressure from the enemy Prince Charles was forced to abandon the English mainland. He sailed on the *Phoenix* to St Mary's, the largest of the Isles of Scilly, landing there on 4 March 1646. This was only thirty miles from Cornwall, but Parliament's dominance of the seas meant it was low on supplies, no food having reached it from England for six weeks.

Lady Fanshawe, the heavily pregnant wife of one of Charles's retinue, noted on arrival: 'Meat and fuel, for half the court to serve them for a month, was not to be had in the whole island. And truly we begged our daily bread of God, for we thought every meal our last.'[8] The king's followers grew sick of the taste of salted fish, one of the islanders' main products.

St Mary's was soon realised to be as militarily vulnerable as it was poorly provisioned. Despite the recent arrival of 300 Irish troops, the garrison was unable to defend the sprawling coastline. Lord Colepeper was sent to France to tell Henrietta Maria that reinforcements must be sent immediately.

Parliament, aware of the prince's vulnerability in his new island surroundings, tried to lure him into captivity. A silky letter was delivered by a rebel trumpeter in early April:

*Sir,*

*The Lords and Commons assembled in the Parliament of England, being informed that your highness is lately removed into the Isle of Scilly, have commanded us, in their names, to invite you to come forthwith into their quarters; and to reside in such place, and with such council and attendants about you, as the two houses shall think fit to appoint.*[9]

Charles waited, and then composed a reply laced with equal insincerity. He thanked his enemies for their kindness, and promised to continue to correspond with them, adding how much he looked forward to any further advice that they might choose to send him.

It was inevitable, the prince's advisers realised, that Parliament would now attack St Mary's, to seize Charles and take him to England as a prisoner in all but name. Even before they had got round to sending the prince's reply, a fleet of two dozen ships had been dispatched to the Scilly Isles under Vice-Admiral William Batten, with instructions to bring him in. With Batten went Colonel Thomas Gollop, a Royalist who had recently surrendered the island and castle of Portland to Parliament. Gollop had promised his captors that he would help deliver the prince into their clutches.

As soon as Henrietta Maria learnt from Colepeper the danger that her son was in, she wrote to Hyde stressing her great concern at the inadequacy of the Scilly Isles as a safe haven for the talisman of the Royalist cause: 'I need not remember [remind] you of what importance to the king, and all his party, the safety of the prince's person is. If he should fall into the rebels' hands, the whole would thereby become desperate.'[10] Not for the last time, Charles's freedom would be inextricably linked to any future hopes that the Royalist cause might cling to in the face of humiliating setbacks.

It was at this point, with his liberty and life in real danger, that Charles produced the letter his father had sent to him from

Hereford ten months earlier. He realised that its terms were precisely relevant to the peril he now faced. In the letter the king had insisted that Charles must never surrender on dishonourable terms, or do anything to undermine the concept of regal authority. This must be the case even if his father's life (or his own) were at stake. Equally, the prince must not risk death, because on him rested the future hopes of the Crown. It was clear that the preservation of Charles's life was the priority now, with the enemy closing in fast.

When the Parliamentary fleet sent to capture the prince on St Mary's was scattered in a timely two-day storm, Charles took the opportunity to flee to Jersey. He arrived there on 17 April 1646, as the sun was going down, the pilot of his frigate mistakenly steering a course that would normally have guaranteed shipwreck. The royal party was luckily spared, thanks to an abnormally high spring tide covering the rocks below. 'God be praised,' Lady Fanshawe wrote, 'his Highness, and all of us came safe ashore through so great a danger.'[11]

It was a silent entry into the harbour. There was no salute of cannon fire, from land or sea. Everyone knew that this visit, far from being part of some triumphant royal progress, was instead uncomfortable proof that the king's cause in England was in a calamitous state. Charles was coming to Jersey as a forlorn refugee.

But the largest of the Channel Islands was a relatively safe place for him to find himself in. Jersey had a good-sized Royalist force, and a network of established defences. The granite Mont Orgueil Castle, on the east coast, had been the site of fortifications since Roman times, and the two wards of Elizabeth Castle, which Sir Walter Raleigh had improved while Jersey's governor at the start of the century, added solid assistance from their rocky islet. There was a further tower at the entrance to St Aubin's harbour that had recently been freshly fortified, and half a mile off the coast of Guernsey, Castle Cornet stood in distant support.

Sir George Carteret, from the ancient Jersey family of de Carteret, was the island's bailiff and lieutenant-governor. Samuel Pepys described this larger-than-life character as 'the most passionate man in the world'. It was a world that Carteret, a seafarer since boyhood, had seen plenty of. Before the Civil Wars he had served with distinction against the Barbary pirates of North Africa, rescuing Christian captives from Salé in modern-day Morocco. In 1643 Carteret captured Jersey for Charles I, ejecting the island's Parliamentary garrison within a month of landing. Two years later, by now a Royalist vice-admiral, he was knighted. Soon after Prince Charles's landing on Jersey Sir Edward Hyde noted that Carteret was perhaps 'the best seaman of England', and certainly 'a worthy and most excellent person, of extraordinary merit towards the crown and nation of England'. Carteret was determined to keep the prince safe.

The neighbouring Channel Island, Guernsey, had a strong Puritan element, and was keenly supportive of Parliament. With this enemy lying less than thirty miles away, Carteret insisted that all of Jersey's regular soldiers and militia publicly profess their loyalty to the Crown. He had an open Bible placed on a drumhead, and as he watched, ten men at a time stepped forward, each placing a hand on the canvas, before being led by a priest through an oath of commitment to the king of England.

Carteret also equipped ten frigates to prey on Parliamentary shipping. This man, who had made his name fighting against pirates, now oversaw a network of privateers, operating in the name of the king. They caused consternation to the enemy at sea, and provided prizes that were sold to fund increased defences and supplies on land.

Anticipating that Parliament would soon send a task force to try to recapture Jersey and seize Charles, Carteret stocked and secured his strongholds. Their stores were filled with salted fish, corn, peas, biscuit and beef. His reserves were so plentiful that he filled the church at Castle Cornet with them, while stripping back its roof to form an additional artillery platform. Further cannon were placed along the island's coast at all likely landing points.

Sir George had two new cisterns, capable of holding more than eighty tons of water, installed in the upper ward of Elizabeth Castle. He established his headquarters there, and had the prince stay with him as his guest. Despite the military threat, and the visiting prince's reduced circumstances, the show of royal ceremony was painstakingly maintained.

We know, from a diarist living on the island, that at dinnertime Charles would hear grace bareheaded, before putting his hat on to eat. He would then sit alone at the head of the table, where silver cutlery had been laid out for him. A priest would stand to his right, while his lords and courtiers remained bareheaded and on their feet behind him while he ate. As he waited for his food to arrive, a kneeling pageboy would help him to wash and dry his hands.

Dinner was offered in a succession of silver serving dishes, containing selections of meat, fish and game, which were placed before him. Food that Charles liked the look of was taken to a carvery, where a taster tested it. Sliced up, it was returned to the prince on a silver platter.

Two pages waited, on bended knee, while he ate. One was constantly ready with a silver dish containing slices of bread. The other was the cupbearer. When Charles beckoned this servant forward, he held the goblet to his master's lips with one hand, while with the other he positioned a second cup to catch any drops before they could splash onto the prince's clothes. There was no stinting on pomp for the prince even when his court was minute, he was effectively in exile, and his dominion was a dot of an island.

Charles remained under Carteret's protection on Jersey from April till June 1646. Already tall, and with the tufts of a moustache sprouting, the prince seems to have had an affair with the lieutenant-governor's daughter Marguerite, who was five years older than him. A key subplot of Charles's life, his pursuit of women, continued as the First Civil War reached its conclusion, and progressed steadily from this point on.

Henrietta Maria was insistent that her eldest son should come to her in France. There she hoped to keep him safe, and under her control, while her husband continued his increasingly hopeless resistance in England. This was very much against the wishes of Sir Edward Hyde and the other conservative advisers travelling with the prince. They wanted to keep him out of the orbit of France, because it was the historic, Roman Catholic, enemy of England. Hyde believed that what the queen was asking Charles to do breached 'the fundamental rules of policy'.[12]

Hyde had planned to be an Anglican priest, until the death of an elder brother left him as his father's potential heir. Becoming a lawyer and a Member of Parliament instead, he remained wedded to the strictest principles of the Church of England. These made him pious in some eyes, but priggish to others. In many ways he seems to have seen himself as the keeper of his young master's conscience.

Furious that her instructions were being ignored, Henrietta Maria sent a delegation to Jersey to insist on Charles's removal to France. It was led by her great favourite, Henry, Lord Jermyn. The distrust of Hyde and his allies for the queen's judgement, and for her inner circle's trustworthiness, was intense. Hyde had developed a particular dislike of Jermyn on a number of grounds, ranging from his promotion of the plan to take the prince to live in France, to his having impregnated a beauty at court and then refusing to marry her. Jermyn was also the hereditary governor of Jersey, and there were strong suspicions that he was planning to sell the island to France.

To the traditional supporters of the Crown, such as Hyde, Jermyn epitomised the sort of insufferable and devious character that the queen liked to surround herself with. 'The English about Her Majesty, most favoured and consulted by her,' recorded one observer, 'were generally subjected to betray her counsels, and were too well known to have little regard to virtue, or to be acted by any settled principle of religion or honour. The old cavaliers did not care to trust any of them, and when they confided their senti-ments, advices, & measures to Sir Edward Nicholas [a leading Royalist in exile, who was often at odds with the queen], they posi-tively insisted that he should not communicate any of them to those confidants of Her Majesty, nor even to the Queen herself, who could conceal nothing from them, but consulted them in all affairs.'[13]

Eventually Charles was persuaded to obey his mother's wishes and go to France with Jermyn. Only one of the councillors appointed by his father accompanied him to St-Germain-en-Laye, west of Paris, where Henrietta Maria resided. The rest refused to do so. The division in the senior Royalist ranks, between the 'Louvre group', who supported the queen and her French leanings, and those traditionalists who saw things in a narrower and more patriotic light, could hardly have been more starkly shown.

Hyde stayed behind in Jersey, where he began to write the early parts of *The History of the Rebellion*, his celebrated chronicle of the English Civil War. He knew that, for now, he had lost the battle for influence over the Prince of Wales to Henrietta Maria, and had to accept that, just like his father, young Charles was 'irresolute'. This was Hyde's polite term for being open to, and acting on, danger-ously bad advice.

Charles left for France in June 1646. He was included in the activities of the French court at Fontainebleau that summer, his future value to the English Royalist movement attached to his liberty, and his eligibility as a royal bachelor.

Henrietta Maria hoped to engineer a marriage for him with her niece Anne Marie Louise of Orléans, Duchess of Montpensier.

'Mademoiselle', as she was known, was three years older than the prince, and not lacking in self-esteem. One of her pleasures was listing her many physical attributes in a journal. She relished the fineness of her height and figure, the glory of her auburn hair, the oval prettiness of her face, while not forgetting the finer details, from the coral bud of her lips, down to the daintiness of her feet: 'There were not wanting those who complimented me on the beauty of my face and form', she wrote, or 'the fairness of my complexion, the brilliancy of my hair; no less admirable, they confessed, than all the riches which bedecked my person.'[14]

To Henrietta Maria, the good looks were a bonus. It was her niece's vast inheritance and royal blood that made her an especially desirable daughter-in-law. But Mademoiselle was more interested in the idea of marrying the Holy Roman Emperor, who had been widowed that May, than in contemplating life with the gauche English prince, whose French was poor, and whose only conversation seemed to be about horses, hunting and dogs.

Besides, while she heard endlessly from Henrietta Maria how smitten Charles was with her, she saw little supporting evidence from her young cousin himself. Mademoiselle wrote: 'Had he spoken for himself there is no knowing what might have been the result, but this I do know, that I was little inclined to listen to proposals in favour of a man who could not say anything for himself.'[15]

The gangly Charles was noticeably ill at ease at the various balls and entertainments that Henrietta Maria forced him to attend. His clumsy attempts to woo Mademoiselle, under maternal duress, soon made him an object of pity at court. Meanwhile, the duchess found him coarse. At a dinner where ortolans were offered up as the finest of delicacies (the tiny songbirds, drowned in Armagnac, were eaten whole, brains, beak, bones and all), Charles was believed to have let himself down by instead gorging on a shoulder of mutton and a side of beef. After eating, the other guests left the royal teenagers together to flirt. But, Mademoiselle would remember with dismay, Charles did not utter a word. After a quarter of an hour of silence, she gave up.

While Charles's awkwardness was upending his mother's matchmaking schemes, the queen in turn upset her son by continuing to treat him like a child. Henrietta Maria insisted that he carry on being bareheaded in her presence, an unusual protocol for a prince of his age and seniority. She also excluded him from important meetings, and insisted on receiving the pension paid to him by the French Crown, so that he was dependent on her for his allowance. Charles's thoughts focused increasingly on getting away from France, and his mother, and doing what he could to fight for his father's cause, as soon as the opportunity arose.

In the spring and summer of 1648 the Second Civil War crackled into life in England and Wales, the king's cause spearheaded by a Scottish invasion from the north on his behalf. That July Charles went from France to The Hague, on the Netherlands coast, to lead a force of English ships that had mutinied against the Commonwealth and declared for the Crown. This fleet was urgently needed to support the Royalist uprising in southern and eastern England. While it prepared for deployment Charles spent time with his younger siblings, Mary, Princess of Orange, and James, Duke of York, who had recently arrived in the Netherlands after escaping from imprisonment in London. Also on hand were two of his first cousins, Princes Rupert and Maurice of the Rhine, who had served as leading Royalist generals in the Civil War.

It was during this month of family reunion and preparation for action at sea that Charles met, and fell for, Lucy Walter.

Lucy was the daughter of William and Elizabeth Walter. Her father was a minor landowner from Pembrokeshire, in south-west Wales, while her mother was from a similar social background, with a small injection of aristocratic blood. Theirs was a poisonous marriage, the diarist John Evelyn referring to both parents as 'very mean creatures'.[16] Taking accusations of her husband's abusive behaviour and abandonment to the House of Lords, Elizabeth achieved a judgement against him in 1641. This ruling was over-turned six years later, in February 1647, when counter-accusations against Elizabeth, including that of infidelity, held sway. Lucy refused to obey the Lords' ruling that she and her two brothers return to their father's household in Wales.

Lucy was a raven-haired, blue-eyed seventeen-year-old beauty, endowed with a shrewdness to match her striking looks. John Evelyn, who shared a carriage ride with the teenaged girl, marked her down in his diary as a 'brown, beautiful, bold, but insipid crea-ture',[17] while James II thought her 'very handsome, of little wit, and some cunning'.[18]

What marked Lucy out for relentless male attention, from a young age, was a pulsating sexual magnetism. So many men desired her that she was quick to appreciate her exceptional bedroom value. It was the start of a livelihood that had Evelyn looking back on her as nothing more than 'a beautiful strumpet'.[19] She would become the kept woman of important and wealthy men, including two of the sons of Robert, Earl of Leicester.

The first of these was twenty-four-year-old Algernon Sidney, a dashing colonel in the rebel army who had been wounded in battle, and who would later declare the execution of Charles I to be 'the justest and bravest act … that was ever done in England, or anywhere'.[20] James II would maintain that Algernon had contracted for Lucy Walter's services with forty gold coins. Others believed her favours had cost him fifty. Either way, it was a small fortune, especially given the brevity of the affair: Sidney was suddenly sent with his regiment to bolster the garrison of Dover Castle, leaving Lucy on her own.

Lucy then moved to the Netherlands, where she was pleased, though probably not surprised, to find herself surrounded by eligible Royalist exiles, wealthy enough to compete for the pleasure of her company. She was soon taken up by Algernon's younger brother, Colonel Robert Sidney. He was a courtier to Prince Charles, with what was to prove the apt title of Groom of the Bedchamber: Robert was Lucy's lover when Charles appeared in the Netherlands to prepare his ships for the expected foray against Parliament.

Some contemporaries believed that Charles was already aware of Lucy's charms, having glimpsed them for himself when younger: 'Her beauty was so perfect that when the King saw her in Wales, where she was, he was … charmed and ravished and enamoured,' a French noblewoman claimed.[21] However, it was Lucy who engineered the meeting with, then the seduction of, Charles in July 1648. At this time, aged eighteen, Charles was, according to an admiring Scot, 'One of the most gentle, innocent, well-inclined Princes, so far as yet appear, that lives in the world [with] a trim person, and a manly carriage'.[22] The account of Madame de Motteville, a French courtier, largely tallies with this generous description, recalling Charles at this time as 'well-made, with a swarthy complexion agreeing with his fine black eyes, a large ugly mouth, a graceful and dignified carriage and a fine figure'. Whatever Charles's physical characteristics, Robert Sidney realised that it would be unwise to compete with the heady attention of his royal master, and stood aside.

During the time the prince spent in The Hague that summer, awaiting the readiness of his fleet, Lucy became pregnant with the first of what would eventually be more than a dozen of Charles's children by various mistresses. Their son, James, was born in Rotterdam on 9 April 1649, ten weeks after the execution of his grandfather Charles I, and nine months after the start of Charles and Lucy's liaison. Gossips pointed out that there had been no discernible gap between the conclusion of Lucy's relationship with Robert Sidney and the beginning of her affair with the prince, and rumours attached to Lucy's son all his life that questioned whether he was in fact of royal blood. Charles, though, always accepted that James was his son, and publicly acknowledged the fact when giving him the title of Duke of Monmouth.

Meanwhile a shortage of funds kept Charles's fleet at anchor, so that his efforts to help his father's cause in the Second Civil War largely came to nothing. When he eventually sailed, his ships harassed and captured a few lesser vessels, before squaring up to the rebel navy in the Thames estuary in August 1648. In the preparations for the battle Charles impressed his men with his insistence on sharing their danger, the courtier Sir Robert Long reporting: 'I must not forget to tell you, the Prince behaved himself with as much gallantry and courage in this business as ever you saw; for when his lords and all the seamen came to desire him to go down into the hold, under the decks, he would not hear of it, but told them his honour was more to him than his safety; and desired them not to speak of it any more.'[23]

But a last-minute storm made engagement impossible. After six fruitless weeks at sea Charles returned to The Hague in September 1648, leaving the Royalist fleet under the command of Prince Rupert of the Rhine. It seems probable that he then resumed his relationship with Lucy Walter. The scandalous liaison had taken place while Sir Edward Hyde, the adviser who sought to make the prince a worthy monarch-in-waiting, was still absent in Jersey. With his moral guardian away, Charles spent time with the more dissolute members of his mother's entourage, including Lord Wilmot.

Hyde would characterise Henry Wilmot as 'A man proud and ambitious, and incapable of being contented; an orderly officer in marches and governing his troops. He drank hard, and had a great power over all who did so, which was a great [many] people.'[24] Wilmot gained Charles's friendship through their shared sense of what comprised a good time. He also won the prince's gratitude by being a willing helper in his romance with Lucy Walter: Wilmot put his carriage at her disposal so she could travel to and from the prince's side with ease.

Hyde was reunited with Prince Charles at The Hague in mid-September 1648, after more than two years' separation. He found his young protégé not only expecting to become a father, but surrounded by a court in exile that was turned in on itself in despair at the recent failure of the Second Civil War. The Scots had been crushed by Cromwell at the battle of Preston, and English resistance to the New Model Army had been firmly stamped out.

In his first speech in the prince's council Hyde voiced his continued deep opposition to future alliances with any powers that were hostile to the Church of England. He delivered his fatalistic view: 'It may be God hath resolved we shall perish, and then it becomes us to perish with those decent and honest circumstances that our good fame may procure a better peace to those who succeed us than we are able to procure for them, and ourselves shall be happier than any other condition could render us.'[25] Continued loss of power was, for Hyde, infinitely preferable to a sacrifice of principles. Nobody worthy of the English Crown, he believed, could lower himself to a shameful alliance with the enemies of the Anglican religion. Anyone who claimed a throne in such circumstances could only keep it for the briefest of times, before inevitable overthrow. If Charles found himself without viable foreign allies, then he must await a turn in fortunes, either through his own becoming better, or those of the rebels deteriorating. Hyde hoped that the Commonwealth's politicians and soldiers might turn against one other, and pull the republican regime apart.

Henrietta Maria and her supporters ridiculed Hyde for choosing to wait for miracles. They preferred to actively plot a return to royal power, and were prepared to contemplate all possible means of doing so.

In the meantime the Royalists of both factions watched in impotent disbelief and despair during January 1649 as their king was taken to London to be tried by a hastily created court, of highly questionable credentials. Prince Charles was determined to have his father released, whatever the cost. He sent a blank sheet of paper to Charles I's captors, to which he had applied only his signature and his seal. This 'carte blanche' signified that there were no terms that he would reject in return for his father's liberty.

When he learnt that his great gesture had failed to save his father from execution, Charles was reduced to terrible, violent sobbing, while, Hyde recalled, 'all about him were almost bereft of their understanding'.

## 2

## *Royal Prey*

*Indeed I think it not the least of my misfortunes that,
for my sake, thou hast run so much hazard; in which
thou hast expressed so much love to me, that I
confess it is impossible to repay, by anything I can
do, let alone words.*

Letter of Charles I to Queen Henrietta Maria, 1644

Charles I had been judged and condemned by a court composed of his enemies. Many of them were military men who had witnessed the wars for themselves, and who had been persuaded that the king was personally responsible for the bloodshed. They tried him for this treason with no time for the formalities of kingship, referring to him as 'Charles Stuart', and cursing him as 'that man of blood'. For his part, the king declined to accept the court's authority to judge him. When he refused to plead 'guilty' or 'not guilty' for a third time, the decision was taken away from him, and he was simply declared guilty. He was sent for beheading outside his London palace of Whitehall, on an icy day at the end of January 1649.

The rest of the royal family also suffered terribly for its association with the king's role in the Civil Wars. Prince Charles's wanderings, punctuated by hopefulness and humiliation, with the enemy constantly snapping at his heels, represented just one part of the trials of the Stuart dynasty at this time.

For all that Charles I adored his wife and doted on his children, once he had declared war on Parliament he exposed them to ever-increasing levels of personal danger. It was the taking of sides in a ferocious conflict, caused by profound political, religious and social tensions, that soon removed the princes and princesses from the supposed sanctuary of royal status. The pampered children of the years of peace became the pawns of war.

The king and his eldest son, Charles, Prince of Wales, put on armour, and led armies against the Crown's foes. To those who fought against the Royalists, they had chosen to step down from their majestic pedestals, and elected to become merely key enemy personnel. Their death on the battlefield could therefore be contemplated as distinctly possible. It was a short step from that thought to one of actively seeking out royal prey.

Meanwhile the Presbyterians and Puritans who dominated the House of Commons had long viewed the French-born queen, Henrietta Maria, with suspicion and distrust. She made no attempt to conceal her zealous Roman Catholicism, and it was clear to all that she exercised considerable control over the king. Yet it was not until 1641, the year before war broke out, that she had first felt in personal danger. Accusations that she was the king's chief evil counsellor, and talk of her possibly being impeached as a consequence, persuaded her to put in place contingency plans for escape.

On Sunday, 16 June 1644 Queen Henrietta Maria gave birth to Princess Henrietta, her eighth and last child, in Bedford House, the finest private residence in Exeter. Henrietta would be one of six of her and King Charles I's children to survive infancy.

The queen had long suffered from ill health. A month earlier her doctor, Theodore de Mayerne, had judged her so fragile that he concluded 'her days would not be many'.[1] Henrietta Maria was left in such a weak state by the delivery that she felt obliged to request a favour of the enemy commander, the Earl of Essex, asking him to guarantee her safe passage to Bath, where she wished to take to the restorative mineral-rich waters. She immediately followed this with a second request, to be allowed to continue on to Bristol after her stay in Bath. Bristol was the most important English port after London, and was held by the Royalists.

Essex could only suspect that, once she was well enough, the queen planned to set sail from Bristol and disappear overseas. He therefore replied that he would be delighted to give her safe conduct, but only if she would go to London – he pointed out that that was, after all, where the best medical advice in the country lay, and added that it would be his honour and pleasure to attend her on her journey to the capital. As for Bath or Bristol, he expressed his regret that he was unable to allow her to travel to either city without Parliament's direction.

Despite the exquisite sheen of the earl's manners, the subtext was clear: Parliament would never contemplate the queen's move to Bath or Bristol, while Essex would do what it took to bring her into his custody, where she could be detained to the advantage of the Crown's enemies, as a highly valuable hostage to be used against the king.

Henrietta Maria was aware that many in Parliament hated her. They correctly guessed that the French princess had only been allowed to marry their Protestant king because Pope Urban VIII wanted to 'procure the reign of popery' in England.[2] Her attachment to her faith had been so unswerving that she had refused to take part in her and her husband's coronation, because it would involve being crowned by a Protestant prelate. Since then she had established ornate Roman Catholic chapels in royal palaces throughout the kingdom, and had formed ties with all manner of apparently dangerous foreigners, including papal envoys. Given this bitter history between queen and Parliament, as soon as Essex refused her request to travel to Bath, Henrietta Maria contemplated her options.

Four weeks later, feeling her health had slightly improved, the queen sailed out of Falmouth harbour for her native France. She was carried on a Flemish man-of-war that had, along with the ten vessels accompanying it, been 'fresh tallow'd and train'd' in order to give her the best chance of outrunning Parliament's roving patrols. She hoped to slip through their blockade on a favourable wind, but a barge with sixteen oarsmen accompanied her ship, ready to spirit her away to safety if the weather calmed.

On the day chosen for the voyage the wind filled the Royalists' sails, and the queen's flotilla sped towards Brest. A rebel frigate fired its cannon at the fleeing ships, but her shots passed wide.

It was all very reminiscent of the queen's arrival in Yorkshire, nearly a year and a half before, in February 1643. Henrietta Maria had spent the early months of the English Civil War in Europe, pawning and selling off her jewels in order to secure soldiers, weapons and money for her husband's cause, at a time when Royalist supplies were dangerously low. After two attempts at crossing to England, during one of which the ship carrying her horses, grooms and coaches had sunk, she managed to land at Bridlington Bay, north of Hull. Four Parliamentary vessels had tailed her, commanded by the same William Batten who would try to capture Prince Charles on the Isles of Scilly in 1646.

The captain of one of the rebel ships had established where the queen would be staying onshore. At four o'clock the next morning, while it was still dark, he and his comrades sailed into the bay and opened fire on Henrietta Maria's lodgings. 'Before I could get out of bed, the [cannon]balls were whistling upon me in such style that you may easily believe I loved not such music,' the queen gamely wrote to her husband.[3] The enemy fire killed some of her attendants, one of her sergeants being cut in two while standing just twenty feet from her. Henrietta Maria only found safety after running through the snow partially dressed, and flinging herself into a ditch that was shielded by a slight rise in the ground. She risked her life again when returning under fire to recover her lapdog, Mitte. The enemy guns blazed away at her for two hours, until a Dutch admiral who had helped escort her to Bridlington insisted that Batten's men cease fire, or suffer the consequences.

The Bishop of Angoulême would chastise the rebels for 'having no respect either to [the queen's] person, or yet to her sex ... nor yet regarding her long sickness, which had brought her even within two fingers of death'.[4] But there was little remorse in London for an attack on a lady whose military efforts saw her celebrated by the Royalist side as the 'she-generalissima'. Besides, because she had refused to take part in the coronation, why should this Roman Catholic Frenchwoman not be treated as just another subject?

When Henrietta Maria made it safely to France, she did so without her infant daughter, having felt compelled to leave Princess Henrietta behind because of the baby's delicacy. She had entrusted her to the care of a godmother, Lady Dalkeith, a noted beauty among Henrietta Maria's courtiers. Anne Dalkeith promised that she would do all in her power to reunite mother and child at the earliest possible opportunity.

Charles I arrived in Exeter to visit his infant daughter in the wake of his wife's successful getaway, and soon after he had personally led the Royalists to victory at the battle of Cropredy Bridge in Oxfordshire. He was determined that the princess be received into the Church of England, and Henrietta was christened in Exeter Cathedral when five weeks old. Her father then rode off again, to lead his side to further success over the Parliamentarians in the south-west. It was the only time father and daughter would ever meet.

Exeter fell to Parliament in April 1646, when Henrietta was twenty-two months old. The victors decided that the young princess must join her sister, Princess Elizabeth, and brother, Henry, Duke of Gloucester, as prisoners in London's St James's Palace. Honouring her promise to the queen, Lady Dalkeith refused to comply, instead keeping her charge with her at Oatlands Palace in Surrey.

By the end of July 1646 Lady Dalkeith realised that Henrietta would soon be forcibly removed from her care. She therefore dressed the toddler as a ragamuffin boy, and disguised herself as a beggar woman, scrunching up a cloth under her clothes to give her the appearance of having a hunchback. Two members of the household were also included in the plan, a man who pretended to be the child's father, and a maid, Elinor Dyke, who was there to help look after the princess throughout the escape.

Lady Dalkeith left a letter behind at Oatlands, begging those remaining there not to let anyone raise the alarm over the princess's absence for three days. She then hoisted Henrietta onto her shoulders and set off by foot with her small party for the port of Dover, nearly 100 miles away.

It was an escape made somewhat harder by the young Henrietta's insistence on telling bemused strangers that she was not, in fact, a boy but a princess. But nobody paid much attention to the scruffy child's claims, and eventually she was brought to Dover, where she and her godmother boarded a ship for France. Arriving there, Lady Dalkeith made good her promise to the queen, returning her daughter to her in Paris, before fainting from exhaustion.

Princess Elizabeth's experience as royal victim was somewhat different.

Princess Mary, Charles I and Henrietta Maria's eldest daughter, was nine years old when she was married in London to the fourteen-year-old William, Prince of Orange, in early May 1641. He was the heir to the Dutch Republic's senior hereditary figure, and part of the marital contract involved a strong expectation that the Netherlands would support the Stuarts in their imminent war.

The next year the queen accompanied her daughter across the North Sea, to settle the girl into her new life, and to help find further support for her husband's cause. They left behind Princess Elizabeth, the king and queen's next oldest daughter. She was seven. She would never see her mother or sister again.

Elizabeth and her younger brother, Henry, Duke of Gloucester, were taken into custody by Parliament at the outbreak of civil war, later in 1642. They were placed under the guardianship of the Earl of Pembroke that October, and were kept at St James's Palace, where the princess had been born and christened during the peaceful years of her father's reign.

Princess Elizabeth had a rare intelligence, astonishing her tutors with her ability in five foreign and ancient languages before she turned eight. When the House of Commons suggested trimming her and her brother's household, early in their gilded imprisonment, the seven-year-old wrote a protest in her own hand that was persuasive enough to convince the House of Lords to overrule the lower house, and leave things as they had been.

1643 was largely a year of convalescence for Elizabeth, after she badly broke a leg. Daily life involved submission to the intense religious programme of her captors, with endless sermons that were meant to win over her soul, but instead numbed her mind. The princess won approval, though, for the natural modesty of her behaviour, and earned the nickname of 'Temperance', a Puritan virtue.

In the summer of 1644 she and Henry were moved to Danvers House in Chelsea, and put in the care of the twice-widowed Sir John Danvers, a disgruntled sixty-year-old courtier who in his youth had been considered one of the best-looking men in England. Danvers's extravagant love for architecture and

Italianate gardens ensured the royal children were accommodated in style.

A succession of other aristocrats sympathetic to Parliament took part in overseeing the royal children. The constant in all these changes was the Countess of Dorset, who had been Prince Charles's governess from the age of one, and who now performed that duty with Elizabeth and Henry until her deteriorating health took its toll.

In the spring of 1645, with the countess retired, the princess and Henry were placed in the custody of the Earl and Countess of Northumberland. They were moved to Syon House in Isleworth, Middlesex. After the surrender of the Royalist capital, Oxford, in June 1646, James, Duke of York, was brought to join them there.

The king and queen were left miserable by their inability to rescue their three middle children, Henrietta Maria writing to Prince Charles: 'Yet my real afflictions do not make me forget your brothers, and that unfortunate Elizabeth. Oh! If before my death, I could see her out of the hands of the traitors, I could die content. To this, at least, I will exhort you, to employ every force, to use every artifice, to withdraw so dear a part of my own heart, this innocent victim of their fury, your worthy sister, from London. Do it, I pray and conjure you, by the spirit of the king, my lord and your father.'[5] But Prince Charles was as powerless to help his siblings as his father had been before him.

Charles I had made overtures to the rebels, and planned kidnap attempts, in the hope of getting Elizabeth and Henry to him at Oxford. But when, after his defeat, the king was imprisoned at Hampton Court, he delighted in travelling the six miles to the Earl of Northumberland's private palace, to visit his three captive children there.

At the end of January 1649, Elizabeth and Henry were taken to say a final goodbye to their father on the day before his execution. Elizabeth's vivid account of this heartbreaking meeting demonstrates an astonishing gift for recall, particularly given the depth of emotions swirling in the fourteen-year-old's mind at such a terrible moment.

She wrote of how her father put eight-year-old Henry, Duke of Gloucester, on his knee, then told him, "'Sweetheart, now they will cut off thy father's head.' And Gloucester looking very intently upon him, he said again, "Heed, my child, what I say: they will cut off my head and perhaps make thee a king. But mark what I say. Thou must not be a king as long as thy brothers Charles and James do live; for they will cut off your brothers' heads when they can catch them, and cut off thy head too at the last, and therefore I charge you, do not be made a king by them." At which my brother sighed deeply, and made answer: "I will be torn in pieces first!"

Elizabeth would remember her father's words of comfort as he turned to her: 'He desired me not to grieve for him, for he should die a martyr, and that he doubted not the Lord would settle his throne upon his son, and that we should all be happier than we could have expected to be if he had lived.'[6] The next day, the king was beheaded, just as he had warned Elizabeth and Henry he would be.

Princess Elizabeth petitioned to join her surviving family on the Continent, but three months later these hopes were dashed. Keen to get her and her brother away from London, 'that they may not be the objects of respect, to draw the eyes and application of the people towards them,'[7] Parliament ordered that Elizabeth and Henry be sent to live with the Earl and Countess of Leicester at Penshurst in Kent. Their hosts were under instruction not to acknowledge the duo's royal blood. Their titles were not to be used, any special treatment was banned, and they were to eat with the Leicesters' children.

Elizabeth's dignity in the wretched role of royal hostage impressed many. John Quarles, an exiled Royalist poet, dedicated

*Regale lectum miseriae*, his lament for Charles I, 'To that Patroness of Virtue and most illustrious Princess, Elizabeth, The sorrowful daughter to our late Martyr'd Sovereign, Charles, King of England'. Elizabeth was, to Quarles and many others, the embodiment of the continuing tragedy of the Stuart cause.

On their brother Charles's landing in Scotland in 1650, to assume the crown there, Elizabeth and her brother were removed to Carisbrooke Castle on the Isle of Wight. This was where their father had been kept secure by Parliament from November 1647 until September 1648, before his journey towards trial and execution in London. It was also as far from Scotland as could be: having the royal children cooped up there stopped them from becoming figureheads for any who might be planning a Royalist uprising in mainland England.

Elizabeth pleaded that her health was too poor for her to be transported from Penshurst to the Isle of Wight, but Sir Anthony Mildmay, who had been part of the king's trial, persuaded the Council of State, the nation's chief executive body, that the security of the nation must come first. On being moved, Elizabeth's delicate health deteriorated. She caught a cold, then consumption. That is the disease that she died of, in Carisbrooke Castle, on 8 September 1650.

Two days later news reached the Isle of Wight that permission had finally been granted by Parliament for the princess and her younger brother to depart for the Netherlands, where they were to be handed over to the care of their older sister, Mary. Instead, Elizabeth's next journey was to an unmarked grave, its whereabouts signalled by her initials, 'E.S.', on a nearby church wall.

Henry, Duke of Gloucester, was told that his older sister had died of a broken heart, because of their brother Charles's submission to the Scots' extreme brand of Protestantism. The Royalists also used Elizabeth's death for propaganda purposes, claiming that she breathed her last while her face nestled on a Bible that Charles I had given her at their final meeting.

James, Duke of York, was taken into Parliamentary hands in June 1646, when the Royalist capital of Oxford fell to Parliament. He was forced to join his siblings, Elizabeth and Henry, in St James's Palace, where he had been born and christened thirteen years earlier. His godparents had been the Queen of Bohemia, the Elector Palatine, and the Prince of Orange. The first two of these had lost their thrones, and the grandson of the third would one day depose James from his. But at the time of his birth the royal family of England was seemingly secure, as well as happily detached from the bloody wars that brought mayhem to swathes of Continental Europe for fifteen years before, and fifteen years after, James's appearance in the world. Soon after his baptism James was given the title of Duke of York and Albany. Aged five, he was appointed lord high admiral of England's expanding navy.

By 1646, James's life had been turned upside down. His father was militarily defeated, unsure of the future, but clinging to his belief that he was central to whatever settlement his war-ravaged kingdoms would reach. His siblings were either captive, fled overseas, or watching in despair from the foreign courts into which they had been married off.

The three royal children confined to St James's Palace were in the care of the 10th Earl of Northumberland, one of the grandest noblemen to stand against the Crown in the English Civil War. Northumberland was a kindly captor, whose own father had wondered what talents he might eventually reveal. The early evidence had not been promising: he had been a sickly child, with no great interest in anything.

Northumberland had turned into a dutiful, dull, but principled man, who had been rewarded with many honours because of his high social standing, rather than through ability. Perhaps as a result, he developed a fanatical belief in the importance of hierarchy, particularly when it involved inherited rank. Sir Edward Hyde, Prince Charles's key courtier, waspishly noted of the earl: 'If he had thought the King as much above him as he thought himself above other considerable men, he would have been a good subject.'[8]

Thanks to such an elevated sense of snobbery governing their captor, the princess and her brothers were treated with full reverence for their royal blood. Northumberland was meticulous about the details of their upbringing, and paid for part of its substantial expense out of his own pocket, since Parliament's allowance was intentionally strict. He was aware that his prime responsibility was to keep his charges safely under Parliamentary control. This was never a side of his duties that he welcomed, but it had proved manageable when his royal prisoners had merely been two young children. The arrival of James, a youth who had been actively engaged in warfare for four years, was a different matter. Security had to be tightened. Northumberland dismissed all of James's retinue, to the duke's disgust and disappointment. He was particularly upset to lose the company of his favourite courtier, a dwarf.

James, unburdened by humility at any stage of his life, was not an easy prisoner. When informed that his father the king had been taken prisoner, he was indignant, asking 'how durst any rogues … use his father after that manner'.[9] When one of those present at this outburst threatened to report his unguarded words to the Earl of Northumberland, James levelled his longbow at him, and might well have loosed off his arrow if he had not been quickly overpowered.

King Charles had heard of plans by some in Parliament to bypass him and his eldest son, and to transfer the crown to James, who they hoped to turn into a puppet ruler. During his visits to his children, the king secretly urged James to do two things: as a guiding principle, to obey his elder brother; and, in the immediate future, to flee abroad. James agreed to his father's instructions, but escape proved an extremely difficult proposition for an adolescent acting on his own. He was caught twice, at which point he was forced to give his word that he would never again try to get away.

Princess Elizabeth encouraged her brother to continue in his attempts at freedom, telling him 'that were she a boy she would not long remain a captive, however light or glittering might be the fetters that bound her'.[10] Elizabeth has been credited with coming up with the ruse that led to James's next escape attempt, but it was more likely the brainchild of an intriguing reprobate called Joseph Bampfield.

Bampfield was a handsome charmer from the south-west of England who had been made colonel of a Royalist infantry regiment when only twenty years old. He had a reputation for resourcefulness, subterfuge and slipperiness, as well as a proven record in the art of escape. When he was made a prisoner of war, his enemies could only hold him briefly before he flitted to freedom. The king, who had used Bampfield's talents as courier and spy during the Civil War, decided he was the best man to extricate his son from St James's Palace, and then get him to safety overseas.

The king wrote to the colonel, stressing the absolute importance to the future of the monarchy of getting the second in line to the throne out of Parliament's control. He recognised that there would be great dangers along the way: 'I believe it will be difficult, and if he miscarry in any attempt it will be the greatest affliction that can arrive to me,' he conceded, 'but I look upon James's escape as Charles's preservation, and nothing can content me more; therefore be careful what you do.'[11]

Bampfield made contact with James through one of the palace's attendants, who engineered a secret meeting between the young duke and his would-be rescuer. By way of credentials Bampfield showed James the letter of instruction he had received from the king. He told James that the escape plan would involve the wearing of a disguise, and measured the boy's height and waist with a ribbon.

James was thrilled at the prospect of possible freedom, and readily obeyed the colonel's directions. These involved his joining his little sister and brother in games of hide and seek in St James's Palace each evening after dinner throughout the following week. There needed to be carved out from James's day an apparently innocent sliver where his absence did not immediately raise suspicion. The children's games provided that cover.

The household, including its guards, quickly became used to James's skill at hiding. Consequently, when on the night of 20 April 1648 the duke could not readily be found, nobody thought much of it. It was assumed that he would be discovered somewhere nearby soon enough, as he had been on the previous six evenings.

But this time, James had made a break for it. After tricking a gardener into lending him a key, he had dined with his younger sister and his little brother before challenging them to their nightly entertainment. Now it was that he went down a staircase to a gate that gave access to the surrounding parkland, triple-locking it behind him with the key he had sweet-talked the trusting gardener into giving him.

Bampfield was waiting on the other side. He wrapped a cloak around the boy, and put a wig on his head, before whisking him away in a coach that carried them to a waiting boat. This was rowed towards a house near the Tower of London where the colonel's lover, Anne Murray, waited.

To keep herself occupied that evening, and assuming that a boy of James's age might well be hungry, Anne busied herself preparing food for the duke. She had a lady's tunic with her for James to wear as a disguise. 'It was,' she would recall, 'a mixed mohair of a light hair colour and black, and the under-petticoat was scarlet.'[12] Anne's tailor had been mystified by the surprisingly unfeminine measurements she had submitted to him, saying that this unseen client had to be the shortest woman with the largest waist that he could remember cutting for.

As time passed, Anne waited with mounting anxiety for the colonel and the duke. Bampfield had warned her that if he and James had not arrived at the steps of London Bridge by ten o'clock, she must assume that the risky plan had failed. If that were the case, she would be in mortal danger of discovery, and must flee for her life.

When she heard church bells chime ten, and the lookout said there was still no sign of the boat, he asked her what they should do. Anne said she must stay, just in case her lover and the boy were running late.

She later admitted that she had in fact assumed the pair had been captured, and that she would soon pay the price for being part of a failed treasonous conspiracy. 'And,' she recalled, 'while I was fortifying myself against what might arrive to me, I heard a great noise of many as I thought coming up the stairs, which I expected to be soldiers to take me, but it was a pleasing disappointment, for the first that came in was the Duke, who with much joy I took in my arms and gave God thanks for his safe arrival. His Highness called, "Quickly, quickly – dress me!"; and, putting on his clothes, I dressed him in the women's habit that was prepared, which fitted his Highness very well.' Indeed, she could not help noticing that he 'was very pretty in it'.[13]

James ate the food Anne had prepared for him. She then gave him a treat for his journey: a Wood Street cake – a fruit cake that was as light in yeast as it was thick with icing. It was a speciality of a neighbourhood of the City of London, and she knew it to be one of the duke's favourites.

James and Bampfield then ran back to the barge, where their oarsmen took advantage of the favourable wind and tide to head towards a waiting Dutch ship, twenty miles away at Gravesend. Before they could reach it, though, the wind turned, convincing

Bampfield that they would be blown back to the shore. James urged: 'Do any thing with me rather than let me go back again!' At last the wind came right once more, and they made it to their ship.

Back at St James's Palace, relaxation at James's assumed skill at hide and seek had first turned to mild concern, before spiralling into panic. The Earl of Northumberland was informed that the duke appeared to be missing, and immediately ordered a meticulous search of the entire palace. When it was found that James was clearly absent, he sent a messenger to William Lenthall, the Speaker of the House of Commons, saying that he feared James had escaped, but that he had no idea how.

Northumberland, his many former offices including a stint as lord admiral of England, insisted that the Speaker immediately send a dispatch to the great seaports of Kent and Sussex, barring any vessel from leaving for abroad until it had been thoroughly searched.

There was chaos in the speaker's office as the clerks bickered over how best to carry out Northumberland's order. They struggled to construct the correct words to help block the flight of the most eminent prisoner in England. Serjeant at Arms Norfoulke, a witness to this clerical pandemonium, later reported that a dozen orders were written out, then rejected, before all were happy with the wording of the final version. By the time the dispatch finally reached its recipients, the duke was gone.

He landed at Middleburg, in the Dutch province of Zeeland, on 22 April 1648, before being carried to The Hague on his brother-in-law's yacht. James had been forced to leave two siblings behind in captivity, but he had gained a third. He was now warmly welcomed into his bravely-won freedom by his older sister Mary, Princess of Orange. At their reunion she threw royal stiffness to the wind, running towards her brother and hugging him tight.

When Prince Charles heard of his brother's daring rescue, he was overjoyed. He of course had no idea that it would one day fall

final act of the English Civil War, bringing to an end a conflict that had claimed the life of one in twenty Englishmen. Cromwell looked now for conciliation and reform, while remaining ready to stamp out further Royalist resistance with his troops, should it surface.

John Bradshaw was prominent among those regicides with a very different view of how things must now be. A lawyer plucked from obscurity to become lord president of the impromptu court that had sent the king to his doom, Bradshaw saw the execution of a tyrannical ruler as a thrilling act that should be celebrated, and then built upon. While Cromwell hoped the king's death would demark a full stop, Bradshaw saw it as a mere comma in the unfurling script of England's electrifying new story.

Those who had overseen Charles I's execution dominated the Council of State, the executive body established the month after the king's death. A replacement for the Privy Council, it was responsible for domestic and foreign policy, as well as the security of England and Wales. Eighteen of its forty-one councillors had been among those to sign the royal death warrant.

All of the councillors and the other regicides could agree on one thing: that the fledgling republic needed to be sustained. But there were others who felt that a unique opportunity for constitutional change had been lamentably mismanaged. They had suffered in the fight against the king, and now expected their aspirations to be honoured. Among them was a radical group known to its detractors as 'the Levellers'.

The Levellers were still working on their manifesto, which they had begun two years earlier, at the time of the king's death. *An Agreement of the People* was intended to be the blueprint for a written constitution, stating the inalienable rights of all Englishmen, and detailing the contract between them and their elected representatives. It demanded equality for all before the law, and that the vote be open to all men over twenty-one, other than Royalists, servants and beggars. *England's New Chaines Discovered*, published immediately after the establishment of the Council of State, was a protest that these hopes had been ignored. The Levellers accused the new government of seizing power from the people. Their leaders were arrested for their effrontery.

But this movement, based on principle, remained dangerous in the months following the execution of the king, and it had support in the army, which had suffered so greatly in the cause against the Crown. Richard Lockier, one of the Levellers' leaders, was captured, then executed by firing squad outside St Paul's Cathedral in late April 1649. This stoked up a wider military mutiny. There were many in the army who had been inspired by Leveller ideas, and who were also furious at arrears in their pay, while being frightened at the prospect of being sent to fight in the graveyard of disease-ridden, boggy Ireland. Cromwell defeated the main mutineer force, in a night attack at Burford in Oxfordshire. While 300 of them were pardoned, three of the ringleaders were shot in the village's churchyard. Even though Cromwell could declare the Leveller threat in the army over by the end of May 1649, there was still much for the new regime to settle before it could consider itself established. A myriad of hopes had been raised by the toppling of the Crown, and not all of them could be satisfied.

Six weeks after Charles I's beheading, kingship was abolished, Parliament declaring: 'The office of a King in a nation, and to have power thereof in a single person, was unnecessary, burdensome, and dangerous to the liberty, safety, and public interest of the people, and therefore ought to be abolished.'[1]

In a further dramatic break with the past, the Royal Seal in the House of Commons was smashed into pieces by a hammer-wielding labourer. Its replacement contained the text: 'In the First Year of Freedom, by God's Blessing Restored.' Ancient liberties, notionally lost under centuries of kingship, were being celebrated and reinstated under the new regime: the Commonwealth.

John Bradshaw's allies included two men who were responsible for the twin struts of the new regime's printed propaganda. The great poet and man of letters John Milton, who now championed the regicides in written duels with their European detractors, was given the title of Secretary for Foreign Tongues.

Meanwhile Milton's friend Marchamont Nedham – a journalist and pamphleteer who had supported Parliament, then sided with the king, before getting firmly behind the new republic – oversaw the influential weekly newsbook *Mercurius Politicus* from June 1650. He took on this important journalistic role at a key moment in the Commonwealth's campaign to make the republic more devout. The Puritan leadership felt this was required in order to secure God's continuing favour. In May 1650 Parliament passed an Act condemning those guilty of incest, adultery and fornication. The incestuous and adulterous could expect the death penalty, 'without clergy' being in attendance at their end. Fornicators received a three-month prison sentence for their first offence. A few months later, the blasphemous joined the swelling ranks of outlaws.

*Mercurius Politicus* produced journalism of the highest class, engaging correspondents throughout Europe, while having access to the republic's all-seeing spy network. Nedham was given a salary of £100 a year, 'whereby he may subsist while endeavouring to serve the Commonwealth'.[2]

The rise of printed domestic news and propaganda was a pronounced feature of the English Civil War. The first such publication, *The Heads of Severall Proceedings in this Present Parliament*, appeared in November 1641, nine months before hostilities began. There was then an explosion of the printed word, with approximately 300 different partisan newsbooks competing for attention during the 1640s and 1650s. Although many faded away after a few issues, several of them appeared with regularity, the most popular having a run of up to 1,500 copies at a time.[3]

Milton and Nedham were both relentless promoters of the king-less state. One of their constant refrains was the merciless mockery of any who proposed that Charles, Prince of Wales – who was sometimes referred to as 'the Young Pretender' – should regain his family's throne. These attacks showed what a terrifying prospect it was for those who had killed the father, should the son return to hold them to account.

The question for those Royalists who had been so decisively defeated in two civil wars, between the summers of 1642 and 1648, was who would provide the manpower to make it possible to challenge Parliament's army, now their own forces had been crushed. The answer to this was most vigorously addressed by the widowed queen.

When Henrietta Maria was informed of her husband's execution, she stood mute and motionless for an age, seized by a shock that she seems not to have come fully to terms with during the remaining twenty years of her life. In the aftermath of Charles I's death she retreated briefly to a Carmelite nunnery. On re-emerging she wore mourning clothes, and would do so for the rest of her days.

Henrietta Maria wrote of her wish to 'retire with only two maids, my secretary, and confessor, to private life, to finish my days with the least possible disturbance, disentangled from the world'.[4] She could not forget, though, the hopes and wishes that her husband had shared with her during the darkest periods of the later years of his rule.

In July 1646 he had written to her: 'And though the worst should come, yet I conjure thee to turn thy grief into a just revenge upon my enemies, and the repossessing of Prince Charles into his inheritances.'[5] Two months earlier he had sent a letter to his eldest son that had equal clarity: 'I command you to obey [your mother] in everything, except religion, concerning which I am confident she will not trouble you.'[6]

Charles was convinced that his wife could be a great support to their eldest son, for he knew how heavily he himself had leant on her throughout the Civil Wars. When the king's baggage train was captured at the battle of Naseby in June 1645, the correspondence unearthed there revealed the full extent of Henrietta Maria's hold over her husband. One letter particularly appalled Parliament. In it, Charles had written: 'I give thee power to promise in my name, to whom thou thinkest most fit, that I will take away all the penal laws against the Roman Catholics in England, as soon as God shall enable me to do it.'[7] One of the main charges levelled against the king by his Puritan and Presbyterian enemies had been that he was secretly sympathetic to Roman Catholicism, thanks to his wife's corrosive influence. This letter conclusively proved the point.

Henrietta Maria knew her husband to be weak, and easily swayed by his advisers. She wrote despairingly of how he was apt 'to take sudden counsels,'[8] many of which, she felt, ran contrary to the Crown's and her family's interests.

This situation had become much more difficult for Henrietta Maria to control after she and Charles parted at Abingdon, for what would turn out to be the last time, on 17 April 1644. She had hugged her husband's knees, begging him to let her stay by his side. But he was adamant that she must go abroad, to secure him aid. Her usefulness in that purpose overrode his thoughts for himself, because, he said, her remaining with him would be his 'greatest consolation'. 'And I found myself ten leagues distant from him,' the queen would recall, 'before I became conscious that I had left him, so much did grief overcome my natural senses'.[9] The great sadness of parting aside, Henrietta Maria was also troubled at leaving her husband far removed from her controlling hand.

The queen was proud to be a child of one of France's great kings, Henri IV, who had been stabbed to death by an assassin when she was less than six months old. She hoped that those who governed the land of her birth would respect her position as one of its princesses, and choose to help her family in its quest for restoration to its royal powers. But the French were embroiled in European conflict, principally the Franco–Spanish War, which had started in 1635 and would rumble on till 1659. They also had to contend with the '*Fronde*', their own civil war, which erupted in 1648, largely brought about by the huge cost of funding France's wars.

Meanwhile Henrietta Maria's brother, Louis XIII, died in 1643. She had hoped he would help her and her husband to overpower the English rebels. Now, she found, France's leading figures were mostly delighted to stand and watch the spectacle across the Channel as their centuries-old enemy tore itself in two.

Henrietta Maria had written to her only surviving brother, the Duke of Orléans, at the beginning of 1646: 'I expect nothing but entire ruin, unless France assists us.'[10] But Orléans was unable to help. He was frequently at odds with Anne of Austria, his young nephew Louis XIV's mother and regent, and with the chief minister, Cardinal Mazarin. Meanwhile Anne and Mazarin's foreign policy was focused on the fight with Spain, with England's discord merely a delicious side dish.

Despite this, Mazarin, the consummate diplomat, seemed to promise much to Henrietta Maria. 'Had I believed Cardinal Mazarin,' she wrote, 'I should have thought he was putting to sea with the most powerful army that had ever left France, for the help of our lost kingdoms.' After being repeatedly let down by him, she concluded bitterly 'that all that he said was only a cheat to quiet me'. But she never gave up hope that France could be persuaded to do the right thing for her and for her family.

When Mazarin funded the Duke of Modena in a failed bid against Spain, Henrietta Maria told him that France's support for her husband would have cost half as much, and that it would have succeeded. 'To which,' she recalled, 'the cardinal made no reply, but took a hasty leave, showing by his mode of treating me, that he no longer recognized me as a queen, and the daughter of a French monarch.'[11]

While Henrietta Maria may have said that she considered herself just 'a poor and wretched widow, in the flood of her miserable emotions', she busily explored all avenues for retrieving her husband's lost crown. These included the possibility of hiring the Duke of Lorraine's forces, or of trusting in the goodwill of Denmark or Sweden. But in the end for various reasons these came to nothing. Ireland and Scotland were left as the most promising springboards for restoring the Stuart cause. The queen and her intimates looked at the Roman Catholicism of the Irish, and the Presbyterianism of the Scottish, and decided the sacrifice of siding with either was a price worth paying, given the magnitude of their ultimate goal.

But the past could not be wished away. Charles I's rule of Scotland had been poorly judged. He had no first-hand experience of Scottish politics, which were enmeshed in the rigidity of the nation's Church – the 'Kirk' – and in the undulating power of the various noble factions. Nor did he appreciate how the physical absence from Scotland of his father (King James returned to his homeland just once during his twenty-two years on the English throne), and then of himself, had left a power vacuum that had, in large part, been filled by the Kirk.

For its part, the Kirk had supreme confidence in its power, seeing itself as the earthly manager of God's wishes. It viewed monarchs as royal magistrates, who served a useful purpose but were unworthy of veneration. The Kirk was happy to hold them individually to account for their human fallibility: a sinner was a sinner, no matter how garlanded his family tree.

Charles I believed with equal passion that the Church must be a spiritual reflection of the hierarchical world of which, he felt certain, he was at the social and political summit. He believed in the importance of bishops, regarding them as being, like himself, selected by God. He also viewed them as powerful allies across his kingdoms: 'the pulpits ... teach obedience [to the Crown]', he wrote in late 1646.[12]

Charles attempted to impose his High Church beliefs on Scotland during the late 1630s, by insisting on the use of the Episcopalian Book of Common Prayer. His high-handedness brought about the National Covenant in 1638. This was an undertaking by the Kirk, on behalf of the Scottish nation, to adhere to the doctrines previously approved by Scotland's Parliament, and to reject any religious interference. While the Covenant acknowledged Scotland's obedience to the Crown, it also warned that, if pushed, the people would fight for their God against their king.

The Covenanters would, essentially, form the government of Scotland from 1638 to 1651, with the 1st Marquess of Argyll – the slight, cross-eyed, redheaded chief of Clan Campbell – as its leading aristocratic light. Charles I had tried to win over Argyll early on, inviting him to London in 1638. During that visit Argyll left the king in no doubt as to his distaste for his religious plans for Scotland. Insulted rather than enlightened, Charles hatched a secret plan for vengeance, approving an invasion of Argyll's lands by Irish sympathisers who allied with the Campbells' bitter enemies, the MacDonalds. These low tactics turned Argyll from a man who was merely at odds with the king's spiritual policies into a livid Covenanter, eager to champion his nation's religious and political freedoms under one banner.

Another leading Covenanter was the lawyer Sir Archibald Johnston, Lord Wariston, who was powered by intense religious convictions. The loss of Wariston's first wife in 1633, when he was twenty-two, seems to have pitched him into a terrible place, from which he emerged with an endless appetite for godliness. Wariston would sleep for only three hours a night, passing his long days in bewilderingly drawn-out prayers and meditations. Dinner guests noted one evening that when he said grace, it took him an hour to reach 'Amen'. While his regular devotions took three hours at a time, he must have surprised even himself when he realised that the prayers he had started at six o'clock one morning had only ended at eight o'clock that evening.

This fanatical piety gained respect amongst other Covenanters, and this readily crossed over into political influence. Wariston's home, near Mercat Cross in Edinburgh, became the meeting place for the leading members of the Kirk, the night before the opening of each annual General Assembly. There they would agree in advance 'the choosing of the Moderator, Committees, and chief points of the Assembly'.[13]

Wariston lent his sharp legal mind to the Kirk as it battled against Charles I's proposed religious settlement for Scotland. Presbyterianism was, to Wariston, 'more than all the world', and 'he looked on the Covenant as the setting of Christ on His throne'.[14] Any who refused to have such beliefs as the cornerstone of their lives must, he argued, be disqualified from public office.

The religious collision between king and Kirk led to the Bishops' Wars of 1639 and 1640. The Scots invaded England, taking Newcastle and threatening advances further south. The urgent need to settle the wars forced Charles to call England's Parliament in April 1640, for the first time in eleven years. Though the 'Short Parliament' lasted just three weeks, a chain of events had been set in motion that eventually culminated in the English Civil War, as Members of Parliament insisted on having a long list of grievances addressed, while the king asserted his independence from the demands of his subjects. This political conflict was exacerbated by the keenly felt religious principles on both sides.

In 1643, with Royalist victories mounting and the loss of the Civil War looking possible, Parliament sought the Scots' help. An alliance was sealed through the Solemn League and Covenant. This agreement guaranteed the preservation of Presbyterianism in

Scotland, and seemed to the Scots to promise that England and Ireland would fall into line once Charles I had been defeated.

A Scottish civil war took place from 1644 to 1647, between the Covenanters and their Royalist opponents. James, 1st Marquess of Montrose, led the king's army, a mixture of Scottish clansmen and Irish troops under Alasdair MacColla.

The charismatic Montrose won a string of remarkable victories with his small force. He repeatedly humiliated the Covenanter leader, the Marquess of Argyll, whose ruthlessness was not matched by either military ability or courage.* It was noted how reluctant Argyll was to engage with the Royalist champion. When he did, it did not go well for him.

The climax came at the battle of Inverlochy, near Ben Nevis, in February 1645. Argyll excused himself from the fight, claiming that he had a dislocated shoulder, and elected to watch proceedings from his boat in the nearby loch. From there he witnessed what was to be the bloodiest defeat his clan would ever suffer. Montrose's significantly outnumbered men cut down 1,500 Campbells. After the battle was lost, Argyll was rowed away to safety.

Montrose's victorious run was finally brought to an end when he was surprised in heavy mist by a large force under Lieutenant General David Leslie, at Philiphaugh in September 1645. This reverse occurred three months after the main English Royalist army had been trounced at Naseby, and added to the escalating despair in Charles I's ranks. Montrose, refused a pardon, went into exile in Norway. The English king now seemed to have no Scottish cards left to play.

Despite this, in the spring of 1646, defeated in England and looking for a way forward, Charles I misguidedly handed himself over to the Scots. He had hoped that the allies of his English enemies would now support him, perhaps out of some underly-

---

* Argyll swore by a Latin saying that translated as 'Dead men don't bite.'

ing loyalty to his Stuart blood, but also because he had been fed inaccurate information about the Scots' attitude to him by the French ambassador to England. The Scots, intrigued but confused by the appearance of their leading opponent in their midst, repeatedly tried to persuade Charles to take the Covenant, explaining that if he did not, they would be unable help him. But the king refused.

Charles had written to Henrietta Maria, earlier that year, saying that he would do anything to get Scottish aid as long as it did not involve him 'giving up the Church of England, with which I will not part upon any condition whatsoever'.[15] While he dug his heels in, citing his unshakeable religious principles, he was also aware of the political importance of his stance: 'The nature of Presbyterian government is to steal or force the Crown from the king's head,' he told Henrietta Maria. 'For their chief maxim is (and I know it to be true), that all kings must submit to Christ's kingdom, of which they are the sole governors ... so that yielding to the Scots in this particular, I should both go against my conscience and ruin my crown.'[16]

Henrietta Maria had agreed with her husband's assessment. She told him, in a letter of October 1646, when the First English Civil War was lost: 'We must endeavour to have the Scots for us, without nevertheless taking the Covenant, or doing anything which shall be dishonourable ... since we have suffered so much, we must resolve to finish with honour.'

The king stuck to his views for several months, with no hint of compromise, leaving the Scots with no choice but to believe him when he said that he was not for turning. They had long made it clear that their God came before their monarch, and in early 1647 they effectively sold him to England's Parliament, on condition that no harm would come to him – he was, after all, their king too.

There were, though, some moderate Covenanters who were open to a compromise with the king. They were party to 'the

Engagement', an agreement that was secretly negotiated in December 1647 while Charles was held prisoner by Parliament on the Isle of Wight. Charles guaranteed these Scottish allies a confirmation of the Solemn League and Covenant in London's Parliament, provided neither he nor any other Englishman was obliged to take the Covenant. There would also be steps towards unification of the two kingdoms, with the Scots being allowed a greater say in the government of England until that plan reached fruition. In return, Charles I was to be rescued from his island imprisonment and taken to London, where a settlement would be forced out of his enemies in Parliament. The main Scottish army would stand poised to invade if the king's and the Engagers' demands were rejected.

Argyll, Wariston and the other hardline Covenanters were against any such alliance, because it would compromise their rigid religious beliefs. They felt vindicated when the Engagers' army was destroyed at the battle of Preston, in August 1648. The Kirk party was now left in control in Scotland. In January 1649 it decreed that any who had agreed to the Engagement must be barred from public office.

The news of the execution of the king at the end of that same month changed everything. It provoked horror throughout Scotland. The Kirk already felt that Parliament had failed to honour its commitment to settle Presbyterianism on England. Now it had also, contrary to its promise, beheaded the Scots' king.

In Edinburgh on 5 February 1649, six days after Charles I's execution, Prince Charles was proclaimed king of Scotland, England and Ireland. War with England was from that point inevitable.

While the Covenanters were quick to proclaim the exiled prince 'King Charles II', they made it clear that he could not actually rule until he had signed the National Covenant, with its guarantees of religious and political union. The following month a delegation of Covenanters travelled to see Charles in the Netherlands, and presented him with a bundle, carefully bound in one form, containing their demands and creeds, with the Covenant at its core.

Charles was startled by the terms offered. 'They presented to him three propositions, demanding that he should banish Montrose & all other malignants and evil counselors from his court; that he should take the Covenant himself & establish it through all his dominions; & that he should bring but an hundred persons with him into Scotland, among which there should be none that had bore arms for his late Majesty.'[17]

Charles's disappointment at the proposals was aggravated by the attitude of his hosts, the deputies of the various Dutch States, who encouraged him to agree to any terms put forward by the Scots. They knew he had nowhere else to turn, other than to Ireland, and that would involve what was, to them, a deeply troubling alliance with Roman Catholics.

But Charles still had hopes that Ireland could prove to be his saviour, because the Royalists there had allied with a Catholic confederacy to form a significant force. The resulting army, commanded by the Marquess of Ormonde, was busying itself in anticipation of an invasion by England's New Model Army. After visiting his mother at St-Germain, Charles returned to Jersey in September 1649, ready to cross to Ireland. But by the time he landed on the island, things had changed very much for the worse. For in mid-August Cromwell had landed near Dublin.

Cromwell soon eliminated Ireland as a possible springboard for the Royalists, tearing through inadequate defences and inferior troops, leaving still unforgotten and unforgiven carnage in his wake. By early 1650, Scotland was the only possible source of military help available to Charles. In February he returned from Jersey to the Continent knowing he had a choice: either side with the Scots, or continue in impotent exile.

It was a question of what compromise he could now accept to win over the deeply distrustful Covenanters. For their part, they already knew quite a lot about him. He seemed to be very far removed from the epitome of humility and religious devotion that they might have hoped for.

# 4

# The Crown, Without Glory

*He that sits on a dunghill today,*
*may tomorrow sit on a throne.*

The Man in the Moon, April 1650

The Marquess of Montrose, the leading Scottish Royalist, was still in exile when the news of Charles I's beheading reached him. He, like the queen, was dumbstruck with bewilderment. When he could at last bring himself to speak, it was to swear an oath of vengeance. He vowed to see that the king's heir was placed on his rightful throne, or to perish in the attempt: 'As I never had passion upon Earth so strong as that to do your King father service, so it shall be my study,' he promised the newly declared king of Scotland, 'to show it redoubled for the recovery of you.'[1] Montrose's unquestioning loyalty would not be reciprocated by his new master.

Charles agreed to look again at the Scottish offering rejected in the Netherlands the previous year. Those speaking for the king justified an agreement with the Scots as 'an effectual means to save Ireland, recover the King's Right in England, and to bring the Murderers of His Majesty's Father to condign punishment'.[2]

Charles encouraged Montrose to return to fight for him in the Highlands. This was in order to put pressure on the Scottish Covenanters there, while Charles negotiated with their representatives in the Netherlands, but Montrose took the royal instruction at face value. He arrived in the northern tip of Scotland with 500 German, Danish and Dutch mercenaries, and some hardy but untrained men from the Orkneys. But the clans failed to rise in his support, fearing the strength of the Covenanters while sensing the weakness of the Crown.

Before he set off for the Netherlands, Charles went to see his mother in a bid to smooth over the differences in the Royalist camp. Lord Byron, one of Charles I's close supporters, wrote to the Marquess of Ormonde on 11 March 1650 that Henrietta Maria and Charles had just spent ten days together in Beauvais. The king was now heading for Breda, while his mother headed for Paris. 'They met with great kindness on both sides and I hope will part so,' wrote Byron, 'and with a full reconcilement of those differences that formerly were betwixt them.' Byron pointed to various figures in Charles's court, including Sir Edward Hyde, who remained set against the treaty with the Scots: '[They] have by all possible means endeavoured to render the treaty we hope for, altogether fruitless to the king.'[3]

A few days later another Royalist in exile, Henry Seymour, reported to Ormonde that Charles was determined on action, even if the Scots proved impossible to negotiate with: 'If the treaty [with the Scots] succeed not his Majesty is resolved to lose no more time in idleness, and therefore must either go to you, or to my lord Montrose into Scotland. His own inclinations lean to the first. But a powerful interest [Henrietta Maria] ... prefers the other, whose game lies another way.'[4]

The negotiations with the Scots lasted from 26 March till the end of April 1650. Charles then capitulated to all demands relating directly to Scotland, but not those that the Scots had pushed for which were connected to England or Ireland. As king of Scotland, he agreed to swear the Oath of the Covenant, and said he would commit to the supreme rule of the Presbyterian Kirk in Scotland.

One of the Scottish delegation, Alexander Jaffray, recorded in his diary the joylessness of the resulting union: 'Being sent there by the [Scottish] Parliament, in the year 1650, for that same business, we did sinfully both entangle and engage the nation and our selves, and that poor young prince to whom we were sent; making him sign and swear a covenant, which we knew, from clear and demonstrable reasons, that he hated in his heart. Yet, finding that upon these terms only, he could be admitted to rule over us (all other means having failed him), he sinfully complied with what we most sinfully pressed upon him – where, I must confess, to my apprehension, our sin was more than his.'[5]

At the same time, news of the alliance gave some English Royalists hope, John Crouch printing in the periodical *The Man in the Moon*:

> *Then cheer up Cavaliers; I hear*
> *The Drums for Charles do beat,*
> *And frozen Hearts half-dead with fear,*
> *Revive with Loyal heat.*[6]

But the sudden submission to the Covenanters' Scottish demands had an immediate, terrible and shameful cost. Charles had agreed, as one of the conditions of Scottish support, to disown his family's great Scottish champion. Deprived of royal patronage, the Marquess of Montrose was now at the mercy of Argyll and the Covenanters.

Charles sent Montrose a letter with confirmation that he had decided to form a pact with his deadliest enemies. It was the ultimate royal betrayal. In the same communication he let Montrose know that he had decided to honour him by making him a Knight of the Garter, the highest order of chivalry in Britain. It was a meaningless gesture. Both men knew that Montrose's life was now hanging by a thread.

Montrose's small force was surprised and routed by his enemies at Carbisdale, forty miles north of Inverness, on 27 April 1650. Despite being wounded in the battle, Montrose managed to escape its ensuing carnage. After wandering the hills without food, being reduced to eating his gloves, he sought refuge in Ardvreck Castle, whose owner, Neil MacLeod of Assynt, had fought alongside him five years earlier. But his host sold his name to infamy by betraying Montrose, and accepting the reward on his head.

On 18 May Montrose was paraded through the packed streets of Edinburgh. He was made to stand in a cart, before being transferred to the hangman's wagon, in which he was forced to sit down, and was bound to his seat for the final leg of his journey to Tolbooth prison, where conditions were famously grim. At this point his eyes are said to have met the squinty glare of his old enemy the Marquess of Argyll, watching from a window on high.

Two days later Montrose was taken to a brief hearing, where he was sentenced to death. Unusually for a nobleman, he was to be denied the merciful swiftness of the axe, and was condemned to being hanged. Such heartlessness was the payback for the turmoil and embarrassment he had caused his enemies during his years of triumph.

On 21 May, the day of Montrose's execution, some of his enemies taunted him for bothering to comb his hair when death was so near. He replied: 'My head is still my own. Tonight, when it will be yours, treat it as you please.'[7]

Lord Wariston watched from a window in his home as Montrose walked to his death, defiant to the end. He had dressed himself in a scarlet cape, silk stockings and ribboned shoes. One observer said he looked more like a bridegroom than a condemned man.

Montrose mounted the gallows, assembled on a thirty-foot-high platform that towered over Mercat Cross. He chose not to pray. In a short statement he said that Charles I 'had lived a saint and died a martyr: I pray God I may end so: if ever I would wish my soul in another man's stead it is in his'.[8]

After the life had been throttled out of him, Montrose's body was cut up. His head was stuck on a spike attached to Tolbooth's upper reaches, and his arms and legs were dispatched to four of the other great cities of Scotland. There they were nailed up high, as deterrents to those who dared to oppose the Covenant. His trunk and bowels were buried in a casket on Burgh Moor, to the south of Edinburgh.

Sir Edward Hyde was on a diplomatic mission to Spain when he learnt that Charles had agreed to the Scots' demands, and that he had subsequently landed at Garmouth, forty-five miles east of Inverness, on 24 June 1650. By this stage Charles had made further concessions, including swearing to both Covenants, and disowning his loyal supporters in Ireland. 'If there be judgement of Heaven upon him,' Hyde wrote, 'I can only pray it may fall as light on him as may be.'

On his progress south to Edinburgh, Charles saw something curious hanging from the gates into Aberdeen. On asking what it was, he was informed that it was one of Montrose's severed arms.

From the outset, Charles found the contract he had agreed with the Scots hard to bear. His hosts insisted on most of his retinue being sent away, because of their 'malignant' nature. Meanwhile, to demonstrate his commitment to the Covenant, he was led through denunciations of his parents, addressing their supposed sins, while also being forced to confess his own many personal shortcomings.

Having humbled himself before God, he was also obliged to debase himself before the Marquess of Argyll. The marquess extracted a promise from Charles that he would receive £40,000 from him if he succeeded in retrieving his English throne.

Argyll was also keen to discuss the possibility of Charles marrying his daughter, Lady Anne Campbell. Charles's father and grandfather had wed princesses from France and Denmark, respectively. For him to have to seriously contemplate marriage to the daughter of one of his subjects showed just how devalued Charles's eligibility had become, by this stage of his exile from England.

The austerity of his everyday life now, with its dour sermons and endless prayers, was far removed from the idle, easygoing court in exile that Charles had become used to. While to the world he exhibited acceptance and charm, inside he was furious at the repeated humiliations: 'The Scots have dealt with me very ill!' he told an Anglican dean.[9]

Oliver Cromwell was recalled from Ireland in 1650, to replace Sir Thomas Fairfax as Lord General of Parliament's army. Fairfax had retired rather than invade Scotland because, he said, 'we are [still] joined in the National League and Covenant'. He refused to attack his old allies.

In late July 1650, in response to the provocation of Charles's presence on British soil and the Scots' promise to place the English crown on his head, Cromwell invaded Scotland with 16,000 men.

It was a testing country to fight in. The Scots held fast behind a defensive line that had Edinburgh at its core. The English, meanwhile, had to contend with a relentlessly hostile landscape. Symptomatic of this was the aggravating presence of 'Mosstroopers', small guerrilla bands of Lowlanders who lay in wait outside the invaders' garrisons, picking off stragglers and disrupting supplies and communications.

Cromwell was one of many in his army to become seriously ill, and it seemed that he and his soldiers would need to retreat unless the opportunity soon presented itself for battle. Even then, the

Scots would heavily outnumber the invaders. Disease and desertion reduced the English to 11,000 fighting men, while the Scottish army was 22,000 strong.

The two mismatched armies eventually lined up to fight in early September, near Dunbar, the port twenty-eight miles north of the border which was Cromwell's main supply point. The Scottish generals, the Earl of Leven and his cousin David Leslie, had established an advantageous position for their troops on the formidable Doon Hill. Cromwell's line of retreat on land had been cut off, and Leven and Leslie expected the English cavalry to make a break for it, leaving their infantry behind to surrender. But things now took a bizarre turn.

The leading Covenanters had already reduced their army's effectiveness. They had insisted that it be purged of eighty officers and 3,000 experienced men, because their religious beliefs were not considered sufficiently godly. The same fanatics now compromised their troops further, ordering an immediate abandonment of their advantageous position on Doon Hill.

Despite the enemy's needless surrender of the tactical advantage, Cromwell was extremely agitated before what would clearly be a pivotal battle: he chewed his lips so furiously that blood was seen dripping down his chin. Before dawn on 3 September he ordered an attack on the Scottish army, which was left disjointed by its new deployment. He started on the enemy's right wing, which his forces overwhelmed before turning on their centre. When that force was also overcome, he set about its left wing. The Scots' large numerical advantage was negated by this three-stage strike. That day the New Model Army – disciplined, professional, and sure that God was on its side – pulled off Cromwell's most startling triumph.

The English lost just twenty-eight men at Dunbar. Leven and Leslie had up to 3,000 killed, and a further 10,000 captured. It was a defeat of biblical proportions, in an age when God's hand was seen in everything. Indeed, there was a suitably Old Testament ring to Cromwell's report to Parliament on the Royalist losses: 'God made them as stubble to our swords.'

Charles could not contain his joy at the defeat of the allies to whom he had been so miserably shackled, and threw his hat in the air at the news. For their part, the Covenanters tried to shift blame for the debacle onto their young king's shoulders. They claimed he had shown a lack of commitment to his religious promises, and divine punishment had been the inevitable consequence.

The Covenanters also rebuked the king's followers. John Middleton was a Scot who had risen dramatically through the army's ranks, from fourteen-year-old pikeman to lieutenant general. He had fought against the Royalists in the First Civil War, but had then changed sides, joining the Engagers and leading their cavalry in the Scottish invasion of England in the summer of 1648. Middleton had been captured at the battle of Preston, but was released on parole. He soon broke that commitment, allying himself closely to the new king of Scotland.

The Kirk party noted Middleton's Royalist sympathies and allegiance to their domestic political rivals, as well as his general debauchery, and in October 1650 excommunicated him. He was only allowed to return to serve in Charles's army after the humiliation of a public penance in Dundee, when he was forced to wear sackcloth and ashes. This was an embarrassment that Middleton would never forget. It was also typical of the heavy-handed treatment meted out to Charles and his followers. The young king was finding it increasingly hard to bear.

A month after Dunbar, Royalists under the Marquess of Huntly attempted a *coup d'état* in support of Charles in the north of Scotland. They intended to bring Highlanders to the king, and so free him from Covenanter control. This design was known as 'The Start', and though it came about with Charles's blessing, it failed because of his indecision.

Leaving Perth under the pretence of participating in a falconry hunting party, the king made a dash for freedom once he had got a fair distance from the city. But his absence was quickly noted, and a force was sent to retrieve him. He was soon overhauled. Two officers who led the pursuit discovered him 'lying in a nasty room on an old bolster above a mat of sedge and rushes, over-wearied and very fearful'.[10] The ignominious end to this escape attempt is of particular interest, given how Charles was to behave exactly a year later, when on the run for his life.

On 1 January 1651, at Scone in Perthshire, the coronation took place that formalised Charles's status as king of Scotland. The Marquess of Argyll, happy to remind the monarch of where true power lay, placed the crown on Charles's head and installed him on the throne.

In reality, though, matters in Scotland were turning in the king's favour. The Covenanters had lost much credibility through their defeat at Dunbar, and Charles had an easy charm that his northern subjects warmed to. He was proving to be a popular king.

Meanwhile, despite their spectacular triumph at Dunbar, the English still had little control over large areas of Scotland. David Leslie clung on determinedly in defensive mode north of the Firth of Forth, with his headquarters at Stirling. But on 17 July 1650 the deadlock was broken when Major General John Lambert played a masterstroke, sending a seaborne expedition into Fife, outflanking Leslie's army. Three days later he defeated the Scottish force sent to meet him at the battle of Inverkeithing. The victory gave the New Model Army control of the Firth of Forth, and cut Charles off from his supporters in the Highlands.

Cromwell now moved his main army north of the defeated Scots. As he did so, he deliberately left the road to England open, hoping Charles would be tempted to lead his men south. Cromwell was confident that the army he had with him, when combined with the forces he had left standing ready at home, could defeat any Scottish force the king could muster. He also believed that the people of England would unite against what would in effect be a foreign invasion, should the king of Scotland take the bait.

Charles was unaware of the trap, and shaken by the enemy advantage gained at Inverkeithing. At the same time he was desperate to get away from Scotland, to regain some of the authority and independence that had been taken from him by the all-controlling Covenanters. He had been an exile since leaving Cornwall for the Isles of Scilly more than five years earlier. Now that he seemed to have been presented with the prospect of a clear run south, the young king dared to dream of a triumphant return to England. He ordered his forces to prepare for invasion, even though his military commanders urged caution.

George Downing had grown up in Massachusetts, and had attended Harvard College, being one of the nine young men who comprised its first year of graduates in 1642. He had since returned to England, to support Parliament as a preacher before switching to military service. From 1650 he was Scoutmaster General of Scotland, in charge of the Commonwealth's agents in that country. He reported to London that 'The generality [i.e. the generals] of the Scots were against the present attempt for England, but the King told them, he would march with such as would follow him: he looks very despondingly, but must adventure all.'[11]

The Parliamentary commander in north-western England, Major General Thomas Harrison, was a religious zealot with complete confidence that he and his Puritan comrades were doing the Lord's work. He was sure that Charles and his army were destined for defeat. Like Downing, he sensed that the enemy's decision to head south had arisen from a place of weakness: the king's men clearly had 'a mighty terror from God upon them', Harrison wrote. He urged 'every good man' to take 'all possible

❦

# 5

# A Foreign Invasion

*The Scottish Armie, which would never bee brought
to fight in their own Countrie, have now left the same
for lost; and are marched into England.*

The Council of State to the Lord Mayor of London,
10 August 1651

Charles entered England near Carlisle on 5 August 1651, at the head of forty-six regiments of Scottish soldiers. They came from all over Scotland, among them Urry's Horse from Aberdeen and Banffshire, the Earl of Home's cavalry and infantry from Berwick, Clan MacKinnon from Skye, MacNeil's Foot from the Outer Hebrides, Lord Drummond's two regiments from Perthshire, and the Duke of Hamilton's Horse from Clydesdale.

But the spymaster George Downing wrote to his controllers in London of the despondency that he detected at the core of this army, and not just amongst its high command: 'They are not above 11,000 men at most; they have very little provision with them; through all the country in Scotland we find their runaways: in a word, nothing was left but a desperate cure, or a desperate ruin, wherewith my heart is filled in the confident expectation of.'[1]

The same sentiment stirred in the breast of Charles's senior Scottish officer, Lieutenant General Leslie. When, in battle, a junior officer rode to Leslie to report 'The enemy is approaching,' it would have been understandable if this fifty-year-old professional soldier had taken a moment to remind himself exactly who it was that he was risking his life against this time. Leslie had, in a distinguished but somewhat relentless career, unsheathed his sword, then ridden hard at Germans, Lithuanians, Poles, Spaniards, Englishmen and fellow Scots.

He had been in command of 7,000 Covenanters when they overcame the 800 Royalists under the Marquess of Montrose at the battle of Philiphaugh in September 1645. A hundred of Montrose's men surrendered on the promise that their lives would be spared. But Presbyterian ministers intervened, telling Leslie that such mercy was folly and urging him to go back on his word. Leslie had all the prisoners shot in cold blood, along with 300 of their camp followers, many of them women and children.

Two years later Leslie defaulted on a similar promise. While besieging an enemy stronghold at Dunaverty Castle in Kintyre, he cut off the water supply, forcing the defenders to surrender. He then ordered the slaughter of 300 prisoners, three of their leaders being shot while on their knees, midway through their final prayers. Others were thrown to drown in the sea, or were cast to their death on the rocks below.

When this effective but brutal soldier learnt that he was to march south, he must have hoped against hope that he would not be forced to fight Cromwell. Leslie had served under Cromwell at the decisive battle of Marston Moor in the First Civil War, where Charles I had lost control of the north of England in a day. The Parliamentary victory there was thanks in large part to Leslie's timely courage and deft, soldierly, touch: the Scots' cavalry charge had tipped the scales in favour of Cromwell's squadrons, and guaranteed the defeat of the Royalist talisman, Prince Rupert. That day, it later became clear, Leslie had helped turn the tide not just of a battle, but of the whole war.

The redheaded, pink-faced Scot, with his dandyish beard, knew as well as anyone, from his own observations on both sides of the battlefield, the supreme level of brilliance that Cromwell was capable of. While he had won with him at Marston Moor, he had lost against him at Dunbar. Leslie appreciated that the Lord General's soldiers, drunk on their sense of godliness, never considered defeat a possibility. As the Commonwealth had boasted two years previously: 'The great God of battle, by a continued series of providences and wonders [has] determined very much in favour of the Parliament.'[2] They saw no reason for that pattern to change.

Leslie had been against the invasion of England by his new king from the start, preferring to continue the attritional defensive war in his homeland. This style of fighting could be expected to provide a constant supply of reinforcements for the king, in a draining and hostile environment for the invading English. Charles's new plan would reverse those favourable conditions.

But Leslie's voice was not loud enough to overturn the king's impetuous urge to try to reverse a year of military disappointment by capitalising on the southern kingdom's apparent vulnerability. Charles was determined to go south, and his impulsiveness trumped Leslie's experience, knowhow, and feeling of impending doom.

On 12 August Parliament passed an Act that noted that 'Charles Stuart' and his forces had been forced to leave Scotland after 'finding their own weakness and disability to continue longer in that country'. The king's army had not so much invaded Scotland, it was declared, but had rather 'fled into England'. The Act stated that Charles had 'been declared a Traitor to the Parliament and people of England', and that anyone who communicated with him, or offered him support of any kind – 'any victuals, provisions, arms, ammunition, horses, plate, money, men, or any other relief what-soever' – would be guilty of high treason, and 'be condemned to suffer death'.[3] It was understood by all that Charles, already declared traitor, would suffer the same fate if captured. But what if he succeeded?

Lucy Hutchinson, the wife of a leading regicide, recorded the panic in the highest echelons of the Commonwealth as news of the Scottish advance reached them: 'The Council of State ... at that time were very much surprised at hearing that the King of Scots was passed by Cromwell, and entered with a great army into England. Bradshaw himself, as stout-hearted as he was, privately could not conceal his fear; some raged and uttered sad discontents against Cromwell, and suspicions of his fidelity.' Eighteen months earlier these men had dared to judge and kill a king. Now that king's son was heading south, with vengeance his spur.

'Both the city and the country,' Lucy Hutchinson recalled, '... were all amazed, and doubtful of their own and the Common-wealth's safety. Some could not hide very pale and unmanly fears, and were in such a distraction of spirit as much disturbed their councils.' Several of these meetings were, she recorded, punctuated with 'raging and crying out'.

Lucy's husband, Colonel John Hutchinson, was an unflappable figure who had kept the Parliamentary cause afloat in Nottingham during the most challenging years of the First Civil War. He was not a man for surrender, or for flexible principles. Taken aback by his comrades' panic, he urged them 'to apply themselves to coun-sels of safety, and not to lose time in accusing others, while they might yet provide to save the endangered realm; or at least to fall nobly in defence of it, and not to yield to fear and despair'.

Colonel Hutchinson set about rounding up all known support-ers of the Crown in Nottinghamshire, to prevent them from join-ing the Scottish army. It was a procedure repeated throughout England and Wales. 'Many gentlemen in the county of Monmouth, suspected not to be friends to the Parliament, are secured, and their horses seized on for the service of the State', the newsbook the *True Informer* reported.[4] In Essex, the Reverend Ralph Josselin recorded in his diary for 29 August 1651 that there was an 'Order to disarm and secure malignants in the County, and to raise volunteers for the security and defence of the same'.[5] All known or suspected Royalists who were still at large had their weapons confiscated, and were forbidden to move more than five miles from their homes. While the threat from the north grew, the Council of State tightened its control throughout England by raising and reinforcing its local militia forces.

There were fears that the Royalists might appear in other parts of England, in support of the Scottish land army. The east coast was seen as being particularly vulnerable. King's Lynn, in north Norfolk, and Lowestoft, in Suffolk, were considered the most likely landing points, while Felixstowe was also 'a place of great concern'.[6] General Blake, in his forty-two-gun flagship *Victory*, was ordered to keep his fleet ready off the East Anglian coast to intercept any seaborne invaders.

At the same time the Council of State wrote to Lieutenant Colonel Edward Salmon, governor of Hull, a city known to contain a large armoury: 'We know that the Scottish army in England has a special eye upon Hull, and has long had designs upon it.'[7] The number of phantom naval invasions keeping the Commonwealth on its toes demonstrates the deep concern that Charles's progress had triggered.

Reports of the king of Scotland's advance into England were eagerly followed around Europe. Michiel Morosini, Venice's ambassador to France, reported secretly to the doge and Senate: 'Such favourable news comes from England that if there was not reason to fear that the queen [Henrietta Maria] announces it designedly, it might be possible to hope for the restoration of the monarchy. The king has entered England with 16,000 combatants, he defeated two corps of cavalry and is proceeding with growing prosperity, various towns have deserted for him, while his forces are augmented by the nobles who keep flocking to him.' Morosini added one significant caveat to his dispatch: 'But he is being followed by Cromwell, and here the Court prefers to hope rather than to fear.'[8] The champion of the New Model Army had set out from Leith with eight mounted and eight infantry regiments, looking to join up with Parliamentary forces converging on Charles from two other directions.

Charles's envoy to Venice was Thomas Killigrew, whose expertise was in the theatre, not diplomacy. He boasted that his king was unopposed on his triumphant march south, and that it was thus fair to 'hope, with the Divine assistance, [that] his Majesty will soon recover his crowns'. Killigrew also claimed that his master was 'supported by all the nobles and leading people' of England.[9] Killigrew chose not to weigh down his pronouncements with detail or evidence.

Sir Edward Nicholas, one of the late king's closest advisers, heard equally upbeat reports, which helped to brighten up his impoverished exile in Antwerp. These also exaggerated the progress of Charles's march south, and the vulnerability of his enemies. Nicholas was right to note, though, that the royal advance 'hath given those at London a notable alarm'.[10]

Similarly optimistic reports reached Bruges, from where Richard Parker wrote home: 'Travellers from London report that Shrewsbury, Chester, Bristol, and Lichfield have declared for the King, and that he was within thirty miles of London, with 15,000 horse; that they are full of fear and have disarmed many of the citizens of London, which I wish we may find confirmed by post.'[11] But the confirmation never came.

The Council of State had better intelligence, which soon soothed the councillors' initial panic. It was noted that 'few come to' Charles, 'and those generally the scum of the people'. Richard

Baxter, a leading English Puritan, put this reluctance to join the invaders down to the Scots' recent defeats at Dunbar and Inverkeithing. This, he believed, 'persuaded all men that necessity forced them [to invade], and they were look'd upon rather as flying than as marching into England; and few men will put themselves into a flying army which is pursued by the conquering enemy.'[12]

The Scots were also ragged, which deterred would-be recruits from believing they would triumph. They were clearly under-equipped for their task, to the extent that their artillery was comprised of guns made of leather, not metal. The Duke of Hamilton, leading his cavalry regiment south, wrote with embarrassment about how 'people were laughing at the ridiculousness of our condition'.

National prejudice also played a part, for the invaders were regarded as strangely alien beings. A Parliamentarian newsbook enjoyed the fundamental problems that Charles's sympathisers in the west of England experienced in basic interactions with the Scots: 'Although there are many in those parts that are disaffected enough to the Parliament, yet by reason of the broad language of the Highlanders, they cannot understand them, and by the reason of the mixture of many other nations in the King's army, they stand off at a distance, and look upon them rather with eyes of amaze-ment, than affection.'

The Scots were believed, after centuries of English propaganda against their fierce neighbours, to be compromised by an inborn savagery: 'It is advertised,' the *True Informer* said, 'that many of the Scots Foot are sick in England, the softness of the southern air not suiting with the toughness of their temper, and complexion.'[13] The wild men of the north were viewed as fish out of water.

False reports whipped up further hostility to the Scots. They were wrongly accused of murdering civilians in Nantwich and Northwich in cold blood. In fact, Charles insisted on the strictest discipline from all his men. When two of his soldiers were found guilty of stealing apples from an orchard, they were executed. But

Parliament's propaganda served its purpose, provoking widespread fury and galvanising resistance. 'The early and angry drums did this morning call forth all our City Regiments into the fields,' recorded a London newsbook, 'where with the hamlets, and the soldiers of the Borough of Southwark, they exercised their army, and made gallant appearance in Finsbury Fields, the Parliament being present.'[14]

There was a similar account from Tothill, near Westminster, stating that: 'London had a rendezvous last week, where were 14,000 horse and foot in the field, at a very short warning.'[15] In a dramatic flourish, the public hangman appeared in front of the troops to burn a declaration that Charles had released, asserting his right to the throne. Then, after the beating of drums and the sounding of trumpets, Parliament's condemnation of the Scottish invasion was read out in full.

Sick and wounded soldiers, billeted in and around London, came forward to offer their services in the protection of the capital. They wanted to assist the regiments under the command of two regicide colonels, John Barkstead and Owen Rowe. Barkstead and 2,000 men had been entrusted with guarding Parliament and the City of London. Rowe, a Puritan merchant who had helped settle colonies in Massachusetts and New Haven, Connecticut, stood ready with his regiment of militia cavalry.

Marchamont Nedham's *Mercurius Politicus* of 28 August 1651 congratulated the English on staying wise to the madness of supporting the Royalist-Scottish invasion: 'What a happiness it is, to live to see this day, wherein we have experience of the noble temper of a Nation! That though many of them be divided in matter of particular interest and opinion; yet they so well understand the general interest of England, that they scorn to embark themselves in such courses, as must of necessity, either debase us under the miserable yolk of a Scottish Tyranny, or vassalise us unto the will of an arbitrary Tyrant; for, had God given over the people to run a-madding after the Royal puppet, we could have expected no other consequence, but endless taxes, and inevitable slavery.'

There was relief in the Parliamentary high command that Charles's army remained almost entirely Scottish. Apart from the disabling of known Royalists across the land, few Englishmen welcomed the eruption of yet more warfare so soon after the bloodiest conflict that the country would ever know in terms of loss of life per head of population. John Milton had warned, nine months after the late king's beheading: 'his son's restorement ... would be so far from conducing to our happiness ... that it would inevitably throw us back again into all our past and fulfilled miseries; would force us to fight over again all our tedious wars, and put us to another fatal struggling for Liberty and life, more dubious than the former'.[16] This was a message that found an audience in many Royalist circles.

Even Oxford, which had offered the late king a level of loyalty unsurpassed anywhere else in his three kingdoms, preferred peace under a victorious enemy to a return to the bloody turmoil that the king of Scotland's invasion now promised. It seemed likely to Oxford's inhabitants that their city would be the chosen destination of the Scots after they had gathered up Royalist reinforcements in Lancashire and Wales on their way south. Oxford was an attractive staging post from which to launch an attack on London, fifty miles to the south-east. As a result Charles I's capital in the First Civil War prepared a force to dispute his son's invasion in what was now the third such conflict.

The Council of State noted with appreciation the readiness of Oxford's scholars to serve the Commonwealth. Fresh fortifications were erected around New College, and throughout August commissions were granted to a range of volunteer officers eager to come to the republic's defence. Captain Draper, governor of Oxford, was ordered to expect the arrival of Colonel Heane, one of the New Model Army's most respected commanders. He was coming with significant reinforcements, and a commission to take over the city's governorship.

Charles had assumed that his charm and physical presence would entice some cities to open their gates to his men as his march progressed. 'The king omitted nothing that might encourage the country to rise with him, or at least to be neuter,' one of his cavalry officers wrote. On approaching Shrewsbury he wrote to Colonel Humphrey Mackworth, Parliament's governor, in flattering terms. He saluted Mackworth as a gentleman, far removed from the rougher element on the rebel side, then demanded that the colonel surrender Shrewsbury's town and castle to him. In return the king promised to pardon him, and 'to grant you presently anything you shall reasonably desire'.

But Mackworth's reply was full of contempt. He addressed it not to any king, but simply to 'The Commander-in-Chief of the Scottish army'. In it he stated: 'I resolve to be found unremovable [as] the faithful servant of the Commonwealth of England: and if you believe me to be a gentleman (as you say you do), you may believe I will be faithful to my trust.'[17] When Parliament learnt of Mackworth's defiant words of loyalty, it sent him a gold chain as a reward.

Contrary to what his English courtiers had promised him prior to the invasion, Charles was joined by few Englishmen of note on his advance south. The 7th Earl of Derby was the most eminent. He was persuaded to join the king at the insistence of his wife Charlotte. The Countess of Derby was the daughter of a French duke, and a granddaughter of the Dutch leader William the Silent, whose obstinate resistance to Spanish domination had been legendary.

The countess had shown resilience during the Civil Wars to match that of her grandfather. In early 1644 she had overseen the successful defence of the family's main residence, Lathom House in Lancashire. Her garrison of 300, which included snipers drawn from the estate's gamekeepers, stood firm for three months against a besieging force of 2,000 Parliamentarians under Sir Thomas Fairfax before being relieved. Even the rebel newsbook *Mercurius Politicus* conceded the countess's great achievement, noting that 'the Amazonian Lady ... hath so dignified her Noble House by those heroic feats of Lathom House'.[18]

The Derbys' vast landholdings included the Isle of Man, which they maintained as a Royalist stronghold throughout the First and Second Civil Wars. The earl now left his indomitable wife in charge of the island while he set off for the English mainland, landing on 15 August and meeting up with the king two days later. With him came 300 men, drawn from all of the Isle of Man's parishes.

Many of the difficulties within Charles's army were personified by the soft-faced, dark-haired, thoroughly decent Derby. During the Civil War he had been given command of the Royalist forces in Lancashire and Cheshire. This leading role was awarded because of his hereditary wealth and influence in the two counties, which enabled him to hand 3,000 men to the king early in the conflict. But Derby had limited military ability. His record included a demoralising defeat at Whalley, in Lancashire in 1643, when his defensive generalship cost the Royalists the day. He also participated, a year later, in the storming of Bolton, where a massacre of a thousand soldiers and townspeople took place. The king had promised this lacklustre soldier governorship of five northern and western English counties, as well as all of those in north Wales, if he would help his invasion now. It was desperate stuff.

Derby's rigid religious views undermined his main task, which was to attract more supporters to the king's banner. He had alienated the leading Roman Catholic Royalists throughout Lancashire at the outset of the Civil Wars because of his undisguised contempt for their beliefs. He did not like the High Church Protestantism that Charles I had championed either. Meanwhile he was unable to accept the Scots as allies, since he still saw them as the instruments of the late king's death. He was an unlikely recruiting officer.

Derby separated from the main royal force in an attempt to whip up more support for the invading army. He appeared before a meeting at Warrington, which had previously been his military headquarters, and urged the townspeople to join Charles's cause. But this approach was rejected by Warrington's Presbyterians, unwilling to side with the earl when he refused to take the Covenant.

By contrast, the generals in Parliament's New Model Army were all by now seasoned and accomplished soldiers, whose more modest social backgrounds were no impediment to high command. Thomas Harrison, in charge of one of the rebel armies in England, was the son of a butcher. John Lambert, who commanded another, was the son of a Yorkshire gentleman. They had both risen through ability to the pinnacle of the New Model Army. These two major generals joined forces near Bolton on 13 August.

Harrison had made himself one of the most feared and hated of the Parliamentary commanders, distinguishing himself at the decisive battles of Marston Moor, Naseby and Langport. Extreme in his religious beliefs, he was buoyed by the clear certainty that God backed Parliament's cause. He trusted that 'the Lord hath now tempted out the enemy from his trenches, fastnesses, and advantages; and we doubt not but He will very speedily discomfit them, and cut this work short in Righteousness'.[19] Harrison also looked forward to the prospect of personal revenge: he had 'got a sore wound' (so severe that, at the time, it was expected to prove fatal) when fighting the Scots at Appleby in Cumbria during their invasion of 1648, which had deprived him of a role in the decisive battle of Preston later that summer. This time he was determined to be present at the final elimination of the enemy's military threat.

Lambert was thirty-two years old during the Worcester campaign, but he had already served Parliament with startling distinction for nearly a decade. An inspirational figure at the battle of Preston, he had performed with equal brilliance during the recent campaigns in Scotland. His close observation of the awkwardness of the remodelled enemy lines before the battle of Dunbar had led to the tactics that won the day so crushingly. Cromwell's poor health for much of his time in Scotland meant he frequently leant on the energetic genius of Lambert, who was two decades his junior. At the same time, the men of the New Model Army admired Lambert for his rare ability, and loved him for his personal courage. He led from the front, and bore the wounds that went with such risk. And it was Lambert's brave and brilliant leadership at the decisive victory at Inverkeithing that had unlocked the Scottish defensive campaign, and persuaded Charles to dream that his march south just might lead to restoration.

Lambert's initial aim, with 4,000 cavalry and dragoons, was to dissuade the Scots from contemplating a retreat by blocking off all possible routes home. At the same time Harrison had taken command of the northern militias, and had given them added backbone and professionalism thanks to an infusion of regular troops. Harrison's brief was wide: 'to stop what he can, and do what further he thinks fit in the counties as he marches'.[20] He was ready to fight, should the enemy turn to engage with him – in fact, he hoped they would. Meanwhile, he and Lambert herded Charles's forces southwards, as Cromwell raced to join up with them. They could then combine to form a force so enormous that the king of Scotland must surely be overwhelmed.

At the same time the lack of enthusiasm that the Scottish general, Leslie, had felt for the campaign from the start had soon become hollow despair. As he led his men ever further from Scotland, into territory that served up surprisingly few reinforcements, he was increasingly aware of England's quiet, deep hostility. When he observed Lambert's men behind him, and Harrison's in front, Leslie guessed that worse was to follow. Cromwell must all the time be closing in, from who knew where.

While he was too professional to shirk his role as the king's lieu-tenant, experience told Leslie that a disastrous end to this ill-judged invasion was certain. In the meantime, he proved incapable of staunching a constant trickling of deserters, and the contagion of despondency spreading amongst his men.

Lambert and Harrison comprised a formidable duo, utterly committed to the destruction of Charles's army. Scoutmaster General George Downing reported, 'Both Major Generals will march night and day till they get to them.'[21] When they combined their forces, they had an army of 12 to 14,000 men. This, secondary, unit was nearly as numerous as the king's entire command.

The major generals remained unsure as to Charles's intended destination. Harrison felt sure it must be Worcester or Gloucester. He was confident that Gloucester would stand firm, its governor being Sir William Constable, an accomplished soldier. Constable also had every encouragement to remain free from Royalist clutches: he had sat with Harrison as a judge of the late king, and had joined him in signing the royal death warrant. Also, as a rebel newsbook of the time reassured its readers, the Gloucester garri-son was 'strongly fortified, and will not be taken either by the flat-tering declarations, or by the threatenings, of the Scots King'.[22]

Harrison was less sure about Worcester, an important city made rich by cloth- and glove-making, which had a history of Royalism. Charles I had twice visited it in the First Civil War, when it had early declared for the king. It had also been the last city in England to remain in Royalist hands during that conflict, its 100-strong garrison capitulating in July 1646. In case Worcester was Charles's destination, Harrison sent 500 Welsh cavalry ahead, to bolster the Parliamentary force there.

The major general had guessed correctly: it was Worcester.

# 6

The Battle of Worcester

*The Pict no shelter now shall find*
*Within his parti-coloured mind,*
*But from this valour sad*
*Shrink underneath the plaid.*

From Andrew Marvell's *An Horatian Ode upon*
*Cromwell's Return from Ireland*, written in 1650

On Thursday, 22 August Charles arrived at Worcester to find only light resistance. It soon became lighter. Harrison's recently arrived reinforcements opted for discretion over valour, and quickly chose escape over death or capture. Troops from the Parliamentary garrison tried briefly to persuade the citizens to deny the king access, but realising the hopelessness of that idea, some fled while the rest surrendered.

The mayor and sheriff of the city, Thomas Lyson and James Bridges, welcomed Charles, and proclaimed him king of Great Britain, France and Ireland. After Lyson had led him through Worcester's streets while holding a sword aloft, Charles addressed English suspicions about his predominantly foreign army. He promised to disband his Scottish soldiers as soon as he had gained his English throne, offered a pardon to those who had fought against the Crown, and ordered all men between the ages of sixteen and sixty to report for a military muster in three days' time, 'with any horse, arms, and ammunition they have or can procure'.[1] The most notable respondent to this summons was Lord Talbot. But he appeared with a squadron of just sixty cavalrymen. The major of this troop was William Careless, a Roman Catholic who knew the surrounding area well. He was rejoining Royalist colours after a long time on the run from Parliament.

The Scots settled into Worcester, happy to recuperate after their 300-mile march. They were exhausted and footsore; many had neither boots nor stockings. Charles had planned to push his army on after a short rest in the city, but he soon appreciated that his men were in no state to continue further. However, Worcester as a defensive position was a great disappointment. Its fortifications were less robust, and its supplies were fewer, than he had expected. 'But,' the Royalists would record, 'His Majesty thought he could not in honour leave them who had so willingly received him, to be plundered by the enemy.'[2] Once they had enjoyed a brief rest, Charles had his men put to work, building a network of outer defences in anticipation of a visit from the enemy.

It was not long in coming. Cromwell's main force had been in the Vale of Evesham, ensuring that the Scots could not head east for London. Learning that Charles and his men were now digging in at Worcester, on 24 August Cromwell joined his men with those of Lambert and Harrison, to form a combined army in excess of 30,000. Further reinforcements were arriving all the time, militia units coming from as far apart as Essex and Somerset.

The *True Informer* reported how Cromwell's mighty force 'advanced with incomparable cheerfulness and courage, to find out their enemies, amazed as much at their resolution as their numbers, are much about Worcester, which city if it should be so inadvised, as to countenance or admit them, believe me, they will repent it at their leisure'.[3] Morale was further improved by the welcome they received from the civilian population, which was happy to supply the Parliamentary force with all that it needed. Meanwhile positive news was coming in from other parts.

On 25 August the Earl of Derby's army of around 1,000 men was defeated. It was attacked at Wigan Lane in Lancashire by a force three times its size, led by Colonel Robert Lilburne, a regicide whose brother was a leading Leveller. While fewer than 100 of Derby's men were killed in the battle, 400 were captured and the rest scattered, pursued by redcoats. What would have been a useful reinforcing army for the king was reduced to nothing.

Derby was among those who fled, after fighting bravely. He had led repeated charges against the enemy, but his raw troops were no match for Lilburne's professionals. The earl was wounded several times before defeat was sure. He then escaped, fleeing in disguise with Colonel Edward Roscarrock, who was also wounded, and two servants. Reaching the market town of Newport, on the border of the counties of Shropshire and Staffordshire, he sought the advice of a friend, Richard Snead, as to where he could safely hide.

Snead took him to Boscobel, a manor house belonging to Charles Giffard, which was tucked deep inside Shropshire's Brewood Forest. The housekeeper there, William Penderel, and his wife Joan tended to the earl's and Roscarrock's wounds. Derby stayed at Boscobel House for two nights. Then, on 31 August, he set off cautiously to rejoin the king, staying briefly with another Royalist household en route.

The Council of State ordered speedy justice against those of Derby's men who had been captured. All the officers and one in ten of the private soldiers were to have 'exemplary proceedings against them, [so] that when the punishment reaches to some, the terror may reach to many, to deter them from the like treasons'.[4] But these sentences would have to wait until the alarm caused by Charles's main army had been dealt with.

The defeat at Wigan Lane marked a crucial turning point for Charles's chances of a successful invasion. Parliamentary sources reported with joy from Amsterdam: 'The news of the Earl of Derby's being routed, and the General's [Cromwell's] approach to Worcester with his Army, hath put them to a stand, and hushed all in a general and serious silence, giving the Scottish King and his Army for lost, though yesterday they recruited their spirits again with a new invention of the king's having taken Gloucester.'[5]

The Earl of Derby, the man tasked with bringing a plentiful supply of English soldiers to strengthen Charles's army, limped into Worcester on 2 September with freshly bound wounds, and just thirty cavalrymen by his side.

Cromwell arrived at Worcester with his army on 28 August. A Royalist wrote with shock of how the republican force had by this stage grown 'to such numbers as made the enemy near 40,000, and the least any of their officers report them was 36,000'.[6] It was, along with the force that Boudicca led against occupying Roman legions, and the sides that clashed at Towton in the Wars of the Roses, one of the largest armies ever to fight on English soil.

Against such overwhelming numerical odds, Cromwell realised that the Royalists would soon have a simple choice: to fight or to take flight. In anticipation that, either way, the king's men would soon be running for their lives, the Council of State decreed that all of its forces that were not actively preparing for battle should stand ready to scoop up the fleeing enemy. 'Because none know which way the Scots will take, when they have entered upon that course,' the Council of State advised its militia leaders in Yorkshire, 'there will be need of many forces in several places. If this work be thoroughly and effectually done, it will very much contribute to a firm and settled peace for the future.'[7]

On the same day the Council of State put their commander in Scotland, Lieutenant General George Monck, on notice that a great victory was expected in England over the Royalist Scots, and that he must 'be in the best readiness you can to entertain any of their stragglers'.[8]

Further south, militia commanders were ordered to 'have your forces ready, and spoil all the fords, and stop the passes, to retard their flight'.[9] Robert Blake, Parliament's admiral, was informed that everything on land was fully under control: 'There are forces on all the passes.' Nobody must be allowed to escape from the coming reckoning, by land or sea.

Seeing the Parliamentarians arrive in such force, Charles was keen to do what he could to stop them settling in outside the city unmolested. 'During the enemy's lying there, the King was very active, and often sent out strong parties,' it was noted, 'but the enemy was so watchful, and lay so strong that, though our men behaved courageously, they could get no advantage of them.'[10]

The Royalists suffered major setbacks in the days before the battle. Charles ordered a night attack by 1,500 of his cavalry, who put on white shirts over their armour so they could be recognised by their comrades in the dark, and sallied out of the city's gates. But a Worcester tailor called Guyse had betrayed the plan to Parliament, and the Cavaliers rode into stiff enemy gunfire before being forced to retreat. As soon as Guyse was identified as the informant, he was hanged.

Cromwell opted to encircle Worcester, and sent Lambert westwards to prod the Royalist defences on that flank. To his astonishment, Lambert discovered that the enemy had failed to complete the demolition of a bridge over the River Severn at Upton. On the far side were 300 of the king's soldiers under the command of Major General Edward Massey, a former hero of the New Model Army who crossed to the Royalist side in disgust at the execution of Charles I. Massey's change of loyalties had seen him derided in a London lampoon as 'a strange, fat, unliked, small-faced fellow'.[11]

However, he had quickly become a favourite of Charles's, joining him first in exile, and then in Scotland. A hugely able and experienced soldier, Massey now let his master down by negligently leaving a single beam intact across the entire length of Upton Bridge.

As daylight broke on 28 August, Lambert ordered eighteen of his best soldiers to cross the girder and establish a bridgehead on the far side. Concerned that they might tumble into the swirling water below, the men sat down to straddle the beam with their legs. They hauled themselves forward with stiff arms, lunge by lunge, praying that their slow and clumsy approach would go unnoticed by the enemy sentries. On reaching the other side, they were quickly spotted. They ran to the village church to make a stand.

The Royalists set the church alight, firing muskets and thrusting pikes in through the windows, while cutting down any who attempted to bolt from the flames. Lambert sent mounted dragoons across the Severn to see if they could rescue his trapped men. Seeing by the dragoons' awkward progress that it was possible for men on horseback to cross the river, albeit with difficulty, he threw in more and more cavalry reinforcements.

Massey appeared from his billet in nearby Hanley Castle to direct his troops. The fighting was fierce, and he had his horse shot from under him. A ripple of grapeshot then caught him in the head, thigh and right hand, leaving him so badly wounded that it seemed certain he would die.

The Royalists had to retreat in the face of overwhelming odds, and leave this western approach to Worcester in enemy hands. From this point on, no reinforcements could reach Charles from Wales or the west of England, two of the most staunchly Royalist areas in Britain. Meanwhile, the king lost the services of Massey, one of his ablest commanders, who was too badly injured to take part in the coming engagement.

\* \* \*

Charles took personal command on the day of the battle. Early on 3 September, he went to the top of Worcester Cathedral with his council of war to inspect the enemy's formations. It was a sparklingly clear morning, with perfect visibility.

It must have been chilling to see tens of thousands of the enemy openly preparing for a major assault. Of particular concern would have been what they spied to the south of the city, where a column of a thousand Parliamentarians was heading for the River Severn with pontoon bridges.

Units commanded by a nest of regicides were on hand to lead the rebels in their two-pronged assault, one of which was made possible by the recent capture of Upton Bridge.

Colonel Richard Ingoldsby was at the forefront of this Parliamentary attack, just as he had been to the fore at the storming of Bridgwater and Bristol. He now held a position with his infantry in front of Powick Bridge. This had been the site, nine years earlier, of the first Royalist victory of the Civil Wars, when Prince Rupert of the Rhine's shock charge against the cream of Parliament's soldiers had given birth to the military reputation of the prince and his brave but unmanageable Cavaliers.

Ingoldsby was a cousin and confidant of Oliver Cromwell's. He had been appointed a judge at Charles I's trial, but had been absent during the proceedings. He subsequently added his signature to the king's death warrant, though he would forever claim that he had been forced to do so by Cromwell gripping his hand hard as he wrote. But the document survives, and Ingoldsby's name appears clearly formed, in an easy flourish that gives no hint of duress.

Also in the front line was the cavalry of Colonel Francis Hacker, whose two brothers were Royalists: one of them had lost his life, and the other a hand, while serving the Crown in their native Nottinghamshire. Hacker had twice been taken prisoner of war, both times refusing his captors' inducements to change sides. A diehard Parliamentarian, he had been placed in charge of guarding Charles I during his trial, a task he had performed with rough contempt for his prisoner: he had recommended the indignity of having two musketeers permanently by the king's side, even in his bedchamber, but the proposal was overruled. Hacker had then been the officer to sign the order to execute the king, and had been present on the scaffold when the axe fell.

Alongside Hacker was William Goffe, a man of intense Puritanism. Goffe's electrifying speech at a prayer meeting of the army in Windsor three and a half years earlier had persuaded many that the king must be tried for treason. He had argued that to fail in this duty would surely lead to the Parliamentary cause being punished by God.

In support of their comrades stood Lord Grey of Groby, commander-in-chief of forces drawn from the Midland counties of Leicestershire, Nottinghamshire, Northamptonshire and Rutland. He was the only son of a peer to sign Charles I's death warrant. Grey's belief in the supremacy of Parliament over the Crown was vividly displayed on his military banner, on which an image of the House of Commons in session was encircled by a series of daggers, gripped tight by determined hands. Lord Grey's fighting motto, when translated from the Latin, read 'Through War, Peace'.

To the other side of the Royalists stood Commissary General Edward Whalley, who had guarded Charles I when the king had been held in Hampton Court for several months in 1647. Charles had broken his word to Whalley, and secretly fled to the Isle of Wight. Despite a civil relationship with his prisoner, Whalley had no compunction in judging him guilty of treason at trial, or in signing his death warrant. Wounded a year earlier at the battle of Dunbar, Whalley had accompanied Cromwell on his recent march south. He now stood ready to help secure the defeat of Charles Stuart and his Scottish invaders.

Colonel Thomas Pride and his regiment had taken a central role in preparing the ground for Charles I's trial, by purging the House of Commons of those Members who might have voted to spare the king. A brewer from London, Pride was one of those who had championed a petition to Parliament in 1648 demanding that Charles be proceeded against 'as an enemy to the kingdom'.

Major General Harrison, who had slowed the Scottish army's march south, had been party to that same petition. Of all those who had judged the late king, Harrison had perhaps been the most harsh and hostile. He had first come to prominence as a major, when he had been identified as one of the 'cluster of preaching officers' whose religious fervour, when added to a natural affinity for soldiery, led to rapid promotion. He now stood in reserve, ready to witness the attacks that, he felt sure, would deliver the *coup de grâce* to the Royalist cause.

Providing the chorus to the Parliamentary attack were the cannon of Major General Richard Deane, who had taken part in all aspects of Charles I's demise, from planning his trial through to the examination of witnesses, as well as helping to choose the hour and location of his execution. Deane's military talents were rare, and in demand: he was now both an admiral and the New Model Army's artillery chief. Once his guns opened their throats to pound Worcester's Fort Royal, which protected Sidbury Gate and the city's south-eastern approaches, it was clear to all that a general assault had begun.

Charles led the resistance to the enemy's twin attack. He tried to stop the two Parliamentarian wings from uniting, sending forward 300 Highlanders under Colonel Colin Pitscottie in an attempt to block 1,000 rebels crossing the Severn. The Scots refused to break, an eyewitness recalling how the grey-coated troops retreated behind their gold and black standard 'with characteristic bravery [and] … disputed every hedge'.[12] But they were eventually killed, captured or scattered.

Cromwell oversaw the progress of the main pontoon, and threw up a second bridge over the River Teme, reinforcing Ingoldsby and Lambert's advances. They pushed against defences commanded by Major General Robert Montgomery, until Montgomery was wounded and his men's ammunition ran out. As the Royalists fled back to the city, Cromwell sent his men in pursuit. He was in that state of euphoria that could possess him in battle, calling on the Lord of Hosts to bring his men victory.

Despite Parliament having more than twice as many troops as the king, the battle of Worcester was in the balance for a while. Cromwell would later call the encounter 'as stiff a contest for four or five hours as ever I have seen'.[13] This was thanks, in part, to Charles's energetic generalship.

While Deane's guns redoubled their efforts against the city's defences, Charles sensed that the pivotal moment of the engagement had been reached. He put himself at the head of a brave counterattack, one of his men later recalling:

*His Majesty behaved himself very gallantly; with his own regiment of horse, and [the] D.[uke of] Hamilton's, he broke a regiment of horse and forced back a considerable body of their horse but at last was overpowered, and our horse ran, though the King strove to make them stand. The King being closely pursued, and our men stopping the passage, was forced to quit his horse, and climb up our half raised mount, and there so encouraged our foot that the enemy retired with loss. The King perceiving the enemy too numerous, and our men worsted, drew them within the walls, where it was long disputed, and then taking a fresh horse, he rode to the cavalry, with the intention of rallying them, and scouring foot from the walls; but it was in vain, for [Lieutenant General] Middleton was wounded, and the chief of the horse officers either dismounted or slain, or I know not where.[14]*

This was the moment when David Leslie and his 3,000-strong Scottish cavalry would have been expected to intervene from their position at Pitchcroft, north of the city. English Royalists would look back on his failure to do so as the epitome of cowardice and treachery, and a dereliction of duty that cost them a chance of victory against the odds.

It seems that when Leslie looked at the desperate fighting in front of him, and the huge numbers of the enemy advancing on Worcester, he judged the day to be already lost. This was, perhaps, a self-fulfilling prophecy, for he had recently said in private of his army that 'howsoever it looked, it would not fight'.

Several days earlier, on reaching Worcester and then learning of the enemy's growing encirclement of his beleaguered and worn-out men, Leslie appears to have extinguished whatever flickering morale he had nursed on the trek south. He knew that this was where everything would be decided, and felt certain that the coming battle would be calamitous. It would doubtless steal the lives of many good Scottish soldiers, perhaps even his own. While risking himself in battle was an integral part of Leslie's profession, he resented the imminent prospect of himself and his men being sacrificed for a scheme that he had marked from its outset as being absolutely and irretrievably doomed.

It was against this context of the Scottish general's dark pessimism that a Royalist would report with disgust: 'David Leslie rode up and down as one amazed, or seeking to fly, for they were so confused that neither threats nor entreaty could persuade them to charge with His Majesty.'[15]

Another of Charles's supporters mourned the absence of the Royalists' late, great general in Scotland, who would never have shrunk from attacking at such a moment, but whose betrayal by the Crown was now so keenly felt: 'One hour of Montrose at the head of the 3,000 horse … had perhaps retrieved the fortune of the day: but Leslie … kept them stationary in the rear, until the infantry, having expended their ammunition, and reduced to fight with the but-ends of their muskets, gave way before the reserves poured in by [Cromwell], and fell back into the city, with the loss of their best leaders.'[16]

While Parliamentary troops poured over the earthworks of Fort Royal, Charles found the roads around him choked with the rising tide of defeat. Arriving at Sudbury Gate he was confronted by an overturned ammunition cart, its oxen lying dead beside it. The king jumped from his horse and scrambled over the cart. He then pulled off his heavy armour in Friar Street, and found a new mount.

When he saw some of his men throwing down their weapons in surrender, he urged them to keep fighting, reminding them of the righteousness of their cause. As it became clear that he could not persuade them to fight on, the king cried, 'I had rather that you would shoot me, than keep me alive to see the consequences of this fatal day!'

Charles was so immersed in the battle that he failed to recognise the moment all was lost. It had already arrived when he announced his intention of leading Leslie's Scots in a final charge. The king's lieutenants explained that there was no point: the men would never obey him, and the day already belonged to the enemy. The rebels had captured Fort Royal, slaying everyone in it, before turning the captured Scottish artillery on Charles's men. Meanwhile, west of the city in St John's, a brigade of Scottish infantry under Major General Thomas Dalyell had surrendered after the briefest resistance, showing the same lack of gumption as Leslie's cavalry.

A small force was formed under the Earl of Cleveland, a veteran cavalry general whose great bravery had been seen at the battle of Cropredy Bridge seven years earlier. Then, his inspired charge had helped to secure victory for the Crown against the run of the action. Now his task was to hold back the enemy, with defeat already certain, while the king tried to flee. Every minute the rebels were delayed would gain Charles more time in which to distance himself from the carnage of the rout.

Nine other officers, including Talbot's Major Careless and Captain Thomas Giffard, joined Cleveland in his holding operation. They led a small body of Cavaliers in repeated charges down Sidbury Street and the High Street, against overwhelming odds. Eventually, with several of their number dead or wounded, the survivors from this brave but bloodied troop either surrendered or fled. Royalist resistance spluttered on in isolated pockets around the city, before being snuffed out.

One of Charles's men who had witnessed him in action, and who was then taken prisoner, wrote: 'What became of His Majesty afterwards I know not, but God preserve him, for certainly a more gallant prince was never born.'

There is a tale, likely true, that the king went quickly back to the Commandery, his lodgings in Worcester, to gather some of his things. His escape attempt nearly ended in failure before it had properly begun, when the enemy's Colonel Ralph Cobbett burst through the building's front door as Charles bolted out the back, leaving his papers behind.

Charles rode out of Worcester through the octagonal bastions and pointed arch of St Martin's Gate. It was six o'clock in the evening, the end of a hellish day, and the start of a journey that promised the king only two possible outcomes: escape, or death.

## 7

# *The Hunt Begins*

*Arrived the news of the fatal Battle of Worcester, which
exceedingly mortified our expectations.*

Diary of John Evelyn, 12 September 1651

Around Europe, news of Charles's defeat was met with a mixture
of shock and resignation. Queen Henrietta Maria had been on the
point of setting off with the French court for Berry when she
received 'the confirmation of defeat at Worcester, which caus'd the
Queen to alter her designs'.

She wrote to postpone a visit to the mother superior of a
nunnery in Chaillot, 'on account of the bad news from England,
which nevertheless I hope is not quite so unfortunate as it is represented. My uneasiness renders me unfit for anything, until I receive
the news which will arrive tonight.' She ended with the plea: 'Pray
to God for the king, my son.'[1]

Sir Edward Nicholas noted that the Duke of York, who was with
his mother at the time, had also chosen to stay behind rather than
remain as a guest of the French court: 'They say it was to expect
here to hear where the King of England was.'[2] If his brother were
dead, James would be the new claimant to the English throne.

While waiting for further news, James remained in Paris with his mother, 'in dreadful apprehension for the King'.[3]

In parts of the Netherlands the result of the battle was at first wrongly reported as a victory for Charles. The English church in The Hague held a service of thanksgiving in the mistaken belief 'that Harrison was killed, Lambert wounded and taken, 3,000 [Parliamentarians] killed ... and the King of Scots was but seven miles from London'.[4]

Charles's sister, Mary of Orange, had been joining in the celebrations at the false report 'that the King had got victory, divided the spoil, and triumphed in the City and Capitol of London, before ever a sword was drawn, or stroke struck'. She chose to reject the follow-up reports that the supposed triumph had in fact been an unmitigated disaster. When forced to accept the truth, she swooned with shock.

Once details of the defeat spread, the focus amongst the Royalists remained Charles's fate. As *Mercurius Politicus* explained: 'The worst act of the tragedy to them is the good King, whether he be killed, or taken, or hidden; whither he is gone, what he will do.'[5]

The senior Royalists in exile struggled to come to terms with the king's failure. Sir Edward Nicholas wrote from Antwerp to Lord Hatton that he was 'here in a doleful condition upon the news of the King's being totally defeated, and his person in so very great danger'.[6] There seemed no future for the Crown's cause if Charles was dead. Even if he was free, he would surely soon be captured. After that would come execution.

The twenty-four-year-old Queen Christina of Sweden had been particularly appalled at the beheading of Charles I. She had commissioned learned attacks on the regicides in Latin, which had been disseminated throughout Europe. But she realised that the result at Worcester made irrelevant her thoughts of helping the Royalists, and shelved plans of sending her fleet to assist the executed king's son.

Ambassador Michiel Morosini reported the scale of the defeat to the doge of Venice from the French court. He said that Charles had been 'forced to seek safety in the mountains of Scotland, with 3,000 horse', and concluded that, without immediate foreign assistance, Charles was vulnerable to 'some accident [overtaking] him, of imprisonment or death. He is the more exposed to this as he has no force to protect him.'[7]

But it was in England that news of the Royalists' trouncing rang loudest. In London Colonel Barkstead lit a bonfire at Whitehall Gate, while his regiment of redcoats discharged volleys of musket-fire in celebration. Thursday, 2 October was marked out as a day on which the victory would be celebrated throughout England, Scotland and Wales.

Meanwhile the details of the defeat became a little clearer. A few hundred of Cromwell's men had died, while between 2,000 and 4,000 Royalists had perished. Cromwell would speak of 'the marvellous salvation wrought at Worcester',[8] and would call the outcome of the engagement a 'crowning mercy'.[9]

The Council of State sent brief headlines about the triumph to its commanders in Scotland, northern England and across the Midlands, and urged them to stand on their guard: 'Some of their horse fled, which our horse are pursuing … It is probable that such as can scatter homewards will endeavour to do so; use your best endeavours to gather them up.' In particular, it was noted: 'As it is probable many of the enemy may endeavour to come to London, endeavour to gather them up, by parties of horse which will send out upon all avenues of the city.'[10]

The day after the battle, the Council of State wrote to Cromwell: 'We have seen your letter to the Speaker, and by that and others, have been informed of the great success given to the forces under your command, not doubting but God will in much mercy finish what remains.'[11]

The crucial part of that mopping-up process would, of course, be the hunting down of King Charles. Either his body must be unearthed from among the slain, or – if he had escaped death – he must be pursued until he was captured.

'Where their King is, God knows,' the *Weekly Intelligencer* mused. 'There are many who affirm that they saw him after the Fort [Royal] was stormed, and that he went out with the Horse that escaped, by the dark protection of the night.' The newsbook gave a description of the fugitive king's clothing, hoping it might assist his would-be captors: 'In the day of the great fight he had on a black suit, it seems not thinking to fight, as on that day, nor dreaming how black it would prove unto him.'[12]

Major General Thomas Harrison was in charge of rounding up the defeated enemy. He and a large force had been held back from the twin assault on Worcester to stand ready for the battle's aftermath. Harrison had loudly and consistently predicted that God would grant his side victory, but the essential point now was to see it through. He relished the prospect of being the harvester of the defeated.

Harrison had proved remarkably effective in rooting out Royalists in Wales following Charles I's execution. One of his enemies would write of this period: 'Major General Harrison [was in command] in Wales; in which employment to characterise his tyranny would swell a volume far exceeding this intended discourse. The laws of the land were not executed in Wales, but Major General Harrison's laws were there in full force.'[13]

The regicides who had risked all in killing Charles I felt sure that the recent triumph at Worcester was a God-given opportunity, if followed up vigorously, to set the seal on the new political order in England. If Harrison could quickly capture Charles, and deprive the Royalists of their natural leader, the future of the republic seemed assured.

Harrison was a man of startling contrasts: a devout Puritan who loved fine things, his reputation for being able to quote at length from the more apocalyptic chapters of the Bible was as well known as the gorgeousness of his clothing. His reputation among his enemies, though, focused on his utter ruthlessness. This trait was driven by a religious fanaticism that saw him enter a state of rapture when in battle. When the Catholic stronghold of Basing House finally fell to Parliament in October 1645, at the conclusion of a trio of bitterly contested sieges, Royalists claimed to have witnessed Harrison kill in cold blood some who had laid down their arms. As he shot an actor called Dick Robinson through the head, he was heard to shout, 'Cursed be he that doeth the work of the Lord negligently!'[14] Perhaps half of Basing's overwhelmed garrison was slaughtered that day, but Harrison's brutality somehow caught the eye more than the rest.

It was Harrison who had been sent to transport the king from his prison at Hurst Castle, on the south coast of England, to London for his trial. Charles I's shocking execution had seen the late king elevated to the status of martyr by his supporters, and tales soon emerged of Harrison's impertinence to the beleaguered monarch in his final days.

The king had been so aware of, and alarmed by, Harrison's dark reputation that on learning that he was the officer in charge of taking him to London, he spent the night in prayer, preparing for imminent death at the major general's hand. When the journey was under way, the king could not resist asking Harrison if he planned to murder him before they reached London. Harrison reassured him that he would do no such thing. If Charles had understood his captor and his beliefs better, this would not have been a comfort to him. The major general was convinced that the tyrant king needed to be tried and condemned publicly for having inflicted such great loss of life on his people. Charles therefore would not be murdered in a corner, as he feared. But he would still need to be put to death.

In January 1649 Harrison sat as one of the king's most enthusiastic judges, barely missing a session. At the conclusion of the trial he rose to his feet with his comrades in a display of unanimous support for the death sentence. He was the seventeenth of the fifty-nine men to sign the death warrant.

After the axe was swung, Charles I's head was stitched back onto his body. His remains were then sent for burial in Windsor. This was considered far enough from London to prevent his tomb becoming a place of pilgrimage for the capital's Royalists.

Harrison oversaw proceedings at the funeral, ensuring that the ceremony was devoid of pomp. He allowed none of the prayers that the king would have wanted at his service, and saw that the coffin was attended by a mere handful of Charles I's most loyal supporters.

Having had a leading part in the execution and burial of the father, Major General Harrison was now placed in charge of the manhunt for the son.

Harrison had everything in place to catch the defeated king and his supporters before the battle had begun. He had as his main support Colonel Robert Lilburne, the man who had recently defeated the Earl of Derby.

A report was printed in Worcester about Parliament's efforts on the day after the battle: 'Yesterday morning, by order from the General, we committed 1,500 horse and dragoons to pursue after the enemy ... who fled in the same way they come thither. Major General Harrison is likewise gone after them, and will we doubt not (through the Lord's mercy) overtake most of them, Colonel Lilburne will, we hope, put a stop unto them ... The King (it is said) went away with not above 12 horse, 'tis thought there is not 1,000 horse of them together ... the number of those that are taken are said to be about 10,000.' While 140 significant officers from his army had already been captured, the king had yet to be found, but, the report continued, 'They are still in pursuit.'[15]

It seemed just a matter of time before the king of Scots was identified, captured and sent for justice. There was, as yet, little concern that he was still unaccounted for. It was expected that Charles's naked remains would be found among the stripped bodies of the fallen, or if sightings of him fleeing Worcester were correct, that he would soon run into one of Harrison's numerous patrols.

PART TWO

# THE ROMAN CATHOLIC
# UNDERGROUND

# 8

## *Whiteladies*

*While we were in this tree, we see soldiers going up and
down, in the thicket of the wood, searching for persons
escaped, we seeing them now and then peeping out of the
wood.*

Charles II's memories, as shared with Samuel Pepys

Even after escaping from Worcester, Charles would not accept
defeat. In the first few hundred yards of his flight from the city he
kept halting his horse, pleading with his senior officers to turn with
him and try to retrieve the day. But they had no time for the
dangerous delusion of the young king. Recognising utter defeat for
what it was, they told him to gallop away from the enemy as fast as
he could.

Charles pulled up at Barbourne Bridge, less than a mile north of
Worcester, and called for his attendants to gather round. He was
just beginning to accept the calamity that had overtaken his army
and his cause. That day had started with him as a reigning king,
and commander-in-chief of a large army. It was ending with him
in catastrophic crisis, his Scottish crown effectively lost in a few
hours, his English one further from his grasp than ever.

He now found himself in the evening gloom, in countryside he barely knew, facing a journey across land whose inhabitants had rejected him when he had had a chance of victory, and who would certainly shun him now he was without hope. At this time of grave danger his main duty must be to obey the central instruction in his father's letter from Hereford of six years earlier: he must keep himself alive. That could only be achieved through escape. But there was no point in simply fleeing – there needed to be a plan.

Convinced that all routes back to Scotland would soon be stopped by the enemy, Charles's first thought was to race for London. He hoped somehow to arrive in the capital before news of his trouncing was heralded to the world. There he could lie low for a while, just one more person in a city whose population exceeded 350,000, before slipping overseas.

But when he proposed London as a goal, his courtiers and generals appeared not to hear him. Instead they continued an argument among themselves over the wisdom of an immediate retracing of the 200 or so miles back to Scotland. It was immediately clear to the king that the Royalist high command was dizzy with defeat.

Only one man heard his bold London plan with approval. This was Lord Wilmot, the high-spirited figure from his exiled mother's court who had helped to facilitate the prince's affair with Lucy Walter.

Henry Wilmot was, at thirty-eight years of age, already a military veteran, having fought for the Dutch as a young man in the Thirty Years War, and then against the Scots in the Bishops' Wars. He had been among the first to swear allegiance to Charles I on the outbreak of civil war, and quickly rose to become one of his more effective generals. The king rewarded him with command of the cavalry, and the title of Lord Wilmot.*

---

* When his father died in 1644, Wilmot succeeded to his Irish title as Viscount Wilmot of Athlone.

Tough and hard-living, adored by his men but envied by some of his colleagues, Wilmot had been wounded three times in battle, and once in a duel. The king realised that his best chance of escape lay in pairing up with this unflappable adventurer, whose company he enjoyed, and whose calmness stood out in the general confusion.

Charles felt the consultation at Barbourne Bridge had gone on long enough. He needed to be on his way – as soon as Worcester was fully secured and pillaged, he was sure that the victors would move on to the business of gathering up the defeated. He turned to Lord Talbot, who had joined him just before the battle, and called on his local knowledge, asking him to point them all northwards. Talbot beckoned forward one of his men, Richard Walker, who had operated as a spy in the area, and told him to act as their guide.

They had not gone far when Major General Massey called out. The grapeshot wounds he had received six days earlier at Upton Bridge were causing him great pain, and he was unable to ride without support. Now the rattling speed of the king's flight made his agony unbearable.

Knowing that he could not keep up with the required pace, Massey declared himself an intolerable handicap, and urged Charles to carry on without him. The king was seen to have tears running down his cheeks as he said, 'Farewell, my dear and faithful friend – the Lord bless and preserve us both!'[1] He then kicked his horse on into the darkness, compelled to leave Massey behind to his fate.

His instinct for self-preservation told the king he must shed the defeated rabble that was still clinging to his side. In a bid to have them scatter for safety, and leave him be, he was heard to shout, 'Shift yourselves, gentlemen! Shift for yourselves!'[2]

Charles had managed to rid himself of most of his unneeded companions after passing Hartlebury, a village ten miles north of Worcester whose main feature was its thirteenth-century castle, which stood in ruins. It had been torn down by Parliament five years earlier, after its Royalist garrison surrendered to the New Model Army without a shot being fired.

As the fugitives spurred their horses on through the landscape of defeat, the focus of many of them never deviated from Scotland as the only possible sanctuary. The whereabouts of their king became a secondary consideration as they continued northwards. Charles was relieved to soon find himself accompanied by just sixty men, picking out side routes of increasing obscurity in order to avoid detection.

They had reached Kinver, nineteen miles north of Worcester, and seventeen miles west of Birmingham, when Walker, the guide, confessed that he was lost. Charles now realised how exhausted he was after a day of fighting, and announced to his companions that all he really craved was somewhere safe to rest for a few hours.

The Earl of Derby proposed Boscobel House, where he had hidden after his recent defeat at Wigan Lane, as a possible haven for the king. Derby listed Boscobel's many attractions: it was tucked away in thick woodland; the people he had encountered there were very much to be trusted; and the owners were Roman Catholics who had built hiding places for their priests.

Roman Catholics had been persecuted during the reigns of Queen Elizabeth and King James. Although England became a Protestant nation in 1559, anti-Catholic legislation had only grown later, as a result of fears for the Crown's safety. It was given particular impetus by a localised uprising in the north of England in 1569, and in response to a plot to assassinate Elizabeth that was unearthed in 1586.

Catholic priests were liable to arrest for high treason. Those who harboured them were considered felons, and risked imprisonment. As a result, 'Catholic houses' such as Boscobel were accustomed to hiding not only their inhabitants' religion, but also those who dispensed it. The king immediately understood that the Roman

Catholics offered him a chance of safety: 'I chose to trust them,' he would later say, 'because I knew they had hiding places for priests that I thought I might make use of in case of need.'[3]

Lord Talbot heard Derby and the king's plan, and pointed out that, by an extraordinary stroke of luck, the owner of Boscobel House was among their number that night. He went to find him, and brought him forward to speak to the king.

Charles Giffard came from a family with a long history of royal service. His ancestor Gautier Giffard (the surname derived from the Norman French word for 'chubby cheeks') had been standard-bearer to William the Conqueror in the eleventh century – William had ridden to Giffard's aid when he fell from his warhorse during the battle of Hastings. Six centuries on, the Giffards remained loyal to the Crown: a cousin, Andrew Giffard, had given his life fighting for the late king. Now Charles Giffard did not hesitate to offer Charles secluded Boscobel House as a hiding place.

Giffard introduced Charles to Francis Yates, one of ten armed men sent to fight at Worcester by Mary Graves, an ardent Royalist who had also supplied the king with the charger he had ridden in battle, as well as the horse he was riding now. Yates was a husbandman, a small farmer, who had been born in Brewood, near Boscobel House. Giffard commended him as the man to get Charles to the house quickly and safely, using little-known byways to avoid detection by the enemy.

Yates set the royal party on its new course, the first leg of which was due east from Kinver. After five miles they approached Stourbridge. This town, a little more than twenty miles north of Worcester, was known for its glassmaking, and French Protestant refugees formed a key part of its skilled workforce. The Royalists seem to have been aware of this Huguenot presence, for they agreed to speak French to one another while passing through the town. This ruse appears to have stopped them from being challenged as they went: they later discovered that Stourbridge had contained a detachment of enemy cavalry on the night they passed through, but it did not confront them.

There had been no time to eat during the day of intense fighting, and the Royalists were ravenous. They had ridden a mile north from Stourbridge when they stopped briefly outside a house and asked its hard-up inhabitants for food. They could only offer Charles a crust of bread and some beer. He consumed both in the saddle.

As they moved off again, Charles quizzed Colonel Roscarrock, who had recently hidden there with the Earl of Derby, about Boscobel House. Everything Roscarrock told him sounded encouraging.

It was while heading north for Boscobel – through Himley, Wombourne and Wrottesley Woods – that Charles learnt that 3,000 of his cavalry had been seen nearby. These were, for the most part, those Scots under Lieutenant General Leslie who had refused to join in the fighting at Worcester. Excited by this news, the royal entourage assumed that the king would rush to join with this force at once, and fight his way back to Scotland. But this was a notion, Charles would recall, 'Which I thought was absolutely impossible, knowing very well that the Country would all rise upon us, and that men who had deserted me when they were in good order would never stand to me when they have been beaten.'

He rode on with the small party of soldiers, courtiers and servants that included Lord Wilmot, the Earl of Derby, the Earl of Lauderdale, and his childhood friend the Duke of Buckingham. At some point during their ride, Yates decided to lead the king and his comrades not to Boscobel, but to another Giffard property that was even more promising as a hiding place.

Whiteladies stood half a mile further inside the dense woodland of Brewood Forest than Boscobel. The half-timbered property was so remote that its lands were used as a safe burial place for the many Roman Catholics who lived in the area. It stood among the ruined walls of an old priory that Henry VIII had forcibly confiscated for profit. Local legend had it that when the last abbess had been pulled, screaming, from the doorway in 1536, she had vowed that her nuns would return one day. Nobody could have foreseen that a king, let alone one fleeing for his life, would get there first.

They reached Whiteladies at three o'clock in the morning of Thursday, 4 September, the day after the battle. They had ridden forty miles or so, but because of the period early on when they had lost their way, they were only twenty-six miles from the battlefield.

The varied occupants of Whiteladies were woken by the loud arrival of the fugitive band. Among them was Frances Cotton, a widow who was a Giffard by birth: her father, John Giffard of Chillington, had built nearby Boscobel House. She lived in the family wing of Whiteladies used by Charles Giffard and his wife when they visited.

In two other sections of the house lived Mistress Anne Edwards, Edward Martin, and a boy called Bartholomew Martin. Another inhabitant of this part of Whiteladies was William Walker, an elderly Roman Catholic priest. Walker secretly administered to the three households, and to the surrounding poor who practised his faith, sometimes with the assistance of colleagues in the area. Whiteladies' straggling footprint was that of a small commune, rather than a conventional home.

The gate to the property was watched by George Penderel, one of Whiteladies' servants. The youngest of five surviving brothers* whose loyalty to Charles would soon be tested to the full, he had fought for the late king at Stow-on-the-Wold, the last battle of the First Civil War.

---

* A sixth Penderel brother, Thomas, seems to have been killed at the battle of Edgehill in 1642.

Recognising Charles Giffard and Francis Yates (who was married to his sister Elizabeth), George opened the gate, asking the pair how the battle had gone. While he heard the first dismal reports of the great defeat, Charles and his entourage pushed past into the hallway, with the king's fine horse being led in to join them inside.

The Royalists immediately set about assessing the options that lay before the king. As they did so, George warned that there was a Parliamentary force stationed just three miles from where they stood, in the village of Codsall. It was commanded by Colonel Ashenhurst, a veteran Roundhead.

Derby asked for George's eldest brother, William, to be sent for from Boscobel House. It was William and his wife Joan who had hidden him and Roscarrock there, and tended their wounds, after the reverse at Wigan Lane. Derby had formed a high opinion of William during his time in his care, and invited him and George to join him and the king in a conference in a side room. Charles ate biscuits and drank sack (sweet sherry) while they talked. Introductions were to the point. 'This is the king,' Derby told the brothers. 'Thou must have a care of him as thou didst me.'[4] William and George must have been utterly amazed to meet the king under these circumstances, but they swore they would do all they could for him.

It was agreed that they needed to know what was happening in the immediate area of Whiteladies before committing the king to an escape plan. William asked George to visit the nearby village of Tong, to find out if any other Royalist fugitives were nearby, and to discover how close the pursuing enemy was.

George returned with the news that nobody from either army had yet been spotted nearby. He brought with him his and William's middle brother Richard, the tenant of Hobbal Grange, a farm near Tong, where he lived with the brothers' widowed mother Jane. Francis Yates used Richard's nickname, 'Trusty Richard', when introducing him to the king.

The first priority was to disguise the extremely tall king with clothes that fitted. Given his uncommon height of six feet two inches, at a time when few men were taller than five foot six, the costume ended up being a composite drawn from the wardrobes of the various people to hand. Charles Giffard told the lankiest of the Penderel brothers, William, to bring his spare clothes to be tried on by the king. These were a tunic, breeches of a rough green cloth, and a deerskin leather jerkin, which replaced Charles's buff coat, inset with rich bands of gold lace, and fine doublet. The Penderels gathered up the king's cast-off attire, and later buried it in a safe place.

Young Bartholomew Martin produced a bristly hemp shirt, known in the local vernacular as a 'hurden' or 'noggen shirt'. Humphrey Penderel, the second-youngest brother, who operated Whiteladies' mill, provided Charles with suitably rustic headgear: a battered grey hat with a raised brim, of a sufficiently generous girth to cover the king's broad head. Another man, William Creswell, offered up his very basic, but flimsy, shoes.

The king's hairstyle was also worked on. Lord Wilmot started on it, but was making such a mess of lopping off Charles's flowing Cavalier locks with a knife that Richard Penderel took over, wielding a pair of farmer's shears with a skilled and practised hand. The king thanked him for doing such a fine job, and particularly for undoing Wilmot's clumsy efforts. The haircut transformed Charles, giving him a simple peasant's plainness. Charles wiped his hands in the coal dust at the back of the fireplace, and rubbed it onto his face as a final addition to his disguise. As one who witnessed the change later recorded, 'Now his Majesty was *à la mode* the woodman.'[5]

It was time for the king to bid farewell to his entourage. He gave the gold coins from his purse to his servants, and Wilmot received his watch. He entrusted his prized blue ornamented sash and its accompanying jewellery, worn as a Knight of the Garter, to Colonel Thomas Blague.

Blague was a fervent supporter of the Crown who had served Charles I, and who named his eldest daughter Henrietta Maria, after his queen. He was also a famously ferocious soldier, who doubled as a royal courtier. Someone who witnessed the colonel's cavalry troop caught in an enemy ambush remembered how he 'behaved himself as manfully with his sword as any man did, slashing and beating so many fresh Rebels with such courage and dexterity'[6] that his men were able to retreat with surprisingly few casualties. If anyone could protect the king's most precious possessions in such bleak circumstances, and hopefully return them one day, it was Blague.

The Royalists departed reluctantly, deeply troubled that they were leaving their king alone in such danger. To do so was against their code. Realising that they themselves might soon be captured, they insisted that he keep whatever escape plans he might have to himself: none of them wanted to live with the infamy of being the man who betrayed his king, if captured and interrogated.

The Earl of Derby in particular wanted to stay by his master's side, but was forced to accept that the presence of another well-known escapee alongside the king would increase the already great difficulty of smuggling Charles to safety.

These Royalists headed off to join Leslie and his 3,000 men, recently seen at nearby Tong Castle, on their trek to Scotland. Charles's assessment that the spirits of the Scottish cavalry had been shattered was very soon proved correct: Leslie's force was so jittery that it was scattered by the sight of a small detachment of Parliamentary militia under the command of Colonel Benjamin Blundell. The Royalist forces' morale was broken, and it was, from this point on, a case of every man for himself.

Day was breaking on 4 September. It was the morning after the great defeat. The king had just said goodbye to all his familiar followers: Buckingham, who had shared his childhood; the loyal men who had followed him from the Netherlands to Scotland; and those who had joined him on the ill-fated march south. These men of note, who were his natural attendants and companions, knew they could offer him no help in his desperate situation. He would have to fend for himself for the first time in his life, relying on the area's Roman Catholics' expertise in concealing hunted men, and the resourcefulness and local knowledge of the humble Penderels.

Richard Penderel led Charles out of one of Whiteladies' secret doors. The king was weighed down by a woodman's bill, a heavy tool for cutting branches, which he carried unsteadily as he walked. They headed into the most remote part of Spring Coppice, a wood half a mile from Whiteladies, where the king was to hide from his pursuers.

Humphrey, George and William Penderel spread out across the neighbourhood, scouting for news so they could warn Charles and Richard of any approaching danger. The brothers were in a habitat they knew well. All of them lived in these woods, tending small-holdings, supported by grazing rights, while supplementing their subsistence farming with the chopping and guarding of timber.

While still within view of the road, Charles saw a troop of enemy cavalry ride by, mopping up men from his broken army. But the redcoats did not enter Spring Coppice. Charles believed this was because they were put off by heavy localised rainfall over that area of the forest.

A short time after Charles had set off, a detachment of Colonel Ashenhurst's Parliamentary troops arrived at Whiteladies, and asked the occupants if they had seen the king or any other Royalist fugitives. People from the nearby village told them that a large body of the king's men had ridden past three hours earlier. They said they thought Charles could well have been among them, but the Royalists had not stopped, so they could not be entirely sure. This information sent the Roundheads heading off in eager pursuit,

Whiteladies soon well behind them. Everyone wanted the glory of capturing the king.

Charles lay low in the wood for many hours that day, as thick rain fell. He used the time to pick Richard's brains. It quickly became clear that the idea of travelling to London was going to need to be reconsidered. Richard knew of a loose network of people loyal to the Crown, but it was limited to the surrounding area, and did not extend towards the capital. If he was to escape, the king accepted, he would need to modify his plan.

The country-dwellers protecting the king were soon under no illusion as to the softness of their royal charge. Charles would later recall that he spent the day without eating, in the wet. But others remembered that, because the rain was heavy and the king was in the open, they took special care of him.

The Francis Yates who had guided the king to Whiteladies had galloped off with the rest of the fleeing Cavaliers earlier that morning. There remained a second Francis Yates, who like his namesake had married one of the Penderel daughters, Margaret. The couple lived near Boscobel, at Langley Lawn. Margaret Yates arrived in the coppice carrying a blanket that she placed under a tree for Charles to sit on. She also brought him a black clay cup which contained a mixture of milk, eggs and sugar, and apples.

Margaret's arrival was unexpected, and Charles was startled when he saw her approach. He asked her suspiciously, 'Good woman, can you be faithful to a distressed Cavalier?' She replied without hesitation, 'Yes, sir, I will rather die than discover you.' Delighted with this reply, the king used a pewter spoon to dig into the food she had brought with her. When he was full, he passed what remained to George Penderel to finish off.

The second Francis Yates realised that the woodman's bill was too weighty an implement for the king to lug around. He swapped it for his broom hook, a lighter option for shoulders unaccustomed to manual labour.

Yates and the Penderels now set to work educating the king in the simple ways of the countryman: he needed to change his outward characteristics, particularly his tone and bearing, if he was to have a chance of remaining at large. He was first given the alias of 'William Jones', a travelling woodcutter. His protectors were pleased at the ease with which he picked up the Worcestershire accent. Charles was a good mimic, and had enjoyed trying out the various regional accents he had encountered on his march down from Scotland.

But it was his way of walking that was the real problem. A lifetime of being on show, of parading at court, and of ingrained haughty deportment, had to be exchanged for the unassuming gait of the simplest of country-dwellers. Charles found this part of his disguise extremely tricky to master, and even harder to remember. He kept falling back into his accustomed stride, which jarred terribly with his rustic appearance. Throughout his time with them his companions gave him repeated hushed reminders to walk like a peasant, not a prince. To fail in this, in front of a perceptive enemy, would render the rest of the masquerade useless.

Yet, despite his life depending on it, this was never a side of things that Charles could master for long – it went too much against his nature. A Royalist colonel who helped the king later in his escape attempt noted: 'In very deed, the King had a hard task, so to carry himself in all things that he might be in nothing like himself, majesty being so natural unto him, that even when he said nothing, did nothing, his very looks (if a man observed) were enough to betray him.'[7]

With the road to London closed to him, Charles considered his options. He asked Richard for details about Royalists who could be relied on. When Richard mentioned an elderly Catholic Royalist friend of his called Francis Wolfe, who lived in the Shropshire town of Madeley, a few miles to the west of where they were, Charles felt that this could be a potential escape route.

Another twenty-five miles on from Wolfe, and they would arrive at the Welsh border. Wales had proved one of the most loyal areas to the Crown throughout the Civil Wars, providing its army with thousands of recruits. Because of his active engagement in the war, Charles had become acquainted with several influential Welshmen during the preceding turbulent decade. He hoped these men would help him if he arrived at their door in his state of dire need.

He also felt that heading towards Wales would be such an unlikely direction for him to have chosen that it would outfox his pursuers. Surely their attention would be taken up with blocking all roads leading north to Scotland. If he could cross the River Severn and then proceed to Swansea or another busy Welsh port, his plan was to find a ship and cross to France or Spain.

In the late afternoon of Thursday, 4 September, Charles went with Richard, Humphrey and George Penderel, and the second Francis Yates, from Whiteladies to Richard Penderel's house at Hobbal Grange. They arrived there around five o'clock. The king delighted Richard and his wife Mary by the charming ease with which he played with their small daughter Nan (a pet name for Anne), dandling her on his knee as they prepared him a bacon and egg fricassee. After eating alone for a while, Charles again invited Richard to join him. 'Sir, I will,' Richard said. 'You have a better stomach than I,' the king teased, 'for you have eaten five times today already.'[8]

After dinner, Jane Penderel appeared. The brothers' widowed mother was plainly mystified as to why her family had been chosen to help the king at this dark time, but she thanked God for the great honour bestowed upon them, and gave her blessing to the distinguished guest.

Francis Yates offered the king thirty silver shillings to help fund him while he was on the run, but Charles took just ten. The assembled family group took their leave of the king on their knees, kissing his hand, expressing loyal good wishes for his escape, and calling on God to protect him. He and Richard then set off into the fading evening light, for Wales.

## 9

~~~

*The London Road*

</div>

*It is thought they have some express from their young
King, since the defeat at Worcester, and many of them
seem to be confident that their King hath a considerable
army in the Marches of Wales.*

Colonel John Jones to fellow regicide Thomas Scott, 1651

As the posse of leading Royalists were leaving the king at
Whiteladies before sunrise on 4 September, Charles had repeated
to Henry, Lord Wilmot, his secret hope of getting to London.
Wilmot had agreed that 'the London Road was his likeliest way to
escape'.[1] The two men arranged a rendezvous, should their separate
journeys succeed in getting them to the capital: they would meet
at the Three Cranes inn in the Vintry, an old ward of the City of
London that lay on the north bank of the Thames. Once there they
would ask for Will Ashburnham, who had been a Member of
Parliament until his expulsion for being a Royalist.

The Vintry was historically associated with Dick Whittington
– the most famous of all the lord mayors of London had championed public works in the ward. Of more relevance to Charles and
Wilmot was its role as the point where imports from France (espe-

cially wine and garlic) were landed. The ward had also become a well-worn launching point for journeys to the Continent: it was where people embarked for pilgrimages to Santiago di Compostela in Spain. Either France or Spain would be acceptable destinations for the two fugitives.

With the Vintry plan agreed, Charles and Wilmot parted. While Richard, William, Humphrey and George Penderel remained to serve and protect the king, their brother John was sent to guide and assist Wilmot, who was travelling with his servant Robert Swan.

Wilmot had had a poor relationship with Charles I. The late king had never forgiven him for voting in favour of the impeachment and execution of his great favourite the Earl of Strafford, in 1641. Three years later Charles I had stripped Wilmot of all his commands, and imprisoned him, after the Royalist cavalry general was found to be engaged in secret unauthorised peace negotiations with Parliament. But Wilmot was a popular leader, and his officers, refusing to believe him a traitor, petitioned the king for clemency on his behalf. Charles had felt obliged to release Wilmot, provided he promised to live in exile overseas.

Queen Henrietta Maria had for some years acted as Wilmot's patron, and she welcomed him into her court in France. This was where his great friendship with the Prince of Wales had developed, and after Charles I's execution it had blossomed further. The young would-be king appointed Wilmot one of his gentlemen of the bedchamber, a court position of great trust and familiarity.

Wilmot had supported Charles's alliance with the Scots, being among those who appreciated that it offered the only possible chance of retrieving the English throne at that time, and had accompanied Charles to Scotland in 1650. Despite his having fought against the Scots since the Bishops' Wars (when he had been taken prisoner of war after a brave but ill-fated cavalry charge), and his evident taste for the high life, Wilmot had managed to ingratiate himself with his Presbyterian hosts. He was one of the very few prominent Cavaliers allowed to remain in Scotland with Charles during his unhappy stay there.

Wilmot had therefore been with his master through the exasperation of exile in France, the humiliations and disappointments north of the border, and the crushing defeat at Worcester. That early morning at Whiteladies, Charles had remained sure of what he had decided so early in his flight from Worcester: that Wilmot was the man most likely to assist his flight to safety abroad.

The greatest problem Wilmot faced was how very well known he was. This hero from Europe's Thirty Years War had long been a figure of dread to the rebels. They had claimed, exactly nine years previously, in the news sheet *Exceeding true and joyfull newes from Worchester*, that they 'slew Commissary Wilmot', 'within half a mile of Worcester'. This had been wishful thinking. The action the propagandists were referring to was Powick Bridge, but Wilmot, though wounded during the sharp cavalry engagement, was far from dead. Within a month he had recovered sufficiently to lead the Royalist left wing at the battle of Edgehill. The twelve-year-old Charles, Prince of Wales, had witnessed his dramatic charge that day with boyish admiration.

The energetic Wilmot had gone on to have a busy Civil War. One of his successes was the battle of Tipton Green, in 1644, a victory that was achieved after he had led a force out of Worcester, marched it thirty miles north, and relieved the besieged Royalist garrison inside Dudley Castle. Wilmot knew the country around Worcester quite well from his wartime exploits. The counter to this, as he looked to get away, was that many in the area could recognise him by sight. A man of such importance (he had also been Member of Parliament for nearby Tamworth) would be very hard to hide.

The task of keeping Wilmot at liberty was made no easier by his astonishingly inflexible attitude. While Charles was quick to blend in, was happy to masquerade as a woodman, and would be easily persuaded to strike out on foot towards the Welsh border, his aristocratic sidekick had standards that he was simply not prepared to compromise. Even though his life was at stake, Lord Wilmot resolutely refused to wear a disguise, because he thought that if he did, he would be made to look ridiculous. Equally, he declined to travel by foot, because he considered walking to be beneath his status as a gentleman.

This made life extremely difficult for John Penderel. On the day after the battle he had been told to look after this leading Royalist, and to keep him safe at all costs. He was also instructed not to share any information about having seen the king, and not to talk to anyone who he did not already know well and trust fully.

John set off with Wilmot and his servant Robert Swan, leading them in an arc thirty-five miles north of Worcester as he looked with increasing desperation for somewhere safe to hide them. But while the king was lurking in Spring Coppice, content to disguise himself as a woodman and to commit himself to the care of the other Penderel brothers and their wives, Wilmot was dressed as he had been during the previous day's engagement, every inch the Royalist military notable. While the king had sent his horse off with his men when they left Whiteladies, knowing it would attract unwelcome and dangerous attention, Wilmot remained on his, which was eye-catching in its magnificence.

Wilmot was also quick to find fault with the various hiding places that John proposed. He rejected Hunger Hill, the property of John Shores, as being too exposed. He did not like the home of John Clempson in Pattingham any better, once he learnt that the village priest was a supporter of the Commonwealth. There were other, unspecified, problems with the sanctuary offered by a man called Reynolds. But the area was teeming with Major General Harrison's mopping-up parties, and the longer Wilmot remained out in the open, the more certain it was that he would be captured.

The trio's first serious brush came not with soldiers, but with civilians. Workers at Brewood Forge looked up on hearing the sound of hooves, and were astonished to see what appeared to be a caricature of a senior Cavalier officer riding past them with two companions. They mounted their horses and set off after them, only to be pulled up short by a Royalist sympathiser who insisted they were making a mistake: the man they were pursuing was none other than Colonel Thomas Crompton, a Parliamentary war hero. The workmen went back to the forge, while Wilmot, Swan and John Penderel waited in a nearby pit until they were quite sure the danger had passed. At another point the three Royalists nearly rode directly into a Roundhead cavalry troop which was coming the other way.

John was soon convinced that remaining at large with his difficult and demanding charge, in an area swarming with hostile forces, was going to take all his resourcefulness, as well as a lot of good fortune, if it was not going to end in disaster.

Just outside the small village of Coven, five miles north of Wolverhampton, they had their lucky break when they bumped into William Walker, the Roman Catholic priest who lived at Whiteladies. John explained the extreme danger he and his two companions were in, and Walker ushered them to the home of John Huntbatch, a Royalist who lived nearby at Brinsford.

While Wilmot and Swan hid, John led the party's horses away to be concealed in stables belonging to John Evans, a neighbour. This gave Wilmot time to examine Huntbatch's home, and to conclude that it could only be a temporary solution. It was bound to be searched soon, because of both its exposed position and its householder's known loyalties: Huntbatch had been threatened with confiscation of all his property seven years earlier because of his attachment to the Crown. Wilmot implored John to find him 'some asylum' where he could feel truly safe.

John was reluctant to leave Wilmot in such a dangerous place, but was persuaded that there was no time to lose. He rode to

Wolverhampton to see what Royalist sympathisers there had to offer, but none of them felt able to help. They were demoralised by the previous day's decisive defeat, and the town was already filled with Parliamentary soldiers, busy conducting searches for the king's men.

Besides, the oldest inhabitants remembered what had happened less than half a century earlier to a pair of local farmers. John Holyhead and Thomas Smart had hidden Robert Wintour and Stephen Littleton, conspirators in the Gunpowder Plot. They had planned to blow up Parliament, along with much of the royal family, but were foiled at the last moment. Wintour and Littleton managed to evade capture for two months, but their luck ran out in early 1606, and Holyhead and Smart were arrested alongside them. The sentence for any who helped someone guilty of high treason was to suffer the established punishment for that crime. They were therefore hanged, drawn and quartered. Memories of the men's terrible screams as they were castrated and disembowelled on butchers' blocks had echoed down the generations.

Returning from Wolverhampton towards Huntbatch's house, still with no plan in place, John entered the village of Northcot. There he spied Mrs Underhill, a farmer's wife who he knew, tending her garden. He started up a conversation with her, and told her that he desperately needed help in concealing some Royalist fugitives. Affronted and afraid, Mrs Underhill said she could not possibly assist him, both because her husband was away, and on account of the many Parliamentarians combing the area. She begged John to leave her in peace.

Just as he was being sent on his way, John looked up to see the wiry figure of Father John Huddleston passing by. He knew Huddleston, a kind-faced man in his early forties, both as an ardent Royalist and as a visitor to Whiteladies, where he shared priestly duties with William Walker, joining him from time to time to say prayers and do holy offices for their fellow Roman Catholics.

Huddleston had been educated at the English College in Douai, a Catholic seminary established in northern France in response to Queen Elizabeth's persecutions. Despite his religious calling, it seems that he had taken up arms for Charles I in the Civil Wars.

John followed after Father Huddleston, but the priest failed to recognise this countryman who seemed so annoyingly eager to engage him in conversation. John started by asking what he was carrying under his arm. It was, Huddleston replied, a parcel containing half a dozen shirts, the gift of a lady in Leamington Spa, kindly sent because he was tutor to her grandson.

John then asked what news the priest might have heard recently. Huddleston responded that the only information he had learnt was very good: 'That the King had got the day at Worcester.' John replied, ''Tis clear contrary,' and related the scale of the previous day's defeat.

Huddleston asked where he had heard such a terrible tale, and John explained that he had learnt it first hand at Whiteladies, which he had left that morning. He told the flabbergasted priest that he had seen the king and his leading men there, and added, 'If I did not know you better than you seem to know me, I should not have been thus bold, for I had commands and cautions sufficient to be circumspect, both what to do and to whom I spoke.'

He then reassured Huddleston, 'I know you right well, for I have seen you very often with your good friend, my old master, Mr Walker, at Whiteladies, whom I left this morning in great trouble to see His Majesty and his friends in that sad and desperate condition – one whereof I have brought to a very near neighbour of yours, a person of quality I believe, for he's a very brave gentleman. There I have left him exposed to all dangers; been at Wolverhampton, in hopes among friends thereabout to have found some place of more safety for him, but am disappointed at all [places] and [am] now going back to see how God hath disposed of him, for if he be not removed this night, he cannot escape.'[2]

Charles painted as a young warrior king in waiting, during his European exile.
Portrait by Philippe de Champaigne (c.1653).

Charles's parents, King Charles I and Queen Henrietta Maria, painted by Sir Anthony van Dyck before the Civil Wars that cost the king his crown and his life.

Lucy Walter, the first of Charles's many mistresses, reclining on her bed in a pose flaunting her famed sexual magnetism.

Sir Edward Hyde (later 1st Earl of Clarendon), who in many ways saw himself as the keeper of Charles's conscience. Resistant to alliances with any who opposed the Church of England, he refused to have any part in Charles's Scottish venture.

James Grahame, 1st Marquess of Montrose, was the Royalists' military champion in Scotland. He served the Stuarts with distinction, but was ultimately betrayed by Charles.

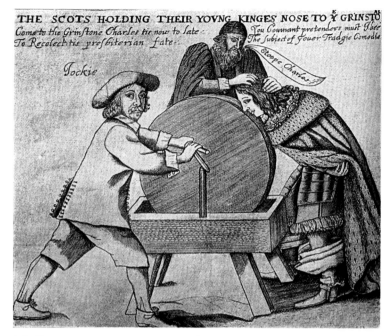

THE SCOTS HOLDING THEIR YOVNG KINGES NOSE TO Ŷ GRINSTŌ

Come to the Grimstone Charles tis now to late
To Recolecht tis presbiterian fate.

You Covnant pretenders must Bee
The Subiect of Your Tradgie Comedie

Iockie

Stoope Charles

A Parliamentary propaganda cartoon, mocking Charles for the desperate sacrifice in principles that his alliance with the Scots forced out of him.

The decisive battle of Worcester was the final engagement of the Civil Wars. American presidents John Adams and Thomas Jefferson visited the battlefield in 1786, Adams calling it 'the ground where liberty was fought for'.

A view of Boscobel, Whiteladies and the Royal Oak, by Robert Streater. All three subjects of this painting provided crucial cover for the king on the run, and have entered the mythology surrounding his escape.

James Stanley, 7th Earl of Derby, was given military commands in the king's army because of his social eminence, rather than through any military ability. He was no match for the able leaders of the New Model Army.

an Orig.ᵍˡ Painting.

M.ᵛᵈᵉʳ Gucht fecit.

Major General Thomas Harrison was put in charge of mopping up Charles's defeated army, and of bringing in the fugitive royal. A zealous Puritan, he had been one of the prime movers behind the execution of Charles I.

Richard Penderel – 'Trusty Richard' – was a key member of the humble rural family that risked all to hide the king during his earliest days on the run.

Father John Huddleston, Royalist and Roman Catholic, helped save Charles's life – and later, perhaps, helped spare his soul.

The two men talked further as they walked. As Huddleston listened with shock and despair to John's account, the pair drew closer to Moseley Hall, the secluded late-Elizabethan building where Huddleston was secretly acting as chaplain to the Catholic household of its owner, Thomas Whitgreave. Whitgreave had fought for the Crown as a captain at the battle of Naseby in 1645, and had been wounded and captured there.

Moseley Hall was a mile from the spot where John had accosted the priest, and six miles from Whiteladies. As they approached it across the fields, John asked Huddleston if he might persuade Whitgreave to take Wilmot in, and keep him safe for a while. Huddleston told him not to say any more on the subject until they could finish their conversation in private.

Huddleston took John into the hall, and showed him to his room, where he told him to wait while he went to find Whitgreave. He caught up with Whitgreave outside, and repeated to him the astonishing news he had heard from John. Huddleston suggested that Whitgreave go with John to Huntbatch's house at Coven, to see how he could help prevent Wilmot from being caught. Whitgreave immediately agreed to the plan.

Whitgreave arrived to find Wilmot in a state of near disbelief that he was somehow still at large, given the closeness of his escapes in the brief period since the defeat at Worcester. He was clearly resigned to imminent capture unless he could somehow be rescued from this inadequate hiding place.

Wilmot was equally despondent about the hopes of the king, and the rest of Charles's right-hand men. He described to Whitgreave the beleaguered state Charles had been in when he had last seen him, and how the other Royalist grandees had scattered in the desperate hope of avoiding being taken, or cut down, by the victorious enemy.

To a Royalist like Whitgreave, the news relayed to him by Huddleston and Wilmot must have been overwhelming in its awfulness. The young king was the great hope of their cause. He had come to reclaim the crown that had been taken so violently from his family. He was now, it was clear, totally defeated. It seemed highly likely that he must either already have been captured, or that, like Wilmot, he was on the point of being so. Either way, it seemed certain that there would very soon be another royal visit to the executioner's block.

Whitgreave promised to do all he could to help Wilmot. He told Huntbatch that he knew of a safe place for Wilmot at a friend's house. He was careful not to give away that Wilmot would in fact be hidden in his own home. There was no benefit in Huntbatch knowing the truth: he might be careless with the secret, or he might be interrogated, and have it forced out of him by Parliament's men.

Whitgreave asked Huntbatch to bring Wilmot and his servant to a prearranged spot on his estate at midnight, when Whitgreave could be sure that his family and servants were all safely in bed. He told Huntbatch to keep to a route that only local people would know, to lessen the chances of detection.

Whitgreave was at the rendezvous at the appointed hour, but to his increasing alarm there was no sign of Wilmot or Huntbatch. He returned home after a long and fruitless wait, convinced that something must have gone very wrong. He was therefore amazed, on reaching Moseley Hall, to find that Wilmot was already there, waiting for him. For some reason Huntbatch had decided to bring him directly there, and by a different route to the one that had been so carefully thought through and decided upon. Seeing the bewilderment on Whitgreave's face, Wilmot was horrified that Huntbatch had inconvenienced his new host so unnecessarily, thoughtlessly and dangerously.

Whitgreave welcomed Wilmot to his home and gave him something to eat before showing him to his bed. Wilmot decided that he would sleep in his clothes, in case he needed to dash for safety in the night, and handed over a purse of precious jewels, which he asked his host to hide with particular care: they were to fund his escape attempt. Wilmot's servant Robert Swan settled down into a makeshift bed near his master's while Whitgreave went outside to see that their horses were secured and their possessions hidden. Whitgreave then showed Wilmot Moseley Hall's finest hiding place. It was a priest hole.

Priest holes were constructed with the utmost secrecy, the normal practice being for the owner of the house and the builder of the hiding place to be the only ones to know where it was, and how it was opened. In Abbots Salford, a large gabled mansion built in Warwickshire in 1602, the priest hole was built at the very top of the building. Few who entered the dingy attic would notice the nondescript oak cupboard standing to one side. But, by pulling out a pin from under one of its shelves, a hidden door would be released, giving access to a four-foot-deep alcove. Once inside, the person hiding would slide a hefty bolt shut behind them.

The most prolific constructor and architect of these 'privacies' in the late sixteenth and early seventeenth centuries was Nicholas Owen, a carpenter from Oxford. Owen was slight – his nickname was 'Little John' – and lame, after a horse rolled on him and crushed a leg. To the outside world he was a simple travelling joiner. He worked at regular jobs in the day, to add to the appearance of normality. But it was at night that he got down to his real role. For in reality, this man, who used the aliases of 'Draper' and 'Andrewes', was the invaluable helper of leading Jesuits. His prime responsibility was the building of places for hiding and escape for persecuted priests. Owen worked across England in grand houses that formed the core of local Catholic underground networks. He took enormous care to make each hideaway distinctive in form and access, so that if one of his installations was discovered it would not help the royal, Protestant, authorities to root out the rest.

Owen had a preference for working inside the interior walls of houses. He also had a gift for thinking in three dimensions, and employed curves in his intricate designs. 'With incomparable skill, he knew how to conduct priests to a place of safety along the subterranean passages, to hide them between walls and bury them in labyrinths of a thousand windings,' wrote Father Matthias Tanner, a historian of the Jesuit order in the seventeenth century.[3] It was difficult, and extremely painful, employment. Owen had accumulated many injuries to his body, brought about by his chiselling away in barely accessible holes, hewn out of thick masonry, while he lay contorted and exhausted, doing the work he believed his God required of him. He was constantly in pain, particularly because of a chronic hernia.

Nicholas Owen was inspired to the heights of ingenuity through first-hand knowledge of what would happen if any of those he worked so hard to conceal were discovered. The authorities captured him in 1594. They knew he was Catholic, but did not realise that this prisoner was the constructor of so many priest holes. He was tortured nonetheless, refusing to give up the names of any of his associates, before a rich sympathiser bought his freedom for a large sum.

Twelve years later, he and three other Jesuits were the subject of a relentless search of Hindlip Hall, in Worcestershire. This followed the Gunpowder Plot, the failure of which resulted in an exhaustive manhunt for all the Catholics connected to the conspiracy. Owen and a comrade had little warning of the search, and were forced to hide quickly in a priest hole in Hindlip's long gallery. They eventually had to give themselves up after eleven days, having long since consumed the single apple they had taken into hiding with them some time before.

On this occasion the authorities knew exactly how great a prize they had unearthed in Owen. Secretary of State Robert Cecil wrote excitedly: 'It is incredible, how great was the joy caused by his arrest … knowing the great skill of Owen in constructing hiding places, and the innumerable quantity of dark holes which he had schemed for hiding priests all through England.'[4] Eager to extract his many secrets, they took Owen from prison to the Tower of London for torture. Father John Gerard (whose eventual escape from the Tower some years earlier was probably assisted by Owen) has left his account of what he was subjected to, as a captured Jesuit priest:

> *We went to the torture room in a kind of procession, the attendants walking ahead with lighted candles.*
>
> *The chamber was underground and dark, particularly near the entrance. It was a vast place, and every device and instrument of human torture was there. They pointed out some of them to me and said I would try them all. Then [the interrogator] asked me again if I would confess.*
>
> *'I cannot,' I said.*
>
> *I fell on my knees for a moment's prayer. Then they took me to a big upright pillar, one of the wooden posts which held the roof of this huge underground chamber. Driven into the top of it were iron staples for supporting heavy weights. Then they put my wrists into iron gauntlets and ordered me to climb two or three wicker steps.*
>
> *My arms were then lifted up and an iron bar was passed through the rings of one gauntlet, then through the staple and rings to the second gauntlet. This done, they fastened the bar with a pin to prevent it from slipping, and then, removing the wicker steps one by one from under my feet, they left me hanging by my hands and arms fastened above my head.*[5]

Father Gerard was suspended by the wrists from the ceiling for several hours, losing consciousness because of the agony tearing through his hands, arms, shoulders and chest, before being brought round by his tormentors. When he was awake, they forced him once more along the same pathway through physical anguish to oblivion. Gerard recalled going through this cycle eight or nine times in a day. He recognised the temptation to end the pain by giving up the information demanded. It was only his belief in God that kept him from doing so:

> *Seeing my agony and the struggle going on in my mind, He gave me this most merciful thought: the utmost and worst they can do is to kill you, and you have often wanted to give your life for your Lord God. The Lord God sees all you are enduring – He can do all things. You are in God's keeping.*

Interrogated in this same way, Owen told his torturers nothing they did not already know: the notes taken during his interrogations show the thin pickings he offered up, to the frustration of the inquisitors. They also underline Owen's unshakeable resolve to shield his comrades' anonymity, and so save them from similar suffering – the same consideration, in fact, that had made him determined to build the best hideaways he could possibly devise.

Owen's anguish was not over. He was stretched on the rack, his torturers binding his torso with a metal sheet to hold his hernia in. But eventually, a contemporary recorded, 'his bowels gushed out, together with his life'. To blacken Owen's name, and to downplay his heroism, the authorities falsely claimed that he had resorted to suicide, a mortal sin to Roman Catholics. They said he had 'ripped up his own belly with a knife without a point'.[6] This, despite his being bound and guarded at all times, and torture having left him incapable of holding anything in his hands. The thought of Owen having the strength or capacity to stab himself with a weapon is absurd.*

\* \* \*

---

\* Nicholas Owen was canonised by Pope Paul VI in 1970.

Moseley Hall's priest hole was a particularly fine one. It was so impossible to detect, Thomas Whitgreave boasted, that he had used it to hide successfully from a recent 'violent strict search' ordered by Captain Henry Stone, the governor of Stafford and a scourge of the area's Royalists.

The priest hole was accessed through a trapdoor in the floor of the small suite of rooms Lord Wilmot was shown to. The person hiding found himself in a space, bound with oak beams and brickwork, that lay behind the rear of the hall's brewhouse chimney. There was a stone seat in the corner, and an inch-wide hole in the wall, set with a pin that could be popped out. Through this, water or broth could be poured through a pipe, to keep the person within alive in case a search was prolonged.

On first being shown this safest of havens, Wilmot said, 'I would give a world my friend were here,' and swore that he would have paid £20,000 to make such a wish come true. As happy as he was to have found such a fine hiding place, he was tormented by not knowing what had happened to the king.

On the evening of Thursday, 4 September, while Wilmot was preparing to set off for Moseley Hall, Richard Penderel led the king from his home at Hobbal Grange to start their night-time trek towards Wales. The going was tougher than Charles had anticipated, and for a man used to the finest footwear in the land, the coarse shoes he had borrowed from William Creswell were painful; the soft skin of his feet was soon rubbed raw.

The cross-country route Richard had chosen meant the two men had to go slowly, but even so they were surprised by the thwack of low-hanging branches and by drop-away ditches, while stumps and ruts tripped them up with sudden violence. At one point, convinced that all was lost, and with his feet blistered and bloody, Charles threw himself to the ground in despair, saying he could not go on – he would rather stay where he was, and be discovered, than take another step. It was a moment reminiscent of his capture a year earlier at 'The Start', when he had been discovered hiding in a sorry state by the Covenanters' men, 'over-wearied and very fearful'.

This time, though, he was fortunate to have a strong and unflappable companion who would not let him give up. Richard managed to talk him into continuing, alternating claims that there was not much further to go with promises that the terrain ahead would be less challenging. Charles stumbled on in the darkness, his chafed feet causing him increasing agony.

The two men's immediate goal was a ferry across the Severn between Bridgnorth and Shrewsbury. A little before midnight, after seven miles of excruciating progress, they approached Evelith Mill, two miles from the market town of Madeley, by means of whose bridge they planned to cross the river.

As they got nearer they could make out the miller, dressed in white, seated in his doorway. Richard suffered a moment of clumsiness when, after quietly opening the gate that led to the millbridge, he let it clap shut behind him. The miller spun round. Making out two figures in the dark, he barked the challenge, 'Who goes there?'

'Neighbours going home!' Richard called back hopefully. But his reply failed to convince.

'If you be neighbours, stand!' the miller said. 'Or else I will knock you down!'

Richard urged the king to keep up with him as he broke into a run. The pair cleared another gate, the miller running after them, cursing 'Rogues! Rogues!' They could hear others spill out of the mill, and assumed that they had joined in the chase. Fleeing for their lives, the king and Richard waded through a brook, before scurrying along the thick, muddy furrows of a lane. Charles would recall that the only way he stayed close to Richard in the darkness was by following the rubbing noise made by his calfskin breeches as he ran.

Eventually Charles shouted out, telling Richard to join him in jumping a hedge. For half an hour they lay still on the other side, hearts pounding, straining to hear if their pursuers were on their scent, until finally they were satisfied that there was nobody coming after them.

It was now a little before one o'clock in the morning. Charles, shaken by the miller's pursuit, was feeling vulnerable. His main concern was the growing belief that nobody would be prepared to put up with a guest of his toxicity. He said that he would hide in a hedgerow near a great tree, while Richard made his way to Wolfe's home in order to assure himself of his reliability.

Richard banged on Wolfe's door. It was opened by the old man's daughter. When Wolfe eventually appeared, Richard kept the king's identity to himself, asking only if he might agree to hide a gentleman escapee from the battle of Worcester. Wolfe was full of regret, but said it was too risky a proposition for him: the Parliamentarians had made it plain that anyone helping fleeing Royalists would pay with their life. The only person he would risk his neck for would be the king himself. Richard went with his instinct, and told the astonished Wolfe that that was in fact the gentleman he was referring to. His composure regained, Wolfe agreed to do what he could.

As dawn on Friday, 5 September approached, Richard returned to the king and told him what had been said. Charles was appalled that Richard had revealed his identity to this stranger so easily. He realised, though, that he had no choice now but to trust Wolfe, and set off for his house, which he crept into from the back.

When Charles met Francis Wolfe, the old man's anxiety was clear to see. Wolfe reported that Parliamentary forces had Madeley and the nearby ferry buttoned up. There were two companies of Harrison's militia in the town, and they were eagerly looking out for Royalists on the run. There was not a single ford across the Severn that he knew of that was not being watched, and every boat along the river had been taken under military control. Added to this was the equally gloomy news that all the hiding places in Wolfe's home had already been discovered, so they were quite useless. Indeed, they would surely be the first places the enemy would look, if and when they returned. Further, the enemy troops were being billeted on households in the locality, which would make it impossible for the king to stay under his roof for any time at all.

Charles washed quickly in the house, then Wolfe took him and Richard to hide in the hay store in his barn, returning later with cold meat for them. The pair lay up there all day, and were joined in the evening by Wolfe and his son, a freshly released Royalist prisoner of war. Over food the four men discussed the king's options, the Wolfes both being quite adamant that there was no possibility of his getting into Wales, because the River Severn was so closely guarded. Contrary to Charles's calculations, Major General Harrison had recognised even before the battle of Worcester had been won that this would be an attractive escape route. Harrison knew Wales and its strong Royalist leanings first hand, from his time rooting out Anglican priests there the previous year. As a result, he had closed down the Anglo–Welsh border with ruthless efficiency.

Charles accepted the Wolfes' advice and gave up on his Welsh plan. He also followed the old man's suggestion that he cover his bright white stockings with green yarn ones, because they stood out too much. Wolfe's wife further refined Charles's disguise, rubbing the juice of walnut leaves onto the backs of his hands, to darken them to something that might pass for a labourer's skin tone.

It was time to move on, before one of Harrison's patrols stumbled on them. The Wolfes gave the two men provisions for their journey, and a little money. They also offered them horses, but it was decided that, despite the biting pain Charles felt at every step, they would be safer on foot. That way they could cut across country, and avoid roads thick with enemy search parties.

With very few options, Charles decided to set off that night on the road back towards Richard's home at Hobbal Grange. It was eleven o'clock on Friday, 5 September, when the king and Richard left the Wolfes, whose maid led them in the dark for the first couple of miles. Charles hoped to find out what had happened to Henry Wilmot once he had got back to Hobbal Grange. If Wilmot had found it as difficult to move on as he had, Charles intended to join with him, and resume their original plan of heading for London together.

## 10

# *Near Misses*

*It is not yet known of any certainty where the Scots King is. If he be not already gotten away into the Isle of Man, it's thought he skulks in some private corners.*

Another Victory in Lancashire obtained against the Scots,
September 1651

After being shown the priest hole at Moseley Hall, and retiring to bed fully dressed, Wilmot had slept well that Thursday night.

In the morning his host, Thomas Whitgreave, sent the priest William Walker to Bentley Hall, four miles south-east of Moseley, and near to Walsall. Bentley's owner, Colonel John Lane, a Royalist who had fought for the Stuarts since the English Civil War's start in 1642, knew Walker well. Whitgreave trusted that Lane would be prepared to listen to what Walker had to say, and would help by looking after and hiding Wilmot's striking horse.

Whitgreave hoped it could be hidden at Lane's home, where the stables were less open to general view than were his at Moseley. Whitgreave's house was near the road, and a neighbouring household had a clear sight of the property. If anyone spied Wilmot's

134

charger, they could not help but wonder where it was from, and whose it was. Bentley Hall had none of these concerns, for it stood quite alone.

What Whitgreave had not known when he sent Walker on his way was that Colonel Lane had served under Wilmot during the Civil War. Lane immediately agreed to help his former superior officer in any way he could, and told Walker to take back the message that he would come to Moseley Hall at midnight. He suggested the rendezvous with Whitgreave should take place in a close called Alport's Leasow, which had 'a great dry pit, covered with many trees'. He could leave his horse there without concern that it would be spotted.

Whitgreave met Lane at Alport's Leasow at the agreed time, and brought him home to Moseley with him to see Wilmot. Lane and Wilmot greeted one another, then Lane wasted no time in revealing the plan he had formed in the few hours since he had become aware of Wilmot's plight.

He urged Wilmot to move to Bentley Hall, which he judged to be safer than Moseley. Apart from the latter's dangerous lack of privacy, Lane pointed out that Whitgreave was a known Catholic, who must surely be under greater suspicion of helping fleeing Royalists than most. Moseley was therefore more likely to attract sudden Parliamentary house searches than Bentley.

As well as holding out the immediate possibility of a safer haven, the colonel was also the bearer of intriguing news. His much younger sister, Jane – the colonel was forty-three, Jane was in her mid-twenties – had recently secured a pass from Captain Stone in Stafford. This document, won from a hostile but powerful figure, granted Jane and a manservant permission to travel to the home of some cousins who lived near Bristol. One of them was about to give birth, and Jane had persuaded Captain Stone that she needed to be on hand to help.

This pass, Lane hoped, might enable Wilmot to accompany his sister, disguised as her manservant. Once they reached their destination he could make his own way the short distance to Bristol, and find a ship to take him abroad.

Wilmot thanked Lane for his kind offer, but said he must stay at Moseley for now because he wanted to be ready to help the king, and he was delighted by the hiding place Whitgreave had provided for him. He encouraged the colonel to keep his sister's pass safe, and to hand. For the right person, it would surely be a godsend.

On the return journey from Francis Wolfe's home, after the attempt to cross to Wales had come to nothing, the king and Richard once again approached Evelith Mill and its fierce occupant. Charles insisted that they give it a wide berth. He was adamant that he and Richard must wade through the river rather than risk another confrontation, and a further hue and cry.

Richard protested that the stretch of water was known to be treacherous, and admitted that he did not know how to swim. Charles, a strong and enthusiastic swimmer, said he would help him over. Entering the water, Charles found it only reached his waist, and he was able to guide Richard across with ease.

Once they reached Hobbal Grange, they decided to carry on for a further three miles to Boscobel House, where the Earl of Derby had urged Charles to head in the aftermath of defeat, and where William and Joan Penderel were live-in housekeepers for the Giffard family.

They arrived at Boscobel at three o'clock in the morning of Saturday, 6 September. The nine miles from Madeley had taken four hours to cover, because of the dark, the roughness of the route travelled, and the state of Charles's feet. The king had, by this stage, been walking for two straight nights, in agony.

Joan Penderel knelt to peel off the wet shoes and stockings, which were heavy with pieces of gravel, then tended to the king's blisters and treated his wounds. She managed to find him fresh stockings, but there were no other shoes that fitted him, so she warmed the ones that had been torturing him by popping warm coals inside them, so they would at least be dry by the time he was forced to put them on again.

The king asked of William, 'What news?' William informed him that Major William Careless was also concealed in the house. It was a name the king recognised as belonging to a brave officer from his crushed army at Worcester.

Careless, who had rallied to the king in the days before the battle, had been one of the Royalists who had charged down the city's streets, risking all while the king made his escape. Indeed, Careless had stayed till the very end: he believed he had witnessed the battle's last fatality before finally riding off.

He had then found himself in an area that he knew well – he had grown up nearby at Broom Hall, in Brewood. Then, during the First Civil War, he had briefly become governor of Tong Castle, which stood a couple of miles from Boscobel, and from Whiteladies.

David Jones, a friend of the major's, had hidden him for a while at Tong Heath. From there he had found his way to Boscobel House, led there by a woman called Elizabeth Burgess.

Careless was another from the intertwined local Catholic gentry families of this part of western England. His loyalty to the Crown had brought him a great deal of suffering, including a spell as a prisoner of war. In the nine months prior to the battle of Worcester, after his release from captivity, he had been lying low in the vicinity, hoping that the day would come when he would be able to help the Stuart cause once more.

Charles summoned the major, who was quite overcome by the sight of his master. He started crying, and the king – tired, scared and vulnerable – joined in the tears. After they had regained control of their emotions, Charles asked Careless for his recommendations as to what he should do next.

Careless was clear in his advice, stressing that the king was in mortal danger: the major had seen the enemy in great numbers, fanning out over the entire area in pursuit of escaping Royalists. Charles's capture was, of course, their prime goal.

Careless advised that hiding either in Boscobel House or in the nearby woodland would prove equally disastrous, given the quantity and the persistence of the enemy: they would surely discover the king in either place before long. In fact, having observed the thoroughness of the Parliamentarians up close, Careless was sure they would return to Boscobel that day.

The one spot nearby where Careless considered that Charles might find safety was in a great oak tree he had spotted on his travels, and had briefly hidden in himself. This oak had been pollarded a few years before, which had prompted it to grow back strong, with an unusually thick platform of lower branches. This lushness was, Careless had noticed, impossible to see through. In addition, the oak grew in a spot blessed with good views in every direction. As both hiding place and observation point, it struck him as the best and only option.

Charles enjoyed a quick breakfast of bread and cheese, with warmed milk and beer. Then, at nine o'clock on the morning of Saturday, 6 September he set out for the hiding place that would come to symbolise his time on the run after Worcester.

Careless led the king to the foot of the oak tree, and the two men climbed up into its dense boughs, using a woodman's ladder lent by William Penderel. They carried with them two cushions from William's home, as well as provisions for the day: more bread and cheese, wrapped in linen, and weak beer to wash it down with.

After settling into the hiding spot, Careless noticed Charles's extreme tiredness following all his exertions, and invited him to lay his head in his lap, while using the cushions as a makeshift mattress. The king slept deeply for the first time in three days, his head so heavy on Careless's lap that the major lost all sensation in one of his legs. On one occasion, as a group of redcoat soldiers were riding beneath the oak, Careless feared that his leg was so numb that he and the king might slide out of the tree and drop into the enemy's path. Unable even to whisper, in case the Parliamentarians should hear him, but no longer able to keep the king secure, the major gently pinched Charles till he woke up.

They waited for a lull in the busy day of search parties, then shared the food and drink they had taken up with them. Meanwhile William and Joan Penderel kept watch on the ground below, Joan pretending to be busy gathering sticks. Several times they spotted redcoats combing the thick woodland, hunting for Royalist prey. At one point they saw an old woman scraping around in the field near them, looking for something to eat, and heard her suddenly shout out, to nobody they could see, 'Master, don't you see a troop of horse before you?' But neither those cavalrymen, nor any of their comrades, climbed up into the branches of the formidable oak, whose heavy, leafy boughs screened the king and the major. At the one instant when an enemy cavalryman started to look too intently at the oak, and seemed to think of examining it closely, Joan Penderel quickly diverted his attention, and the moment of greatest danger passed.

In the evening Charles and Careless came down from the oak, and returned to Boscobel House. Charles sat in a hidden corner of the garden, drinking wine brought for him by Richard Penderel from Wolverhampton. In this secluded spot, so far removed from the stress of the day, William Penderel took the opportunity to shave Charles, and trim his hair some more. They stayed in the garden till it grew dark.

Meanwhile, also on Saturday, 6 September, Humphrey Penderel, the miller, went to Shifnal to pay some taxes due to the military. While there he asked Captain Broadways, the tax collector, what he had heard about goings on in the area. Their conversation was interrupted by the sudden appearance of a Parliamentary colonel, who demanded to know of Broadways if he had followed up reports that the king had been seen at Whiteladies. Broadways said he had heard the rumour that Charles had been there, but knew nothing further. He then motioned towards Humphrey, and told the colonel that this man would know more on the subject, since he was an inhabitant of the house in question.

The colonel, excited by this coincidence, interrogated Humphrey sharply, but the miller did well. He conceded that Charles, as he supposed everyone had heard, had indeed passed through the property. But, he added, it would have been quite impossible for the king to have stayed on there, undiscovered, because the three families that all called Whiteladies home could agree over nothing: there was not a chance of such a disparate group keeping the king's hiding place secret, if he had chosen to shelter under such a divided roof.

The colonel reminded Humphrey of the £1,000 bounty on the king's head. Humphrey was unmoved. The colonel rudely dismissed him, saying Parliament would capture the king within a day or two, with or without the help of the likes of him.

When Humphrey returned to recount this tale, it was the first time that Charles learnt of the enormous price on his head. He felt despondent, knowing what a temptation such a fortune must be to anyone, let alone a family scraping a living from the land: at this time a craftsman in the building trade was earning roughly £25 per year, and £1,000 could have bought just short of 200 head of cattle.

The Penderels had not mentioned it to their guest, but the day before, one of them had been approached by someone who had been present at Whiteladies when Charles had first put on his woodman's disguise. Were the brothers aware, this man enquired, where Charles was now, for he had just learnt that £1,000 was being offered for his capture. This Penderel brother, determined to keep the king safe, managed to persuade the would-be bounty hunter that it was too late to claim any such reward: they were already guilty of helping the king, and if they now confessed as much, they would both be executed for treason.

Careless reassured the king that those few who knew his whereabouts would never contemplate his betrayal, even for a reward 100 times greater than that on offer. This declaration of infinite loyalty set Charles's mind at rest.

At the same time that Charles was coming to terms with the size of the price on his head, Parliament was redoubling its efforts to find him. There had, early on, been great excitement at the capture of 'a tall young Gentleman', but on examination he proved not to be the king.

A few days after the battle, the Irish and Scottish Committee, which was responsible for deciding what to do with the flood of Royalist prisoners, urged the House of Commons to 'publish their pleasure concerning those who harbour and conceal any person who has been in arms for Charles Stuart, and for encouragement of such as shall apprehend, or discover ... the said Charles Stuart'.[1]

Inaccurate reports came in from across England as to the king's progress. From Cheshire, it was stated: 'Now (blessed be God) most of the enemies of this Commonwealth, that got off from the fight at Worcester, are all killed and taken: but Charles Stuart, their Captain General, hath again narrowly escaped, and out run them all, being habited in mean apparel, with only four men to attend him: he is gone towards Scotland with a great and panic fear, by reason of his disaffection of the country towards him.' They said that he had got as far as Didsbury, near Manchester, where he had been attacked and nearly killed by Clubmen – civilians who armed themselves in order to defend their communities from the excesses of both sides in the Civil War. 'However,' the report continued, 'there is all diligence used for the waylaying and intercepting of him before he gets over [the river] Tweed.'[2]

Major General Harrison and his squadrons had no idea where the king was, but they had no doubt that he must be in a desperate state, and that he would be captured soon. They had too many people looking for him for any other outcome to seem possible.

While Charles could grasp the temptation that a sum as vast as £1,000 represented, his general appreciation of the value of money was that of a pampered prince. Unaware of the great luxury that meat was to a family such as the Penderels, the king asked if he could have some mutton for his Sunday dinner the next day. His hosts were keen to oblige, but had nothing so costly in their larder. It is said that William and Joan Penderel had last tasted meat at the christening of their eldest child, several years earlier.

William had no livestock of his own, and so, rather than disappoint the king, he chose to turn thief. He crept out into the night to steal a sheep from a flock belonging to one of Boscobel's tenant farmers, William Staunton. Careless ran it through with his dagger before he and William skinned it and hacked it up, before presenting the king with a hindquarter. Charles cut slices off the joint into collops, which he seasoned and pricked, then fried in a pan. He would later boast that he had been senior cook during the preparation of this delicious dinner, while Careless had been a useful under-cook. The tactlessness of his request for a meat that was such a rare luxury was, for now, lost on him.

With the king having eaten his fill, the vexed question arose of where to hide him that night. It was decided he should stay where the Earl of Derby had felt safe during his brief time there in late August, after his men had been routed at Wigan Lane.

At Boscobel there were two priest holes. One could be reached from the main bedroom, which had a sliding section in the lower part of its wooden panelling. In the floor inside was a trapdoor, leading to a space five feet two inches deep, four feet six inches long and three feet four inches wide – too small to be comfortable for a six-foot-two-inch man to stretch out in, but then, it had not been designed with comfort in mind. From this, it was possible to walk down steps inside the great chimney that led to an exit into the garden. This exit was impossible to see from the outside, since it was swathed in creepers.

The second hiding place was higher up in the house. Its entry point was a square hole at the top of a staircase leading up to an attic area known as 'the gallery'. Unlike the cramped, windowless sleeping space below, this had the benefit of space and light.

As Charles hid up in Boscobel, the Penderel brothers busied themselves on his behalf. Richard went to Wolverhampton to buy provisions for the king, and to ask George Mainwaring, a contact of Major Careless, if he could harbour two, nameless, Royalists on the run. Mainwaring replied, with regret, that he was unable to do so, but suggested an approach be made to a gentleman he was sure could help: Thomas Whitgreave, of Moseley Hall.

Wilmot, who was already at Moseley, was unaware that Charles had set off from Whiteladies on his unsuccessful journey towards Wales. On the evening of Friday, 5 September he sent John Penderel to Whiteladies to tell the king that he had found an excellent hiding place with Thomas Whitgreave. John was directed to do all he could to encourage Charles to join him there, but when he arrived at Whiteladies he was told that the king had already left.

This is one of many instances when it is as well to remember to place the events in this tale against their backdrop. This was an age with severely limited communications. While that was often of benefit to the king during his travels, because it prevented his enemies from structuring and seeing through a comprehensive search for him, there were also occasions when the inability to communicate threatened to upend the escape attempt.

This was such an occasion. Nobody had any means of knowing that the king's Welsh plan had come to nothing, and that he was adrift in a hostile landscape, more in need of Wilmot's company than ever. Instead, an unavoidable reliance on out-of-date news, shared in good faith, now threatened to part the king and his right-hand man for good.

John Penderel returned to Moseley and told Wilmot what he had just heard at Whiteladies. Pleased that Charles had apparently identified and taken a chance of reaching safety, Wilmot felt released from the obligation of waiting in the area in case the king needed his assistance. His loyalty must now be to himself. He told Colonel Lane that he would, after all, be delighted to make use of his sister Jane's pass, and asked the colonel to send his and his servant's horses across to Moseley Hall.

Feeling sure that he would not see the king again on English soil, Wilmot thanked Whitgreave for all his great help, acknowledging that without his assistance he would certainly have been captured. He then sent John Penderel home to Whiteladies, after expressing gratitude for his great loyalty and energy from the time he had guided him away from Whiteladies till this, the moment of final farewell. Wilmot and his servant then rode to Colonel Lane's at Bentley Hall, with the aim of collecting Jane's pass and riding with her towards Bristol and, if all went well, a ship to France.

John Penderel returned to Whiteladies the next day, Saturday, 6 September. While there was still no sign of the king, Richard's wife advised John to head straight away for Boscobel House. There he found Charles with Major Careless, despondent about his chances of escape.

John transmitted Wilmot's message, bidding the king to join him at Moseley Hall. This was a ray of hope, and was received with great excitement by Charles. He was eager to join up with his friend, and put in motion the plan of getting to London, then overseas, with a man he had identified from the start as the perfect escape companion.

Convinced by Careless that staying on at Boscobel in the meantime would lead to his certain capture, he headed off with the major to hide in the oak tree for the day, feeling certain that he would soon be by Wilmot's side. He had no way of knowing that Wilmot was no longer at Moseley Hall.

On Sunday, 7 September Major General Thomas Harrison wrote a report to Parliament listing the many successes his troops had already enjoyed while mopping up pockets of the enemy as they fled. He was pleased to report the utter destruction of the Scottish force, before reminding his comrades in London of the God-given nature of their victory: 'The Lord grant that the Parliament (whom He hath thus further honoured, and owned in the eyes of all the world) may improve this mercy, entrusted to their management, according to the will of God, in establishing the ways of righteousness and justice: yet more relieving of the oppressed.' There was no place in Harrison's world order for corrupt or ungodly kings: 'All his enemies shall be made his footstool,' the major general wrote, with complete certainty.[3] That would include the highest-born in the land.

At daybreak on that same day, John Penderel arrived once more at Moseley, this time as the king's messenger. He found Thomas Whitgreave and Father Huddleston on horseback, preparing to ride to Whiteladies. While taking a walk together even earlier that day, they had decided to travel there to find out more about the recent extraordinary goings on at the house, first-hand.

As soon as he drew close to them, John asked Whitgreave and Huddleston where Lord Wilmot was. They replied that he was no longer there, but had set off for Colonel Lane's house, before heading for Bristol. Penderel vented his despair at the cruel turn of events: 'Then are we all undone, for His Majesty is now forced back to Whiteladies, weary, wet, enduring there hunger and cold all day long in the woods, no place to harbour him at night but some poor cottage or other, with dangers worse than all other hardships who hath sent me to my Lord to procure his speedy remove, not resolving which way to remove, nor we able to advise.'[4]

He explained that when the king had reached Boscobel, and joined up with Major Careless the previous morning, the mood had been grim: nobody could think how to help him, and he had grown 'very melancholy'. It had only been John's report that Wilmot was at Moseley Hall that had brought Charles out of his gloom. The king still believed, John said, that he and Wilmot could make good their escape together.

As they digested another piece of astonishing news, Whitgreave and Huddleston were conscious that Penderel must be exhausted. He had been busy running urgent errands between Moseley, Whiteladies and Boscobel, without a break, for most of the previous twenty-four hours. Before that he had endured the stress of trying to keep the uncontrollable Wilmot safe. But his work was not done yet.

Whitgreave and Huddleston realised that they now had to act, in person. They could commit nothing to paper, with the king's safety in play, and interception of a letter likely to result in his capture. They also knew that Colonel Lane did not know John Penderel, so would be unlikely to trust him, especially given the general upheaval that all were experiencing after the battle of Worcester. They decided they must accompany John back to Bentley, to speak with Lane, and see if there was a way of bringing about the reunion of the king and Wilmot.

On arrival at Bentley, Whitgreave and Huddleston discovered to their relief that Wilmot had yet to set off from the house. Whitgreave explained to Lane that he could vouch for John Penderel, who had come to see him and Huddleston after recently spending time with a very eminent person, whose name could not be disclosed at this point. Whitgreave said that it was essential that John be immediately taken to Wilmot, so he could pass on to him a message of the utmost urgency from this anonymous source.

Lane immediately took John to Wilmot. On hearing the message from the king, Wilmot quizzed John about Boscobel: where it was, what the hiding places were like, and if the enemy had searched it yet. Everything he heard convinced him that it was far too dangerous a place for Charles to remain in. He told John that the king must be brought to Moseley Hall as soon as possible.

John asked Thomas Whitgreave and Father Huddleston to describe where exactly at Moseley he and his brothers should bring the king to. He estimated that they would be able to get him there at around midnight that Sunday night; or certainly by one o'clock the next morning. After receiving clear directions, he headed off to find his brothers, so they could prepare the king for his journey.

John returned to Boscobel to report to Charles the thrilling news that Wilmot was at Bentley, but that he was moving back to Moseley to meet up with the king there, that night. It was now a matter of getting the king the eight miles to Moseley, without his having to walk there on sore feet. The Penderels had cast around for a horse. A friend called Mr Stanton, who lived in nearby Hatton, would have lent his, but somebody else was already borrowing it at the time. With no alternatives, Major Careless persuaded Humphrey Penderel to let his old mill horse, weary from years of lugging packs and provisions, carry the king that night. A worn-out bridle and saddle were found.

Charles said he would just take Careless and John Penderel with him, but the consensus was against this. The Penderel brothers insisted that they all come, to protect the king on such a dangerous expedition. They also convinced Charles and Careless that the major was too well known in the area, as a prominent Royalist, to be included in an already extremely risky journey. Charles said goodbye to Careless, and wished him luck in his own escape.

So it was that, at eleven o'clock that Sunday night, Charles left Boscobel for Moseley. The five Penderel brothers, accompanied by their brother-in-law, the second Francis Yates, led the king through the darkness. The members of this makeshift royal escort were all armed with clubs, pikestaffs or scythes, and some also had pistols.

They advanced in a basic defensive formation, two men in front, two behind, and one either side of the mounted king. Despite it being so late, they kept to little-known paths. The way was rutted, and several times the old mill horse lost its footing. Charles called out to Humphrey, who was leading his horse, to take greater care, otherwise he would fall. Humphrey replied that while his nag was used to carrying heavier loads than the king, it was unaccustomed to having 'the weight of three kingdoms on his back'. This quick-witted comment, coming at a time of high tension and danger, had them all chuckling for some time.

The seven men safely reached Pendeford Mill, two miles short of Moseley Hall, at which point the Penderels told Charles he must walk the remainder of the journey, as they felt the safest way from that point was along a footpath that was too narrow for the horse. Humphrey steered the nag into a ditch, so the king could dismount with greater ease. He then proceeded on foot, with a walking stick taking some of the weight off his feet.

Charles at last approached Moseley Hall at around two or three o'clock in the morning of Monday, 8 September. As he began to head for the house, with Francis Yates and Richard and John Penderel, it suddenly struck him that he would not see the other three again, so he turned back.

'I am troubled,' he apologised, 'that I forget to take my leave of my friends; but if ever I come into England by foul or fair means, I will remember you, and let me see you when ever it shall so please God.' William, Humphrey and George kissed the king's hand, wished him well, and disappeared home, unaware of what would happen to Charles now, but sure that they had played their part in at least giving him a chance of escape, and survival.

# 11

# Reunion

*If you hear anything of the King, be pleased to
communicate it.*

Sir Edward Nicholas to Sir George Radcliffe

Whitgreave and Huddleston had waited till the rest of the
Whitgreave family were in bed before taking up separate stations
outside, awaiting the arrival of Wilmot from Bentley, and of the
king from Boscobel.

Wilmot met up with Whitgreave as arranged, on time, by his
dry pit. Whitgreave took Wilmot back up to the bedroom he had
so recently vacated, with its adjacent priest hole. But Wilmot,
impatient to know if the king had arrived, was unable to relax. As
it grew ever later, and the expected time of Charles's arrival slipped
by, Wilmot began to fret terribly. It seemed that, yet again, he and
his master would miss one another.

Wilmot knew that he must stay inside, near to the safety of the
priest hole, in case an enemy search party appeared and surprised
him out in the open. He persuaded Whitgreave to wait outside in
the orchard, urging him to let him know as soon as he spotted
anyone drawing near.

Eventually, three hours after Wilmot's prompt appearance, Whitgreave made out some shadowy figures approaching. He informed Wilmot that he thought his friend was about to arrive, and Wilmot told Whitgreave to stay beside the orchard door, to greet him when he came. Meanwhile Wilmot waited inside, at the bottom of the staircase, holding a torch.

Charles, Francis Yates and Richard and John Penderel advanced through the garden, entering by a heavy wooden door whose iron-studded design the king would always remember. He now saw Thomas Whitgreave, and would later recall noticing that he was in frail health.

For his part, Charles looked nothing like Whitgreave's image of a king. 'When he came to the door,' Whitgreave later confessed, 'with the Penderels guarding him, he was so habited, like one of them, that I could not tell which was he, only I knew all the rest.' It was a brief welcome, Whitgreave recalling: 'I could scarce put off my hat to him, but he discovering by the light the stairs, immediately went to them, where his Lordship expected him, and took him up to his chamber.'

Father Huddleston was waiting upstairs, and he subsequently remembered his first impressions of the king's clothing: 'The habit that the king came in ... was a very greasy old gray steeple turned hat, with the brims turned up, without lining or hat-band, the sweat appearing two inches [deep] (through it) round the band-place; a green cloth jump-coat, threadbare, even to the threads being worn white; and breeches of the same with long knees down to the garter; with an old sweaty leather doublet, a pair of white flannel-stockings next his legs, which the King said were his boot-stockings, their tops being cut off to prevent their being discovered; and upon them, a pair of old green yarn stockings, all worn, and darned at the knees, with their feet cut off; which last he said he had of Mr Wolfe, who persuaded him thereto, to hide his other white ones, for fear of being observed. His shoes were old, all slashed for the ease of his feet and full of gravel, with little rolls of paper between his toes; which he said he was advised to, to keep them from galling. He had an old coarse shirt, patched both at the neck and hands, of that very coarse sort which in that country go by the name of nogging-shirts … He had no gloves, but a long thorn-stick, not very strong, but crooked three or four several ways, in his hand; his hair cut short up to his ears, and hands coloured, his Majesty refusing to have any gloves when Father H. offered him some, as also to change his stick.'[1]

Whitgreave took the two Penderel brothers and Yates to get something to eat and drink before they set off home again. They were still tucking in when Huddleston appeared, telling Whitgreave that he must, please, come upstairs at once.

Whitgreave entered the chamber, and saw Wilmot and the king talking. Charles was heard to ask after his other leading followers, who had dispersed after the defeat, 'What is become of Buckingham, Cleveland, and others?' But Wilmot, cocooned since Worcester in the protective web spun by John Penderel, had no answers to the question.

Wilmot then noticed that Whitgreave and Huddleston had entered the room and, with great solemnity, announced a point that they had both fully grasped already: 'This gentleman under disguise, whom I have hitherto concealed, is both your master and mine, and the master of us all, to whom we all owe our duty and allegiance.'

Wilmot and Huddleston knelt before the king, and kissed his hand. Whitgreave came forward, also kneeling, before throwing his arms around his royal guest's knees in joy. Charles beckoned to the men to stand. Whitgreave remembered the king telling him that Wilmot had already given him such a warm report of his loyalty and bravery that he would never forget it. Charles then asked, 'Where is the private place my Lord tells me of?' Whitgreave showed the priest hole to the king, who declared it the best he had ever seen.

Charles then told Wilmot, Whitgreave and Huddleston to join him in his room. The king sat on his bed, and ate biscuits while drinking sweet Spanish wine. He started to suffer from a nosebleed – something, he reassured Huddleston, that he often experienced, so it was of no concern to him. He dabbed at the blood with a rough rag from his pocket, before Huddleston swapped it for a fine handkerchief.*

Charles asked Huddleston and Whitgreave to remove his shoes. Huddleston closely inspected the mess that confronted him: 'His shoes were cut and slashed, as well over the toes as behind in the heels, to give ease to his feet, grown tender with his uneasy night's marches on foot; much gravel got into his shoes, which were as wet within as without. The stockings he had then on were a pair of white flannel stockings next his skin which His Majesty said he used with his boots with green embroidered tops; which they were glad to cut off, having no other ready to use. Over them were a pair of old sad gray stirrup stockings, much darned in the knees, the heels … cut off; which in his march toward Wales, he was advised to draw over his own, to obscure the whiteness of his own, which gave too great a show. On the night that Mr Huddleston came to turn off His Majesty's own stockings, he found little rolls of paper between them and his feet; and marveling thereat, His Majesty told them he was advised to put white paper between as remedy, the most excellent remedy for the chafing of his feet.'[2] Huddleston was silently appalled – this bad advice must have made the king's suffering even greater.

The priest placed a cushion under Charles's feet, and carefully dried them off. He then slipped clean warm stockings and slippers onto them, after which the king sprang up and joked that he now felt so reinvigorated that he was ready to lead another march. 'If it would please Almighty God to send him once more an army of

---

* The priest would keep the rag as a royal relic, and eventually sent it to a relative, a Mr Brithwayte, who venerated it.

10,000 good and loyal soldiers and subjects,' Whitgreave remembered the king declaring, 'he feared not to expel all those rogues forth of his kingdom.'[3] It was humorous fighting talk from a young man who must have felt certain, in his quieter moments, that no English army would ever again rise for his family's thrice-defeated cause.

Huddleston looked at the king's shirt and found it in a miserable state. He asked Wilmot if he might be permitted to change it. 'Yes, by all means,' Wilmot replied, adding that he would be pleased to have a fresh one as well, since he had been wearing his since before the battle.

Huddleston was happy to offer a pair of tow-coloured shirts from the batch of six that he had received three days earlier, at the time he had bumped into John Penderel and been brought into the royal conspiracy. He aired them both, giving one to the king and the second to Wilmot. Whitgreave also gave some of his clothes to the king, including a pair of boots.

The men chatted for an hour, before Charles announced that he was eager to take to his bed for a good night's sleep. It must have been after four o'clock in the morning, on Monday, 8 September, when he lay down to rest on a pallet in the priest hole.

Wilmot now took the opportunity to talk to Whitgreave alone. He told him that he or Huddleston would always be near enough to the king to pass on news of any sudden visits by the enemy. But he wanted Whitgreave to be very clear on one further point: 'If it should so fall out that the rebels have intelligence of your harbouring any of the king's party, and should therefore put you to any torture for confession,' he instructed his host, 'be sure you discover me first, which may haply in such case satisfy them, and preserve the king.'[4] Wilmot may well have been infuriating because of his vanity and his inflexible ways, but the king had chosen his companion well when it came to raw courage.

* * *

After sunrise that day all the household servants were sent off on errands, except a kitchen maid. She was a Roman Catholic, who was trusted with more of her master's business than her colleagues. But not even she could be allowed to know the true identity of the extra guest she must now cook for. She was told that she was going to have to secretly get more supplies because a Royalist relative of Father Huddleston's was hiding upstairs after fighting at the battle of Worcester. Like all the servants, she was ordered not to venture to the top of the hall – the reason given was that Huddleston was unwell, and must not be disturbed. Only three people ever saw the king, or knew he was there, during his stay at Moseley Hall: Father Huddleston, who stayed with him throughout; Thomas Whitgreave; and Mrs Alice Whitgreave, Thomas's mother.

Alice had brought Roman Catholicism to Moseley when she married her second husband, Thomas's father. As she was first introduced to the king in his chamber at the top of her home, she kissed his hand. He returned the gesture with a salute. The young king and the elderly widow would greatly enjoy each other's company during his stay.

Alice would spend much of her time supervising the servants and checking on the quality of the food that would be served to her hidden guest. She ladled his food out herself in the kitchen, and passed it to her son. Thomas then took it upstairs to the door into Huddleston's rooms, from where the priest would carry it to the table where the king ate. Sometimes Charles invited the widow and her son to eat with him.

Apart from the Whitgreave family and Huddleston, the motley household included three boys that Huddleston was tutoring. These were Thomas Paling and Francis Reynolds – two of Whitgreave's nephews – and Sir John Preston, the thirteen-year-old son of an aristocratic Royalist cavalry colonel who had been mortally wounded in battle six years earlier. The Preston family estate had been confiscated by Parliament and given to one of its supporters. The Prestons and the Huddlestons were strongly linked through both their Catholicism and their shared roots in Lancashire and Cumberland.

The boys were excused lessons, and instead were allotted a window each from which to watch for any strangers approaching the house. They were not informed of the king's presence, but must have known they were on sentry duty for a reason. Young Sir John Preston joked to his two companions during supper one evening, 'Eat hard, boys, for we have been on the life guard and hard duty this day!' As Whitgreave noted, this was 'more truly spoken than he was aware', the life guard being the regiment dedicated to the monarch's personal protection. 'The best soldiers of all could not be more diligent or exact than those three lads,' Huddleston would remember.

On Monday, 8 September Whitgreave went into the centre of Wolverhampton to see what news he could gather. He was also tasked by Wilmot with contacting Colonel Lane, so his horses could be brought back from Bentley to Moseley. When they were delivered, Wilmot rode to Bentley to tell the colonel to come the following night to collect the king, and take him from Moseley to Bentley.

Charles spent that Monday night in bed while Huddleston watched over him, and Whitgreave kept guard in the passage outside. Meanwhile the good sense of having moved him to Moseley was immediately proven: Parliamentary forces arrived at Boscobel later on the day the king had left, to search the house for fugitives.

Most of the next day he spent either lying on a bed in Huddleston's room, or sitting in Whitgreave's study, above the front door of Moseley Hall. He enjoyed chatting with his two companions, and peering out of the window. At one point his attention was drawn to the sight of a band of desperate beggars shuffling into view. Studying them more closely, he realised with shock that these pitiful figures were some of his own soldiers, 'all of them stripped', Huddleston remembered, 'many of them cut, some without stocking or shoe, scarce so much left upon them as to cover their nakedness, eating peas out of reaps and handfuls of straw in their hands, which they had pulled up in the fields as they passed, roots and raw coleworts [bitter cabbages] cast out of gardens for hogs, and gathered up by them in the ways as they passed, to preserve themselves from famine, not daring to call at any house, scarce to beg bread or touch anything but what was given them by good people of pity. Some of them His Majesty knew, pointed at, and said they were Highlanders of his own regiment, and one of them an officer.'[5]

The sight of these pathetic remnants of his army set Charles to thinking aloud: 'There he told us of the Scottish usage, and of his march from thence to Worcester, and of the flight there, and enquired of us how this country and the gentry stood affected, and who were against him.' Many of the names he heard belonged to Catholics.

Later Charles noticed a book in the study. It was a copy of *Manual of Controversies*, a catechism written by the contemporary Catholic theologian Henry Turbeville. After reading some of it, he declared that he would take it with him on his travels.

In the middle of that day, a troop of Parliamentary cavalry passed through the village of Moseley. John Penderel spotted them, but decided not to bother the king with the news, because he could see that they were not coming to the hall, and (as he later said) he had no wish to ruin Charles's lunch with a needless alarm.

The same day a much more menacing event occurred. Whitgreave was standing watch by one of the windows while Charles took a nap, when he was troubled to see a neighbour running as fast as he could towards Moseley Hall. The man blurted out his message to one of the Whitgreaves' maids, who then went to the bottom of the stairs and shouted, 'Soldiers! Soldiers are coming!'

The king jumped up from his bed and ran to the priest hole, where he hid with Huddleston. Whitgreave secured it from the outside, then left the house to confront and distract the search party. But as soon as the Roundheads saw Whitgreave, they fell on him. They knew him to have fought against them at Naseby in 1645, and now accused him of having returned to Royalist colours at Worcester a few days earlier. 'But after much dispute with them,' Whitgreave recalled, with relief, 'and by the neighbours being informed of their false information, that I was not there [at Worcester], being very ill a great while, they let me go.' Once Whitgreave was released from his roughing up, he was considered above suspicion. This enabled him to travel a little from his home, gather information, and buy supplies for the house.

He remained outside the hall until he had seen the last of the search party leave the area. He was later told that the redcoats had brought with them a famous priest-catcher called Southall. Priest-catchers were often from a military or spying background, and they worked with informants to track down Roman Catholics. It was a business: their best tool was bribery, while success entitled them to a reward of a third of any money forfeited by the captured. During the eleven years leading up to the summer of 1651, these bounty hunters had caught fifty Catholics. While some were reprieved, the rest were exiled or executed.

Southall had peeled off from the main search party and gone to pay a visit on the nearby blacksmith, in the hope of a helpful lead. Everyone knew that, because of his everyday contact with travellers passing through, the blacksmith was the figure in any community who was most in touch with the goings on of the outside world; gossip was nearly as much a part of his repertoire as the hammer and the anvil. The Moseley blacksmith, a man by the name of Holbeard, was busy shoeing a horse when Southall appeared and asked him if he knew where the king was. If he did, Southall promised, he would receive a £1,000 reward. Holbeard told him he could not help, since he had no idea of the king's whereabouts. Southall moved on, as near to claiming the enormous reward as he would ever be.

On the same afternoon Wilmot sent word that Colonel Lane would come that night to collect the king. Charles asked Father Huddleston for one last favour before he went: he wanted to see the Catholic chapel hidden in Moseley's eaves. Charles reassured Huddleston that he had nothing to fear from his request, and promised that when he won his throne back he would ensure that Catholics had no need to hide their prayers or their preachers. After looking round the chapel, Whitgreave noted with pride that Charles said 'it was a very decent place'.

Around midnight, Colonel Lane and Whitgreave rendezvoused, Whitgreave's nephew Francis Reynolds holding the colonel's and the king's horses. Whitgreave led Lane to a stile at the corner of his orchard, where he was to wait for the king.

Inside Moseley Hall, Charles took his leave of the trio who had kept him safe, thanking Alice Whitgreave, Thomas Whitgreave and Father Huddleston for their loyalty and kindness. Mrs Whitgreave handed 'some raisins, almonds and other sweetmeats' to the king, some of which he sampled then, before putting the rest aside for later.

While Parliamentary troops scoured the countryside for the man they were desperate to capture, inside this mansion three Royalists sank to their knees in deference to their king. They prayed aloud that God might protect him from his enemies. He saluted Mrs Whitgreave, and promised Father Huddleston and Thomas Whitgreave that he would never forget all that they had done for him.

Charles walked with Whitgreave and Huddleston towards Colonel Lane, and the four men continued to where the two horses were being held. It was a cold and drizzly night, so Huddleston insisted the king take his cloak with him, as well as some money.

When the king mounted his horse, Whitgreave and Huddleston knelt and kissed his hand once again, uttering more words of hope and encouragement. He and Colonel Lane then disappeared into the night.

Father Huddleston would later note that 'all the persons employed in this work, within the knowledge of Father H, were Roman Catholics but Mr Huntbatch'.[6]

# PART THREE

# A LEAGUE OF GENTLEMEN

# 12

# Heading for the Coast

*It is constantly reported, and believed, that the Scots
King is dead, and the late Queen of England is of the
same belief, and doth mourn for him.*

Weekly Intelligencer, September 1651

On Monday, 8 September the *Weekly Intelligencer* reported on
Major General Harrison's progress as he harvested Royalist fugitives while continuing his relentless hunt for the king: 'After such
a field of our enemies, which this great victory had mowed, and
taken ... about 10,000 of them, Major General Harrison hath since
gleaned no less than fourteen hundred of them in one place, and
letters this day advertise that some hundreds more have been gathered up in another, so that (some of the chiefest of them being
made sacrifices for the establishment of the Commonwealth) we
hope after this harvest, to enjoy many happy years of peace and
plenty.'[1]

If that dream of a settled and prosperous future were to come
true, it was essential that Charles be caught. While he remained
unaccounted for, speculation was beginning to mount as to what
might have happened to him. 'It is this day reported,' the *Weekly*

*Intelligencer* pronounced, 'that the Scots King attended but with twelve men, is fled back over Warrington Bridge, endeavouring to return by the same way by which he came; but such is the vigilance of Colonel Lilburne, that it will be almost impossible for him to escape; others are extremely confident, and will not be gainsaid but that he is fled toward North Wales, and being a lost man, will do his uttermost to get into the Isle of Man to make his moan there.'[2]

The next day, *Mercurius Politicus* noted how the English people had risen to help Harrison's men in the apprehending of fleeing Scots: 'That part of the enemy that took Preston Road for Lancaster, were overtaken by commanded parties of Major General Harrison … Not any of these scattered remnants can escape through, but have been stuck in the hands of the country people, by hundreds and fifties.'[3]

John Penderel went to discuss arrangements for the journey with Jane Lane, the colonel's handsome younger sister. She was, the diarist John Evelyn would write, a lady blessed with 'an acute wit'. Jane sent John back to Charles with some boiled walnuts, which she urged the king to rub on his face and hands, to obscure the whiteness associated with gentle living. As Charles had already learnt from earlier protectors, dark skin was the inevitable consequence of toiling outdoors.

Colonel Lane took Charles to Bentley that night of Tuesday, 9 September, accompanied by John Penderel. Once there, the king adapted his disguise. Out went the simple clothes of a countryman, and instead he put on a sober grey suit, more befitting the status of a trusted manservant. For this journey Charles took on the alias of 'William Jackson', the name of a son of one of the Lanes' tenants. He carried ten or twelve silver shillings – anything more would have aroused suspicion if he was stopped by the enemy and forced to turn out his pockets.

On Wednesday, 10 September, Colonel and Jane Lane rode to a field beside Bentley where they met up with the king just before dawn. John Penderel now parted with Charles, who would set off on the next leg of his life-or-death adventure in the hands of Mistress Lane. For the first time in his escape attempt, there would be not a single Penderel brother on hand to help the king. The departure of John, who Father Huddleston would later judge to have helped the king even more than his siblings had done, must have been a poignant moment.

Jane assured Charles that she knew the country they would be crossing intimately, and had many friends along the route who could help in an emergency. The king was shown to a strawberry roan gelding, and Colonel Lane quietly took him aside to give him a quick lesson in the etiquette he should display towards his lady companion. As was customary for a senior manservant at the time, the king was to ride at the front of a double saddle shared with his mistress.

Jane's mother came to say goodbye to her daughter. There was an awkward pause when Jane turned from her parents to the horse and then stood looking expectantly at Charles. 'Will,' said Colonel Lane, 'thou must give my sister thy hand.' Charles tried to remember his recent instructions, but instead 'offered his hand the contrary way', which made old Mrs Lane exclaim in good-humoured despair, 'What a goodly horseman my daughter has got to ride before her!'⁴

They set off for Long Marston in the Vale of Evesham, where they planned to break the journey to Bristol. With them went Henry Lascelles, a trusted cousin of Jane's who had served as a cornet in Colonel Lane's regiment, and who was aware of Charles's true identity. Also in the party were Jane's sister Withy, and brother-in-law John Petre. They were from Horton in Buckinghamshire, and were heading for Lord Paget's house near Windsor. The Petres planned to go their separate way on reaching Stratford-upon-

Avon. They had no idea that the very tall attendant who rode with Jane was in fact their would-be king.

Lord Wilmot rode out half a mile ahead of the king and his companions, accompanied by his servant Robert Swan and by Colonel Lane. As usual, Wilmot had not allowed himself to suffer the indignity of a disguise. Instead, he had a hawk on his hand and spaniels at his heels. If challenged, he planned to say that he was a gentleman called Morton, who was out hunting. Despite the feebleness of this premise, it is only fair to note that, yet again, Wilmot was happy to meet any oncoming dangers first. Indeed, his riding out from Bentley provides almost the perfect snapshot of him: stubborn to the point of stupidity over the need for concealment, but at the same time endlessly brave in his devotion to his king.

Having travelled by separate routes, the two parties would meet up at Abbots Leigh, the house near Bristol that Captain Stone had specified as Jane's destination on his invaluable pass. In the meantime Wilmot and Swan rode towards Packington Hall in Warwickshire, where Wilmot had a friend who could be relied upon to hide him. He was Sir Clement Fisher, who had served as a captain in Colonel Lane's regiment in the Civil War. Wilmot would then move on to the home of John Winter in Dyrham, north of Bath.

Charles encountered a problem early on in his journey. Within two hours of setting off, after passing through Rowley Regis and Quinton, his horse shed a shoe. Repairing to the nearby wool town of Bromsgrove, they sought out a blacksmith. Once the man had set about shoeing his horse, Charles fell into conversation with him, asking what news he had heard from other parts recently. Worcester was only sixteen miles away, so the king would have been confident that fallout from the previous week's battle would be in the blacksmith's arsenal of gossip.

Charles would later recall, with mischievous delight, the unfiltered thoughts that the Bromsgrove blacksmith shared with him:

'He told me there was no news that he knew of since the good news of the beating of the rogues, the Scots. I asked him whether there was none of the English taken that joined with the Scots. He answered that he did not hear that that rogue, Charles Stuart, was taken, but some of the others were taken, but not Charles Stuart. I told him that if that rogue were taken he deserved to be hanged more than all the rest, for bringing in the Scots. Upon which he said that I spoke like an honest man, and so we parted.'

The party resumed its journey. At Wootton, just short of Stratford-upon-Avon, they could make out ahead of them a troop of Parliamentary cavalry, the men dismounted, the horses chewing grass. John Petre panicked, revealing to the others that the enemy had roughed him up on more than one occasion, and that he would not suffer the same treatment again.

With Petre refusing to ride on, Charles quietly pleaded with Jane Lane to persuade all the party to continue on their way together, otherwise he was afraid that the enemy would become suspicious, and ride to see why some of their number had suddenly turned to avoid them. It was all in vain: the Petres separated from the group, and rode off in a different direction to Stratford-upon-Avon.

Fortunately for the king, the cavalrymen proved more interested in making the most of their break than in investigating the splitting up of a small knot of travellers. Maybe it was because Charles's group had women in its number. Jane, Charles and Lascelles passed through the enemy unit, exchanging pleasantries, and were able to carry on without any further excitements.

They safely reached the home of Jane's cousins John and Amy Tombes in Long Marston, where they were to spend the night. It had already been decided that they would not share Charles's identity with their hosts. He was introduced as the servant William Jackson, and was sent to lend a hand to the household staff.

Charles was shown to the kitchen. It was an alien environment for a king. The cook told him to help with the meat that was being prepared for dinner that night. She pointed him towards the jack – an antiquated piece of domestic machinery that helped turn the spit – thinking that would be the best place to deploy his helping hand.

The king was stumped. Although always interested in gadgetry and mechanics, he could make no sense of the contraption that now confronted him. After a pause, he gave it a heave, but succeeded only in sending it spinning in the wrong direction, the workings screeching in protest at their rough treatment.

The furious cook came over to scold him. 'What countryman are you, that you know not how to wind up a jack?' It was a question that could have provoked panic, but Charles kept calm. 'I am a poor tenant's son of Colonel Lane, in Staffordshire,' he claimed. 'We seldom have roast meat, but when we have, we don't make use of a jack.' The cook still clucked away in a fury, but without doubting that what the clumsy young man had just told her was the truth.

Charles's reply shows not only commendable unflappability, but also observational intelligence. He had, by this point of his escape attempt, spent enough time witnessing the hand-to-mouth existence of the poorer rural element to understand something of their economic, and dietary, reality. Even though there was no longer a Penderel by his side, the lessons they had taught him remained invaluable. He had learnt a lot since insensitively ordering mutton for his dinner when a guest in a poor man's home.

On Thursday, 11 September the party continued on to Cirencester, where they appear to have spent the night in an inn called the Crown. The next day they rode a further forty miles, through Chipping Sodbury, to reach the destination allowed by their military pass.

Abbots Leigh, three miles west of Bristol, had a tantalising view over the Bristol Channel. It was the home of George Norton and his heavily pregnant wife Ellen. The Royalist party arrived there in the evening, their hosts again unaware of Charles's identity. But this was a large country house, with a correspondingly sizeable staff, and the king's carefully contrived anonymity was about to receive a major challenge.

Charles was astonished and deeply troubled to find that the butler of the house was a man he knew from many years back. His name was John Pope, and he had been part of the domestic household that the king knew during his boyhood at the Palace of Richmond. Pope had later enlisted in the Royalist cavalry, serving alongside Charles at Lichfield in Staffordshire, where he had seen the then Prince of Wales up close. Given the context of their meeting now, though, Pope at this stage failed to recognise his former master.

As part of a prearranged plan, Jane Lane announced on arrival that her servant Jackson was recovering from a fever, and asked Pope to take him somewhere quiet, so he could rest. This was an effective way of removing Charles from exposure to all of the house's many visitors, servants and tradesmen; he was put in Pope's quarters, where he was attentively looked after by Margaret Rider, one of the Nortons' maids.

In the morning Charles went downstairs to share a servant's breakfast of bread and butter, with ale and sherry. He was joined by Pope and two others, one of whom began regaling the small group with a detailed account of the battle of Worcester. Charles feared that this man may have been fighting for Parliament, but gentle enquiry revealed that he was in fact one of his own men: he had served in Charles's Guards' Regiment under Major Broughton, an officer the king knew well (and who, Charles was unaware, had been captured when fleeing from Worcester).

Charles could not resist asking the raconteur what sort of man the king really was. The Royalist gave an exact description of the king's clothes and horse on the day of the battle, before addressing his mighty height, telling 'Jackson' that Charles was 'at least three fingers taller' than even he was. The king quickly withdrew from the room, fearing that the storyteller might at any moment realise his true identity, and blurt it out.

Pope accompanied him as he exited into the hall. At that moment Ellen Norton passed by, and Charles removed his hat in a sign of courteous respect for the lady of the house. It was then that the king felt the full glare of Pope's eyes on him, as they devoured his features. Pretending not to notice, or to be concerned by, Pope's obvious interest, Charles went for a walk outside.

On his return he was met by Henry Lascelles, who was in a highly agitated state. 'What shall we do?' Lascelles asked. 'I am afraid Pope knows you, for he says very positively to me that it is you, but I have denied it.' Despite Lascelles's protestations, Pope remained utterly convinced that Jackson was the king. Charles asked Lascelles if he thought Pope trustworthy. His dependability was, Lascelles said, beyond doubt. Charles had already formed the same opinion, and told Lascelles he had better bring Pope to him immediately.

The king straight away admitted to Pope who he really was, and told him what a relief it was to stumble across such a stalwart supporter at a time when he needed faithful friends more than on any other occasion in his life. Pope declared himself equally happy, but also very concerned. He explained that there were some in the Nortons' household who were enemies of the Crown. But now that he knew for sure that Jackson was his king, he vowed that he would do anything he could to keep him safe.

Charles took immediate advantage of the offer, sending Pope into Bristol to see if there were any ships that were preparing to set sail for France or Spain. Pope returned with the disappointing, and surprising, news that none were due to leave for either country in the coming month.

Charles now informed Pope that he was expecting Wilmot's imminent arrival at Abbots Leigh. Pope warned that this was out

Henry, Lord Wilmot, was Charles's chosen sidekick when it became clear that he must try to escape from the enemy. Wilmot's refusal to adopt a disguise did not help proceedings, but his bravery and loyalty were endless. He would be rewarded by Charles with the title of 1st Earl of Rochester.

Charles with Major William Careless, famously hiding in an oak tree while enemy patrols scoured the surrounding woodland for the defeated king. Charles would later recognise Careless for his 'singular fidelity', and would insist he change his name to 'Carlos' (the Spanish for Charles) in memory of his courageous service.

The Royal Oak today. It is a descendant of the original tree, which could not survive the plundering of souvenir-hunters, desperate for a memento of what seemed to be a miraculous tale of escape.

Charles riding with Jane Lane on a strawberry roan horse. Jane had secured a pass from a Parliamentary official that enabled her to travel with a manservant towards Bristol. Charles took this opportunity to head for the coast in disguise.

### ⇨ By the Parliament.

## A PROCLAMATION

FOR THE

Discovery and Apprehending of *CHARLS STUART*, and other Traytors his Adherents and Abettors.

Hereas CHARLS STUART Son to the late Tyrant, with divers of the English and Scotish Nation, have lately in a Trayterous and Hostile maner with an Army invaded this Nation, which by the Blessing of God upon the Forces of this Commonwealth have been defeated, and many of the chief Actors therein slain and taken prisoners, but the said Charls Stuart is escaped : For the speedy Apprehending of such Malicious and Dangerous Traytors to the Peace of this Commonwealth, The Parliament doth straightly Charge and Command all Officers, as well Civil as Military, and all other the good People of this Nation, That they make diligent Search and Enquiry for the said Charls Stuart, and his Abettors and Adherents in this Invasion, and use their best Endeavors for the Discovery and Arresting the Bodies of them and every of them ; and being apprehended, to bring or cause to be brought forthwith and without delay, in safe Custody before the Parliament or Council of State, to be proceeded with and ordered as Justice shall require, And if any person shall knowingly Conceal the said Charls Stuart, or any his Abettors or Adherents, or shall not Reveal the Places of their Abode or Being, if it be in their power so to do, The Parliament doth Declare, That they will hold them as partakers and Abettors of their Trayterous and Wicked Practices and Designs : And the Parliament doth further Publish and Declare, That whosoever shall apprehend the person of the said Charls Stuart, and shall bring or cause him to be brought to the Parliament or Council of State, shall have given and bestowed on him or them as a Reward for such Service, the sum of One thousand pounds. And all Officers, Civil and Military, are required to be aiding and assisting unto such person and persons therein. Given at Westminster this Tenth day of September, One thousand six hundred fifty one.

*Wednesday the Tenth of September, 1651.*

ORdered by the Parliament, That this Proclamation be forthwith Printed and Published.

Hen: Scobell, Cleric. Parliamenti.

London, Printed by *John Field*, Printer to the Parliament of *England*. 1651.

Parliament's proclamation for the discovery and apprehending of Charles Stuart, listing his treachery and offering the huge reward of £1,000 to whoever captured the defeated king. It was disseminated in print, and read out to crowds across the land.

Colonel George Gunter was one of the great heroes of the tale. He provided total commitment and sharp focus to the business of getting the king to safety, and believed he had been involved in a matter that had been decided by God.

COL. LANE who
saved KING CHAS II.
after the Battle
of WORCESTER.

Colonel John Lane – Jane Lane's older brother – had served under Lord Wilmot during the Civil Wars. He was among a band of Royalist regimental commanders who kept the king out of the enemy's clutches.

Thomas Whitgreave was a well-known Royalist, who had fought at the battle of Naseby. He was roughed up by Parliamentary redcoats while hiding the king, because they were convinced he must have been involved in the battle of Worcester. His home, Moseley Hall, contained priest holes that Charles hid in.

Oliver Cromwell and John Lambert were two of the great military figures of the New Model Army, who delivered repeated and comprehensive defeats to those Scots who chose to support the doomed Stuart cause.

The priest hole in which Charles hid at Moseley Hall, and which he declared the best he had ever seen.

Bentley Hall, in Staffordshire, stood in quiet isolation. Colonel Lane, Bentley's owner, insisted the king move there, rather than remain at Moseley Hall, which was overlooked by neighbours and was known for its Roman Catholic inhabitants.

The *Surprise*, a 60-ton coal barge, was captained by Nicholas Tatersall. At the Restoration she was renamed the *Royal Escape*.

The Restoration of Charles II at Whitehall on 29 May 1660. The magnificent return of the young king could not have been further removed from his last time on English soil, as a desperate fugitive.

Charles II in middle age – charming, lazy, and addicted to pleasure. His rule was controversial, and punctuated by disaster. He would look back at his time on the run as the high point of his life.

of the question: Wilmot must not come to the house, because many people there knew him by sight, and several of these were his enemies. He volunteered to wait for Wilmot at a safe distance from the property, and intercept him. After doing this successfully, Pope took Wilmot to an inn, to pass the time till nightfall. He then guided him secretly through the darkness to Abbots Leigh, and led him to Charles's room.

Charles consulted with Pope and Wilmot as to his next move. He decided to head for Trent House, four miles north-west of Sherborne in Dorset. It was the new home of an old acquaintance, Francis Wyndham, and his wife Anne. She was from the wealthy Gerrard family, and they had been married five years. The Wyndhams had moved to Trent earlier in 1651, having amicably split the inheritance of four Dorset estates with Anne's sister and co-heir.

The Wyndhams were part of a strong Royalist network, connected by marriage and blood. Francis was a brother-in-law of John Winter, with whom Wilmot had so recently been staying in Gloucestershire. Anne's sister was married to Bullen Reymes, a Royalist infantry colonel who had fought in the south-west on Charles I's behalf, and who had been imprisoned in Taunton Castle the previous year because of his continued loyalty to the Crown. Francis's eldest brother, Sir Edmund, had led the defence of Bridgwater Castle in the summer of 1645, while his feisty sister-in-law Christabella had been wet-nurse to Charles as a baby, governess to him as a boy, and his first lover as a youth. It was she who, with bared breast, had taken a potshot at Cromwell shortly before Bridgwater fell to the New Model Army. To complete the bonds of loyalty to the Crown, Edmund and Christabella's son, Sir Hugh Wyndham, was a Cavalier colonel known to Charles since childhood.

Francis Wyndham's record of loyalty to the Crown was impressive in its own right. He had served under Charles I as a colonel from 1643, when he had been made governor of Dunster Castle, near Minehead in Somerset. Charles had briefly stayed there with Wyndham in May 1645. Four months later, when the Royalist military cause was beyond repair, Wyndham and his garrison were holed up in a siege. So stubborn was their resistance that Colonel Robert Blake, the Parliamentary commander, ordered Wyndham's mother to be placed directly in his line of fire. Blake's sappers had failed to bring about Dunster Castle's surrender with their subterranean explosions, but Blake hoped the threat of his mother's imminent death would persuade the garrison commander to yield.

But Blake had failed to take into account Elizabeth Wyndham's courage. She was defiant in the face of death, urging her son to do his duty and fight on for the king, whatever her fate. Impressed by such bravery, Blake spared her. Dunster Castle eventually fell after 160 days of defiance, Francis Wyndham being allowed to surrender on generous terms. It was one of the last Royalist strongholds to succumb to the inevitable.

The circle entrusted with the king's safety remained necessarily tight, as the search for him was still intense. When the king had briefly stayed as Francis Wyndham's guest six years earlier, he had done so as an honoured and fêted prince. Now he was attempting to cross country thickly infested with the enemy, his status that of the most hunted man in the country.

On the evening of Monday, 15 September, the night before his departure for Trent House, it seemed the king's plans of moving on would have to be shelved. Ellen Norton's pregnancy ended in heartbreak. She went into labour, but suffered a stillbirth. She was not only distraught at her loss, but also dangerously ill. Clearly Jane Lane would be expected to attend to the cousin whose pregnancy had given her a reason to travel so far from home.

Charles knew that, despite the Norton family's dreadful loss, he had to leave Abbots Leigh as soon as he could. The excuse of his needing to rest while recovering from illness could not hold for much longer. The more he mingled in this household, which it was known contained some who were his enemies, the greater the risk of his being identified, captured and executed.

It was Charles who thought of the necessary ruse to get away from the house. He had a letter composed that purported to come from Jane Lane's sixty-six-year-old father, telling her that he was seriously ill and feared he was about to die. His final wish was that his daughter should come to him to say her goodbyes, and receive his blessing. Pope presented the letter to Jane at dinner. She carried off the pretence of profound shock convincingly, sobbing at this latest terrible family news.

On the morning of Tuesday, 16 September, thirteen days after the defeat at Worcester, and four days after their arrival at Abbots Leigh, the fugitives set off for Francis Wyndham's home in Dorset. They broke their journey by spending the night in the manor house of Castle Cary, a market town in Somerset, twelve miles south-east of Wells. Castle Cary's church had been stripped of its lead roof by Parliamentary soldiers six years earlier. The rebels had peeled it back and melted it down to make musketballs to fire at the Royalist garrison defending Sherborne Castle.

Charles's host that night was Edward Kirton, the steward of Castle Cary, who worked for one of the Royalists' leading generals, the Marquess of Hertford. Hertford had been Charles's governor in the early 1640s, and was a loyal servant of Charles I, remaining with him throughout the trial for his life. He had then acted as one of the late king's pallbearers at the modest funeral in Windsor that followed. The younger Charles would later declare that Hertford was 'an extraordinary person, who hath merited as much of the king my father and myself as a subject can do'.[5]

Moving on from Castle Cary, Charles reached Trent House on Wednesday, 17 September. Francis and Anne Wyndham lived there with their three-year-old son. Their home was set in a largely

Parliamentary community, next to the village's thirteenth-century church, St Andrew's.

The Wyndhams were waiting in a field for the king to arrive. When Charles spotted the colonel, he shouted out, 'Frank! Frank! How dost thou do?' Wyndham started to cry – he had heard that the king had been killed at Worcester, and had not dared to believe otherwise until now, when he could see Charles for himself. Jane Lane and Henry Lascelles left the king at Trent and continued on their way.

Charles was now reunited with Wilmot, and the two of them met with their host to discuss options for escape. Wyndham proposed that his friend Giles Strangwayes, another Royalist colonel, might be able to advise the king on which harbour to head for to get away abroad. Wyndham duly rode the ten miles to Strangwayes' home, but Strangwayes proved unable to help. He was aware that the Parliamentarians were watching him very closely, and that if he were seen near any of the ports it would arouse strong suspicion. It was better if he played no part, because he would only prove a liability if he did. Assuming that the king was in need of funds, Strangwayes sent him all the money he had – £100 in gold pieces – and his apologies for not being able to do more.

Feeling sure that the king was safe at Trent House, where some of his family knew his true identity, Wyndham decided to scout out the ports himself, pretending to be 'Captain Norris'. He had two contacts that he hoped might help. They were both in Lyme Regis, which at that time was a busier port than Liverpool, thanks to its steady traffic with Continental Europe, and its key position between Bristol and the English Channel.

Lyme Regis had been described by the sixteenth-century local historian John Leyland as 'a pretty market town set in the roots of an high rocky hill down to the hard shore. There cometh a shallow brook from the hills about three miles by north, and cometh fleeting on great stones through a stone bridge in the bottom.'[6] This picturesque spot was something of a precious jewel to the Parliamentarians, having gained fame in 1644 when its garrison of 500 men, assisted with enthusiasm by the town's inhabitants, had survived an eight-week siege by 4,000 Royalists commanded by one of Charles I's nephews, the much-feared Prince Maurice of the Rhine.

This successful resistance had been achieved despite Lyme Regis having few fortifications, other than earthworks that had been quickly constructed. A lot of this work was completed by women of the town who had disguised themselves as men, to convince the Royalists that there were more soldiers ready to meet them than was the case. After the fighting began, the women remained active, ferrying ammunition and reloading muskets. When the Royalists rained fire arrows onto their houses, the townspeople stripped their roofs bare to prevent the flames from spreading.

But it was the combination of Lyme Regis's devout Puritanism and its maritime knowhow that truly saved the day. Twenty-four preachers encouraged the town's defenders to stand firm against the king's 'malignant' army, pointing out that a significant part of the Royalist force were Roman Catholics, from Ireland. This stiffened the townspeople's resolve, whipping up their hatred to such a pitch that an Irish woman found wandering the beach after the Royalists had departed was butchered, and her body fed to the sea.

By the end of the eight weeks the Royalists had suffered 2,000 casualties, to the town's 120. Parliament granted Lyme Regis an annual payment of £1,000 in grateful recognition of its stubborn resistance, which had sucked the impetus out of the Royalists in the south-west, while keeping hold of a crucial port.

It was this hotbed of Puritanism that Wyndham now hoped might save the king. While it transpired that one of the Lyme Regis sailors he had had in mind, Captain Gregory Alford, was on a voyage to Portugal, the other was on hand.

William Ellesdon was, as Captain Alford would recall somewhat disapprovingly, 'newly married to a very rich but rigid Presbyterian'.[7] Wyndham had no intention of sharing the king's identity with Ellesdon, as he was very aware that Ellesdon's brother John was one of the area's many stalwart Parliamentarians. He therefore told him that his need was to get a couple of anonymous gentlemen across the water as quickly as possible, and implored him to sort out a merchant ship immediately. It must have the appearance of a working vessel, while its true purpose would be the smuggling of two men who needed to get to safety.

Ellesdon sent one of his staff to the customs house to see which captains had logged their vessels as being bound for France. The entry that stuck out was that of Stephen Limbry, an importer of wine who was one of Ellesdon's commercial tenants. He was the master of a thirty-ton merchantman which was soon to set sail for the French port of St-Malo.

Ellesdon rode with Wyndham the mile and a half along a coastal path from Lyme Regis to the nearby village of Charmouth, where they found Limbry at home. They said they had something to speak to him about, and asked him to join them in the village's inn.

Wyndham explained that they needed to get a pair of gentlemen across the Channel in secret. The exact destination was not important, Ellesdon explained – it could be anywhere in France. As to the reason for the men's sudden wish to get overseas, Ellesdon said that it was to do with marriage and money: one of the gentlemen, 'having married a great fortune, was troubled by her father and friends, and so they would go into France for some time'. Ellesdon promised to pay Limbry £25 on his vessel's departure, and a further £25 once he had heard from the two gentlemen that they had made it safely to France. Limbry agreed to the deal.

All the arrangements were made, and a rendezvous was arranged at a spot that Ellesdon pointed out to Wyndham from the shore. 'And indeed,' Ellesdon wrote later, 'a more commodious place for such a design could hardly be found, it lying upon the shore a quarter of a mile from any house and from any horse or footpath.' He told Wyndham that Limbry would have his ship sail out of Lyme Regis at five o'clock that Monday evening, and that it would then pause at the allotted point so the two gentlemen could be rowed across a nearby creek, board and be on their way to safety.

Wyndham returned to Trent House with 'hopeful tidings' that passage to France was secured, and a plan was in place. After the previous disappointments, with neither London nor Wales proving to be possible exits overseas, it seemed that Charles was finally within touching distance of freedom. Many of his followers had not been so fortunate.

## 13

# Processing the Prisoners

*Such of them who in the battle escaped death lived but
longer to die, for the most part, more miserably.*

Thomas Blount, *Boscobel*

One of Charles's first questions to Wilmot when they had been
reunited at Moseley Hall had been what had happened to the other
great men of his cause. While Wilmot had not been able to answer,
the truth emerged as the two men moved between Royalist hiding
places, and learnt more of what had been going on outside the
bubble of their escape attempt. The news was dire indeed.

The Duke of Hamilton, one of the senior aristocrats of Scotland,
with a potential claim to the English throne, was the most prominent Scot not to make it out of Worcester alive. His elder brother
had been beheaded in 1649, after being captured fighting for
Charles I the previous year. Now it was his turn to suffer the consequences of an ill-fated foray into an England protected by the
professionalism of the New Model Army, inspired by the brilliance
of Cromwell.

Leading a counterattack on Perry Wood, Hamilton was shot
through the leg. He was then subjected to a grisly amputation, after

178

which he lay in agony in the Commandery, the building that had been Charles's headquarters during his twelve days in Worcester. Hamilton would join the long list of Worcester's fatalities nine days after the battle. His followers were refused permission to remove his body, and he was buried under the high altar of Worcester Cathedral.

The city had paid dearly for welcoming Charles Stuart into its walls. It was violently looted on the night of victory. Those officials who had greeted the king so wholeheartedly on 22 August were soon identified, tried and hanged. As these men lost their lives, so the city lost its dignity, and its defensive lines. On 16 September the Council of State ordered that the walls of Worcester be torn down, and 'laid so flat that they may not be in a posture to be again made defensible'.[1]

Now it became clear that Parliament had had various informants in place, transmitting information about Charles and his army from inside Worcester's walls. On 6 September the Council of State gave rewards to those who had informed them of goings on in the Royalist stronghold in the run-up to the battle, sending particular thanks 'to the little maid mentioned by Major Salway in his narrative to the House [of Commons]'.

Meanwhile the city had a shroud of death hanging over it. Marchamont Nedham's *Mercurius Politicus* gloated that Worcester had 'indeed become a sad spectacle, and was very noisome by reason of the multitudes of dead carcasses, both of man and beast (for the fight was very fierce, and the slaughter of the enemy great) till care was taken for their removal (by God's blessing) to prevent infection'.[2] In the meantime the dead were laid out, John Aubrey hearing that 'The penes of the dead stripped bodies 2 or 3 days were all erect.'[3] 'Death erection', or 'angel lust', can occur in the corpses of men who have met a sudden and violent end.

\* \* \*

Lady Fanshawe, who had noted the scarcity of provisions when she had accompanied Charles to the Isles of Scilly in the spring of 1646, now wrote to one of her children: 'Upon the day of September following was fought the battle of Worcester, when, the King being missed, and nothing of your father being dead or alive for three days was heard of, it is inexpressible what affliction I was in. I neither ate nor slept, but trembled at every motion I heard, expecting the fatal news.'

While the king's fate remained a mystery, she soon read the name of her husband, Sir Anthony, among a list of prominent prisoners of war in a Parliamentary newsbook. Later she was advised that he was being brought to London, and that she would be able to meet him before he was sent for imprisonment pending trial.

She waited in a room in Charing Cross on the agreed date. 'At last came the captain and a soldier with your father, who was very cheerful in appearance; who, after he had spoke and saluted me and his friends there, said: "Cease weeping; no other thing on Earth can move me. Remember, we are all at God's disposal."'

Sir Anthony stressed that being taken prisoner was one of many things that could happen in times of war. He was proud that he had managed to burn his private papers before being taken, and was sure that this action would save 'the lives and estates of many a brave gentleman'. After lunch with his wife he was escorted to Whitehall, where he was kept in solitary confinement in a small room overlooking a bowling green.

Ann Fanshawe worked out where he was being held. 'During the time of his imprisonment I failed not constantly to go, when the clock struck four in the morning, with a dark lantern in my hand, all alone and on foot, from my lodging in Chancery Lane … to Whitehall at the entry that went out of King's Street into the bowling ground. There I would go under his window and softly call him … Thus we talked together; and sometimes I was so wet with rain that it went in at my neck and out at my heels.'[4]

Sir Richard Fanshawe was interrogated repeatedly. The combination of the grim conditions in his cell, and the exertions of the 'cold and hard marches' he had endured since his capture, meant that he became seriously ill, perhaps with scurvy. He was saved from death by Oliver Cromwell, who liked Fanshawe, and advised Ann to get a letter from a doctor explaining how sick he was. Cromwell used this document to persuade his comrades to release Fanshawe from captivity, on a bail of £4,000.

The foremost Englishman to be captured in the days immediately after the battle was not so fortunate. The Earl of Derby had been deeply reluctant to leave Charles's side at Whiteladies. Derby had reached Newport in Shropshire, where he surrendered to Captain Oliver Edge, from Colonel Lilburne's regiment, on the promise that his life would be spared. Edge received a reward for catching such a prized enemy, one of several he accumulated during Harrison's mopping-up operation.

Derby was sent to Chester, and was held in Chester Castle. While there, he heard that the Council of State had written from London insisting that he should be 'brought to trial, [and] made an example of'. Realising that his life would soon be taken from him, Derby wrote to his wife on 10 September: 'I will not stay long on particulars, but, in short, inform you that the King is dead, or narrowly escaped in disguise; whether [one or the other is] not yet known.' He outlined the utter destruction of the Royalist army, with all its noblemen killed or captured, and its rank and file imprisoned or sent overseas. There was little point, he assured her, in her continuing the defence of the Isle of Man in this hopeless, kingless, state.

The earl signed off his parting letter with love for his family, and revulsion at the cauldron of hate and destruction that his country had become: 'God almighty comfort you and my poor children,' he wrote, 'and the Son of God, whose blood was shed for our good, preserve your lives; that by the good will and mercy of God, we may meet once more upon Earth, and last in the Kingdom of Heaven, where we shall be for ever free from all rapine, plunder, and violence; and so I rest everlastingly.'[5]

Derby was court martialled by a board of officers who had, to a man, fought against him during the Civil Wars. Proceedings began at the end of September. The first of the four charges brought against him was 'That he had in a most traitorous and hostile manner, been aiding, abetting, to Charles Stuart, son of the late tyrant.'[6] His attempt to rely on the mercy guaranteed him at capture by Captain Edge proved worthless. His judges decided that 'Quarter for life belongs only to such as are … enemies, not to such as are … Traitors to their Country; The Earl is a Native of England, and therefore being taken fighting against England, cannot be accounted a competent enemy, nor in reason expect an exemption by Quarter.'[7]

Despite Cromwell requesting that his life be spared, Derby's fate was sealed: he was sentenced to death. The place of his execution had been secretly decided before the court martial had even begun. He would be transported forty-five miles north-east of Chester, to Bolton. The officers of the court martial congratulated themselves on this choice, 'wherein the just judgement of God upon this man is very remarkable, that in the same County where he first raised Arms, drew the first blood, and had done so much mischief, yea, and in the very same Town, where by his means so much blood had been spilt … it should be so brought about by his righteous providence, that he should now come to have his blood shed there upon a Scaffold before all the world, by the hand of a public Justice.'[8] He was beheaded in Bolton on 15 October.

There can be no doubt that the death sentence would also apply to Charles on his being captured. Although commonly referred to as 'the King of Scots', he was, like Derby, a native Englishman. Furthermore, he was one who had already been declared traitor by name. In such circumstances, no trial would be necessary: the authorities would simply need to establish his identity. The only fit consequence for his sin, of breathing fresh life into the calamitous civil wars that had cost the lives of hundreds of thousands of Englishmen, Scots and Irishmen, would be public justice in a fitting setting. Like his father he would be condemned as a 'Man of Blood', and like his father he would be publicly beheaded.

Charles's good instincts kept him out of his enemies' reach. His decision, on his ride from Worcester to Whiteladies, not to join his 3,000 men fleeing north, was sound. Parliamentarian newsbooks recorded scarcely credible victories by small bodies of their men against large units of defeated Royalists: 'On Thursday last there marched by our town about 1,000 of the routed Scots, who rendez-voused on Congleton Moor, there taking up their quarters for the most part of that night, lying in their close order,' ran one such report. There they were attacked by 300 irregular Parliamentary troops under a Major Gibson: 'He fell on them with his men in their Rear, killed about 300 and took above 100 prisoners with little loss: for indeed so great is the spirit of fear amongst them, that 10 men will chase 100.'[9] Judging by what happened to the 3,000, if he had joined them on the doomed trek back to Scotland, Charles would have been captured or killed; or, for that matter, captured and then killed.

One of those cavalry officers taken in the chaos of full retreat wrote from prison in Chester soon afterwards. He addressed the hectic period that started with the certainty of imminent defeat inside the cramped Royalist position in Worcester, and ended with his own capture, 125 miles north of the rout: 'Towards the evening all things appeared very horrid, alarms being in every part of the city, and a report that the enemy had entered one end of the town, and we of the horse trampling one up against another, much readier to cut each other's throat than to defend ourselves against the enemy. In this confusion we at last got out of the town, and fled as far as we could, our two Lieutenant Generals [Leslie and Middleton] being, as appeared the next morning, at our head. We had no guide, so we often lost our way, but yet reached Newport [in Shropshire], 30 miles this side of Worcester, the next morning, and there thought to have refreshed ourselves, and marched quietly for Scotland.'[10]

But this was no time for quiet. The Council of State's pre-emptive decision, once it had become confident of victory at Worcester, to block up the ways back north to Scotland, had proved its worth. The imprisoned Cavalier recalled the relentlessness of the enemy, whether uniformed or not: 'There wanted not considerable forces in every place to [con]front us, and we were so closely pursued, in the day by the army and garrison forces, and in the night by the country [folk], that from the time we came out of Worcester, until the Friday evening that I was taken prisoner seven miles from Preston, neither I nor my horse ever rested. Our body consisted of 3,000; in the day we often faced the enemy, and beat their little parties, but still those of us whose horses tired or were shot were lost, unless they could run as fast as we rode. In the night we kept close together, yet some fell asleep on their horses, and if their horses tarried behind, we might hear by their cries what the bloody country were doing with them.'[11] Many were bludgeoned to death.

Leslie and Middleton were among those to lose their horses, most likely to exhaustion. They managed to buy fresh ones, but after that point they were suspected of abandoning their men, the anonymous prisoner in Chester recalling: 'On [the] Thursday night [after the defeat] Lieutenant Generals Middleton and Leslie left us, or willingly lost us, but with all the haste they made, both of them, and Sir William Fleming, are here prisoners.'

Major General Harrison's men held a steady and impenetrable net across northern England. The operation in which Leslie and Middleton were caught by 800 Parliamentary cavalry and dragoons was described in a jubilant report from Lancashire written by the commanding officer, Colonel John Alured, another signatory of Charles I's death warrant:

> *Sir,*
>
> *It hath pleased the Lord to give a great mercy to us in the delivery up of a great many of the leaders, and chief of the Scottish forces into our hands. I marched on a dark rainy night, in rough and tedious way, to the town ... called Ellel, where we had intelligence that most of the Scots commanders lay, which were found to be true, and have taken there these Prisoners, in this enclosed list, nominated ...*[12]

This list included the two Scottish lieutenant generals, two earls, five lords, and many other Scots of great note. As *Mercurius Politicus* gloated: 'I believe now, all the nobility of Scotland that are at liberty may all sit upon a joint-stool.'[13]

The architects of the rolling victory saw this as a time to celebrate God's blessing, and to reward those who had played a significant part in it. The Council of State would vote '£30 a piece to be paid to Lieutenant Robert Milnes, and Captain Lieutenant John Key, for their good service in taking Lieutenant General Leslie, and Lieutenant General Middleton, after the rout of the Scottish army at Worcester'.

That was considered quite a bounty. At the same time, it puts in context the £1,000 reward for catching the elusive Charles Stuart.

There were so many Royalists taken after Worcester – perhaps 10,000 – that the cities where they were first held were choked with them. The cathedral at Worcester was made into a pen to keep hundreds of Scottish prisoners under guard; after they were moved on, Parliament gave a grant for cleaning the place, to get rid of the terrible stench.

The New Model Army soon had prisoners of war in York, Chester, Lancaster, Stafford, Derby, Leicester, Shrewsbury,

Nottingham, Warwick, Liverpool and Carlisle. In Chester there were so many detainees that once the castle and the church were full, private houses were converted into temporary jails.

The first task of the Parliamentary officers was to sort the Scots from the English. The Englishmen who had fought for Charles were kept back for special treatment, for, as Derby had discovered, they were viewed not simply as the enemy, but as contemptible homegrown traitors. The Scots were merely defeated foreign invaders, to be treated cruelly, but not mercilessly. Nineteen of the senior Scottish officers were escorted to Windsor Castle, where they were kept under separate constant watch. The journey south was tougher for the men they had led.

The Council of State asked Cromwell that those Scottish prisoners destined for London should be marched in a way that was 'not too speedy, so that we may be the better prepared to dispose of them'. Various options were looked at to provide a sufficiently large prison compound, including the tiltyard at Greenwich and the East India Company's shipbuilding yard at Blackwall. The latter had the advantage of being surrounded by a twelve-foot-high wall.

The regicide Colonel Barkstead was instructed to see if the artillery ground in Tothill Fields, where the militia had recently paraded before the battle of Worcester, might be suitable for holding 4,000 of the Scottish prisoners. This was marshy land between Millbank and Pimlico, historically associated with necromancy – communication with the dead. It was suitably bleak, and large, and was approved for the task.

En route, the 'Scots, Highlanders, or Redshanks', as Parliament referred to them, were made to sleep on Hampstead Heath, before being led through Highgate, Islington and Kingsland (now Dalston, but then a wooded area with few inhabitants, where the young Samuel Pepys 'used to shoot a bow and arrow'). On their way to London they had relied on people's kindness for food. The oatmeal bags they carried with them on campaign, that held a week's worth of oats (used for making porridge, oatcakes, and a rough but calorific raw oat paste), were long empty. Now they ate tough biscuit given to them by strangers as an act of charity.

On the Saturday the Scottish prisoners were escorted through the City of London, passing through Aldgate, then along Cheapside, Fleet Street and the Strand. After that, as a Royalist called James Heath noted in his *Chronicle of the Late Intestine War*, they were 'driven like a herd of swine through Westminster to Tothill Fields'. It was reminiscent of a scene from a triumph of Ancient Rome, the barbarians paraded before the gawping, jeering citizens of a conquering republic.

Another eyewitness to this humiliation of the defeated revealed the contempt for the Scots that was prevalent in England at the time: 'For the most part they were sturdy surly knaves,' he told his readers. 'Keep them under, and they may serve for nasty, stinking, vassals. I leave to every indifferent person that hath beheld them to judge what a condition they had been in if such a generation as this had prevailed and become their masters, or cut their throats, of which they made themselves so sure many of them brought their wives and bairns in with them. Yet were so many of our Scotified Citizens so pitiful unto them, that as they passed through the City they made them (though prisoners at mercy) masters of more money and good white bread than some of them ever see in their lives.'[14]

This contingent of Scots prisoners and their dependants were turned out into Tothill Fields. Food was bought for them in bulk. It was enough to keep them from starvation, but not to fill their bellies. The very basic bread and cheese of this prison diet was costing the Commonwealth more than £56 per day, and there were concerns at how such a great expense could be maintained for long. A shed was built for the sick and wounded to shelter in, with the rest forced to live in the open autumn air like farm animals. Straw was provided at the end of September 'for their lodgings'. It was all relentlessly grim and unhealthy – an estimated 1,200 of the Scots who were imprisoned at Tothill were also buried there.

It was a similar tale of extreme hardship in the north. Sir Arthur Hazlerigg had been instructed by Parliament to take the 2,300 prisoners in his custody from Durham to Chester and Liverpool, so they could be transported as forced labourers to Ireland. He felt compelled to report to London how terrible conditions had been among the captured: 'When they came to Morpeth, the prisoners being put into a large walled garden, they ate up raw cabbages, leaves, and roots ... which cabbage, as I conceive, they having fasted, as they themselves said, near eight days, poisoned their bodies; for, as they were coming from thence to Newcastle, some died by the wayside; and when they came to Newcastle, I put them into the greatest church in the town: and the next morning, when I sent them to Durham, about seven score were sick, and not able to march, and three died that night, and some fell down in their march from Newcastle to Durham, and died.'

Hazlerigg was at pains to say that the Scots 'wanted not for anything that was fit for prisoners', and boasted that 'there was never the like care taken for any such number of prisoners that ever were in England'. He had broths made for them from oatmeal, beef and cabbage, and provided enough coal to make a hundred fires, but they could not shake off the flux – dysentery. Hazlerigg believed the Scots were themselves responsible for their susceptibility to this illness, for 'they were so unruly, sluttish, and nasty, that it is not to be believed; they acted rather like beasts than men; so that the marshal was allowed 40 men to cleanse and sweep them every day'.

He also despaired at the Scots' treatment of their fellow prisoners, 'for they were exceeding cruel one towards another. If a man was perceived to have any money, it was two to one but he was killed before morning, and robbed; and if he had any good clothes, he that wanted, if he was able, would strangle him, and put on his clothes.'[15] Hazlerigg reckoned he had suffered the loss of 1,600 Scottish prisoners through death, mainly because of sickness and wounds, but the rest to violence.

Meanwhile the effectiveness of Harrison's operation was astonishing. The *Diary*, a Parliamentary newsbook, would record with satisfaction on 29 September: 'We cannot hear of one man come into Scotland of all the army that was defeated at Worcester.'[16] The result of this was that for some time many in Scotland refused to believe the news of a massive defeat put about by the English soldiers in their land. They wanted to hear from their own people what had happened, but Parliament's strict guarding of the route north meant defeated eyewitnesses could not get home with the terrible news – not just of the battle, but also of what was happening to those Scots captured in its aftermath.

Meanwhile, the womenfolk of those who had marched south, not to reappear, were distraught at the vanishing of so many of their men: 'Here is old (or rather new) howling among the ladies in Scotland,' Parliament's propagandists noted, 'for their husbands, fathers, sons, friends, that are slain and taken in England and Scotland.'[17]

The future, for many of the taken Scots, involved years of indentured labour, during which they were treated little better than slaves. A thousand of them were sent to help drain the malaria-infested fens of East Anglia. Their task was to control the waterways so they could be used for transport, and also to prevent these fertile flatlands from being flooded each winter. This hard manual toil was deeply unpopular with the local inhabitants, whose livelihoods of fishing, wildfowling and reed-cutting were threatened by the improvements, and who rioted in protest. But the project was favoured by a commercial body called the Gentleman Adventurers, to whom it promised great wealth. Their work had been disrupted by the Civil Wars, but the end of the conflict, and the supply of cheap prison labour, meant that it could now resume. At the same time Parliament benefited, by farming out the policing and feeding of some of its multitude of captives to a third party. The Gentleman Adventurers had to pay a £10 forfeit for each escapee.

On 22 September, the Council of State agreed that Oliver Cromwell should oversee the transportation of all the Scottish prisoners beneath the rank of lieutenant, or cornet of horse, from Liverpool, Chester, Stafford, Shrewsbury and Worcester, to Bristol, to await transportation abroad. Prisoners were kept in poor conditions, and received meagre daily provisions. They died at the rate of thirty a day before the ships had even left harbour. One imprisoned Scottish minister was to be sent with every 200 prisoners, at no charge, for spiritual counselling, and these preachers were to be 'free from servitude' when relocated.

Two thousand prisoners were sent in chains to do forced labour in the New World. The Reverend John Cotton wrote to Cromwell, explaining how it would be for these men: 'They have not been sold for slaves, to perpetual servitude, but for six, or seven, or eight years.' Those selling them for these stretches received around £30 per man, against transatlantic transport costs of about one-tenth of that sum. It was a lucrative trade in conquered human cargo.

The ship *John and Sara* would take 272 of these Scottish prisoners across the Atlantic to Massachusetts. There they were sold by Thomas Kemble of Charlestown, north of Boston, and worked mainly as unskilled labourers in Hammersmith, the ironworks on the Saugus River, which had started production of pig iron and grey iron in 1646. Others went to work in sawmills in New Hampshire and Maine. Many others were sent to toil in the West Indies and Ireland.

In the face of their terrible battlefield losses, and the garnering of so many prisoners, leading Scots back home were quick to make peace with the victors. On Wednesday, 1 October, reports were sent to London that many of the gentry and clergy of western Scotland had been to visit Lieutenant General George Monck, Parliament's military commander in their country. They said they were eager to make amends with the government in England. The *Weekly Intelligencer* reported, in a bemused tone, how these men 'allege, or at least pretend, that they have all along opposed the late proceedings of the King, and have protested against them'.[18] The Scots said they recognised that this latest victory against them was God's punishment for having allied their country with the Royalist 'malignants', and that they had no interest in 'increasin[g] the indignation of the Almighty'. They threw themselves on the Commonwealth's mercy, in total submission.

Despite the huge numbers of captives, the Commonwealth knew from the beginning that there were more to be brought in, if victory were to be taken to its ultimate point. On 8 September, five days after the battle, the Council of State urged its militia forces throughout England and Scotland to maintain their high state of watchfulness for fugitives: 'Many stragglers from the rout and slaughter of the army may endeavour to hide themselves [in your counties, so] be very diligent to apprehend all such, and keep them in safe custody.'

A few days later, on 13 September, in order to encourage everyone to join the search for Royalists, the Council of State announced that all horses and weapons taken from each Royalist prisoner should be given to his captor. Nobody – whether regular soldier or local official – could deprive the brave citizen of his rightful prize.

On 16 September, further encouragement was sent out to the commanders of the militia in the north to watch all roads, so 'that those who obscure themselves may be apprehended when they attempt to escape home'.[19] On the same day, three commanders further south were reminded of the remaining enemy still on the run: 'As some of them do for some time obscure themselves, hoping, after the enquiry for them is over, to pass into their own country, order a watchful eye to be still kept upon the ways and passages for their apprehension.'[20]

Two of those caught by this time were men who had been with the king at Whiteladies. Charles Giffard, who had readily agreed to the Earl of Derby's suggestion that the king hide in his house at Boscobel, was captured and held in an inn at Bunbury, in Cheshire. He managed to escape.

Meanwhile the first Francis Yates, the small farmer from Brewood who had guided Charles through back roads to Whiteladies on the night of defeat, was caught and identified as having helped the king in his flight. The Parliamentarians repeatedly interrogated him, determined to find out where he had taken Charles, but he refused to talk. Realising that he would not give up the information, and eager to set an example to others who might be tempted to assist the king, Yates was hanged in Oxford.

Even as the vigorous search for fleeing Royalists continued across the land, there was a need to celebrate the victory that had scattered the Commonwealth's enemies so dramatically and decisively. Before the battle, the very survival of the new republic had been in question. Worcester put paid to any such worries in a day. Victory on such a scale also established who was going to be its leading light.

At ten o'clock on the morning of Friday, 12 September the lord mayor of London, his aldermen, the sheriff and the recorder met at the Guildhall in their scarlet robes. They knew Cromwell was returning, and set off in their carriages to greet him. They met the conquering hero in Acton, where the recorder read out profuse praise and congratulations from the City of London before Cromwell continued towards the capital. He was cheered on his way by members of the Council of State, who had so recently questioned his trustworthiness as they quaked at the thought of royal retribution for their part in the death of Charles I.

By the time Cromwell's carriage reached Hyde Park Corner, there were 300 coaches following in his wake. At Knightsbridge the Blue Regiment of the militia, drawn from eight wards of the City of London, saluted the Lord General. In Piccadilly, Colonel Barkstead's redcoats stood to attention. Cannon thundered their gratitude from St James's as Cromwell reached Charing Cross. Throughout his progress, volleys of musket-shot from the troops mixed with cheers from the London crowds. 'As the General passed by,' an admiring scribe wrote, 'the people all along as he went put off their hats, and had reciprocal respects returned from him.'[21]

While the public acclamation of his military victory was relentless, Cromwell insisted that he was only the instrument of God, performing His will, and striking down His enemies. But Hugh Peter, the leading firebrand preacher of his time, who combined his role as Cromwell's unofficial chaplain with command of a fighting regiment, confided to friends that victory at Worcester changed Cromwell forever. Before, he had been humble. But afterwards, Peter noted, Cromwell was more 'elevated'. Although he remained God-fearing, Worcester gave Cromwell confidence that he had been marked out to do great things. Nineteen months after this, his final battlefield victory, he would enter Parliament with a troop of musketeers and forcibly expel its members. Eight months after that, he would accept the title he would keep for life: that of Lord Protector of the Commonwealth of England, Scotland and Ireland.

# 14

# Touching Distance

*The King's misfortune and the uncertainty of his
personal safety renders me so confused in all my faculties
that I am at this time especially most incapable of giving
any advice.*

Sir Edward Nicholas to the Marquess of Ormonde, October 1651

Everything seemed firmly in place for the king to manage his
escape from England: Stephen Limbry's services had been secured;
his merchantman would leave Lyme Regis, and stop briefly off
Charmouth, so Charles and Wilmot could climb aboard; then they
would sail on to France. It was hard to see what could go wrong,
provided the pair could remain at large in the meantime.

On Monday, 22 September, Charles set off from Trent House for
Charmouth, posing as the servant to Juliana Coningsby, a cousin
of Francis Wyndham. It was the same ruse that had worked when
he had shared a saddle with Jane Lane. With them went Wyndham,
Wilmot, Wilmot's servant, and an employee of the Wyndhams
called Harry Peters.

There was a fair that day in Lyme Regis, so Peters was sent ahead
with five shillings to give to Margaret Wade, the landlady of

Charmouth's inn, the Queen's Arms. Wyndham wanted to secure the two best rooms there before the place became filled with revellers.

Ellesdon planned to join up with the Royalist party as it headed for Charmouth, at Wilde, a tucked-away country retreat that belonged to his father, but was occupied by a tenant. To explain away the anticipated influx of the king and his party, Ellesdon told the tenant that he was expecting the imminent arrival of a group of friends travelling on the carriage from London.

Half an hour later, Charles and his companions arrived at Wilde. Ellesdon reassured Wilmot that he had been through every detail of the plan with Limbry so carefully that there could be no snags. The crew had been told that Wilmot was a merchant by the name of Payne, who needed to get to St-Malo with his servant to sort out some business difficulties caused by a corrupt agent. Ellesdon would later claim that Charles was so pleased with what he heard that he gave him a gold coin, promising to give him more when he was in a position to reward him properly. In Ellesdon's version of events, he then headed back to Lyme Regis to oversee final arrangements with Limbry and his ship.

Meanwhile the royal party headed for the inn at Charmouth. Charles and Wilmot stayed in the reserved rooms, expecting to be sailing for France in a matter of hours. While they looked forward to freedom, Wyndham and his servant went to the small creek on the shore, as planned, to wait for the boat from Limbry's ship that would ferry the king and Wilmot aboard. But after several hours it had not appeared. It was a season of very extreme tides, and after the tide turned, Wyndham realised that the chance had passed. He returned to the inn with the deeply disappointing news.

Who was to blame for the plan's failure? According to Ellesdon, it was Limbry. He claimed that Limbry had kept his wife in the dark about his dangerous commitment to smuggle two strangers aboard his ship. She only found out when she asked him why he was setting off with his sea chest unexpectedly. When he revealed his plan, she was both furious and frightened. In this version of events, Mrs Limbry had been at Lyme Regis's fair that day, where 'she had heard the proclamation read, wherein £1,000 was promised as a reward for the discovery of the king, and in which the danger of those also was represented that should conceal his Majesty or any of those that were engaged with him at Worcester, and apprehending that this gentlemen [sic] might be one of the party'.[1] For this reason, Ellesdon concluded, Limbry's wife forbade him from travelling that evening. Ellesdon claimed that he was even locked inside his own home by his wife and daughters, and that they threatened to go to Captain Macy, commander of an infantry unit in Lyme Regis, if he insisted on trying to see his mission through.

Captain Alford's recollections are quite different, and are supported by the written testimony of other witnesses: Samuel Pepys seems to have set great store by Alford's words, since he kept them with his chosen key sources. They reflect significantly less well on Ellesdon, while exonerating Limbry. Alford wrote his account of this part of the escape thirty-three years later, at which time he was serving his second term as mayor of Lyme Regis.

Alford said that the reason the Lyme Regis escape attempt failed was because Ellesdon failed to make the promised £25 down-payment for Limbry's efforts. According to Alford, Limbry was already upset with Ellesdon for withholding nine shillings, needed to make the plan's initial arrangements, after their first meeting. This was the version of events that Limbry would swear to before witnesses in the presence of a Master of Chancery.

Alford maintained that Limbry joined Charles and his party at the inn in Charmouth where they were waiting prior to departing for France. Limbry had gone there to collect his first payment of £25 from Ellesdon before setting off on the voyage. In Alford's account, Limbry 'failed not to be there, and came several times to the house where the gentlemen were with the lady, Mrs Coningsby ... and demanded of the people of the house if Mr Ellesdon were come. The King spoke with the master, who assured him the ship was ready; but still he lingered to see when Mr Ellesdon would come to fulfill his agreement. And it being very late at night, the master finding that Mr Ellesdon never came, who had not paid (nor never did any other) one penny of the money, the master retired there three times, and never came again to the King.'[2]

Over the years Limbry, whose Royalist sympathies were long-established (Ellesdon conceded that he 'had ever the repute of being well affected to his Majesty'), would repeatedly explain and justify his actions to acquaintances: 'That Stephen Limbray [sic] often told Captain Fookes that if Elesdon [sic] had paid him but £10, he had carried away the King; and so he told Mr Thomas Plucknell, who spake it at Bridport the 22nd of January, 1683, before the Lord Bishop of Bristol; and Mr Jones doth affirm that the master often told him that if Elesdon would have given him but £5, he had proceeded.'[3]

Left in limbo in a hostile landscape, Charles and his companions decided to ride to somewhere safer, hoping to establish what had gone wrong, and to repeat their escape attempt the next night. But the king's horse was found to have a loose shoe. The local black-smith, by the name of Hamnet, was summoned. While he was there, he tended to all the other horses too. Looking at the hooves of Lord Wilmot's mount, Hamnet remarked out loud, with obvious interest, that the markings on the shoes showed that they came from in or around Worcester. There must have been an uneasy hush among the Royalists as they waited to see what the black-smith concluded from that discovery.

But Hamnet completed his task without further comment, was thanked and paid, and then left without apparently showing any great concern. His suspicions, however, had very much been aroused by the Worcester connection. Being aware of the ongoing search for Royalists fleeing from their recent defeat, he went to report what he had just seen to the Reverend Benjamin Westley, the parson of Charmouth, and an enemy of the Crown.

Westley, a pious man, was not immediately available, for he was deep in prayer. When he eventually finished his devotions, he heard the blacksmith's intriguing report, and then sent word to the Parliamentary forces in Lyme Regis that a party of suspected Royalists had been spotted in his parish. Captain Macy was dispatched from the town, with ten or twelve cavalrymen, to detain and question the suspects, and find out who they were. By the time they arrived, though, Charles and his party were gone, and Macy could find no hint of the direction in which they had travelled. In fact they had headed east for Bridport, a town known for its Royalist leanings.

As Charles rode into Bridport with Francis Wyndham and Juliana Coningsby, he saw to his horror that the town's unusually wide streets* were swarming with redcoats. Fifteen hundred of them were there, under Colonel James Heane, one of the New Model Army's foremost fighting men. They were preparing to head for Weymouth, where they were to join up with six companies of the regicide Sir Hardress Waller's infantry regiment, and sail on to attack Jersey. Carteret's stronghold still stood firm as one of the last Royalist bastions.

Wyndham, startled by the sheer number of the enemy on view, asked the king what they should do. There was only one thing to do, Charles replied: go to the best hostel in town and find rooms there, because that was where he felt sure Wilmot would head for, given his uncompromising love of the finer things in life.

---

* Bridport was a centre of rope production, for the navy and for the gallows. The town's famously wide streets were put to use in support of this industry, with ropes being hung across them to dry.

The courtyard of the George inn was packed with enemy soldiers. Wyndham accompanied Juliana Coningsby inside, pretending to be her servant, eager to help her settle into her room, and sending an order to the kitchen for a shoulder of mutton to be prepared.

Charles, meanwhile, continued in his role as the groom, and took the party's horses to be rubbed down by the ostler. Far from being intimidated by the sight of the enemy all around him, the king seems to have made a point of being a nuisance, knocking into several redcoats on purpose as he led the horses to the stables. Once there, he asked the ostler to give them some feed. As he worked, the ostler talked openly about having been a Royalist soldier, 'and cursed the Parliament's soldiers that were then in the house'. He then looked thoughtfully at Charles, and said, 'Sure, sir, I know your face.'

Charles instinctively knew that he had to interrupt the other man's thoughts before he worked out who he was, and quickly asked the ostler if he had always lived in Bridport. No, came the reply, he had not. The ostler, happy to talk about himself, revealed that his name was Henry Hall, and that he hailed from Exeter, where he had until recently worked at an inn that, as he described it, Charles realised he knew. It was next to a house that belonged to George Potter, a Royalist merchant (who was Captain Alford's father-in-law). Charles had stayed with Potter briefly during his stint as Royalist commander in the south-west in the First Civil War. Realising that Hall had probably spotted him back then, Charles said, 'Friend, certainly you have seen me there at Mr Potter's, for I served him a good while, above a year.'

This satisfied Hall's curiosity. 'Oh – then I remember you a boy there,' he replied, relaxing, before suggesting they enjoy some beer together. Charles, anxious to get away before the ostler's memory was jogged further, said he sadly could not take up the kind invitation just then, as he had to prepare dinner for his master. But he promised he would be back to see him again on the return leg of his and his master's journey to London, three weeks later. Then he would definitely make time for that beer.

A little later Wilmot arrived in Bridport, and also braved the infusion of enemy soldiers. He soon worked out where Charles and his companions were lodging, before checking himself into another inn.

Charles's party stayed up in their quarters, ensuring that the only person to see them was an old serving woman who brought them their mutton. They gave her what was left of the meat, a treat that she took the precaution of hiding under the room's portable lavatory when she left, so nobody would deprive her of any of it.

Wilmot and the king's party set off separately, all pretending to head towards London, before meeting up. Wilmot reported that there had been some misunderstanding between him and Ellesdon, and that he hoped the ship would arrive on time, at the agreed place, the next night.

Charles was cautious, and insisted that they did not return to the same waiting place as the previous night, in case it had been compromised. Instead, they went to another inn called the George, in the village of Broad Windsor, four miles inland. It was a place that Francis Wyndham knew. He trusted the landlord there, Rhys Jones, because he had worked for friends of his.

Again, because of the preparations for the assault on Jersey, Broad Windsor was swarming with redcoats. The only room available was a small one at the top of the inn, with one bed. Charles and his companions would have to share the space.

That night one of the other guests went into labour, her cries of pain persuading the rebel troops who were staying in the inn to move on to other quarters. The Royalists spent the evening of Tuesday, 23 September there while Harry Peters, the Wyndhams' servant, went to Lyme Regis to check on the ship's readiness.

He returned with deeply disappointing news. Stephen Limbry, sure that whatever mission he was being sent on was a dangerous one, although he was unaware of the king's part in it, had told Ellesdon that he was not prepared to risk his life. The Charmouth plan, so well planned, so promising, and so tantalising, had ended in failure.

There was nothing for it but to return to Trent House, Francis Wyndham's home. Charles set off again, Juliana Coningsby behind him, with time to wonder what might have been, with just a modicum of good luck, and to worry that his best and perhaps only chance of freedom had just passed him by.

It proved extremely fortunate that Charles had kept on the move, because a quarter of an hour after he and his companions had left Bridport, Captain Macy and his cavalry troop rode into the town. They were still hunting for the suspicious group with those horseshoes with the tell-tale Worcester markings. Macy made enquiries at the George inn, and was told that guests answering his description had set off down the road to London. The Parliamentarians charged off in pursuit, not stopping till they reached Dorchester, fifteen miles away.

It is possible that this was the point at which Ellesdon gave in to the temptation of the huge reward on Charles's head. He seems to have set off from Lyme Regis after Macy's posse had departed. Not far out of town he came across a man he knew, Thomas Taylor, and said to him, 'Now, Mr Taylor, there is a £1,000 promised for anyone that can discover the King.' Ellesdon made it clear that he knew where the king might be found. But Taylor later swore that he dismissed the suggestion with disgust: 'I would not do it if it were to gain the World,' he said, before riding on.[4]

Undeterred, Ellesdon appears to have carried on alone in pursuit of the king and the reward. He rode to Pilsdon House, the home of Sir Hugh Wyndham, which was five miles from Lyme Regis. Sir Hugh was Francis Wyndham's uncle, and Ellesdon was convinced that this was where the king would have been taken to hide. He said as much to Sir Hugh, who was furious at the impertinence of his uninvited guest, and sent him swiftly on his way.

Soon after that, perhaps after receiving a tip-off from Ellesdon, Captain Macy appeared at Sir Hugh's house with his troopers. They were no longer merely on the trail of suspected Royalist fugitives, but now openly declared that they were there to arrest 'Charles Stuart'. Excited at the prospect of catching such a uniquely valuable prize, they roughly searched every room of the house, local tradition recording: 'They burst in upon the astonished family with some heat, and commenced their blundering proceedings by declaring that one of the young ladies of the house was Charles Stuart in disguise. When this error had been corrected, they placed the old baronet, his lady, his daughters, his manservants and his maid-servants in the hall under guard, while they set to work to search every cupboard and loft in the house ... The indignant maids watched the soldiers ride sulkily away, while the young ladies mourned over the dainty gowns and laces which had been tumbled out of any wardrobe that could shelter Charles Stuart.'[5] But Charles was already some distance away.

# 15

# Still Searching for a Ship

*There are strong probabilities that Charles Stuart and
the Duke of Buckingham were in or about Staffordshire,
some days after the victory at Worcester, and probably
they may still be in those parts under disguise.*

The Council of State to Captain John Ley, 13 October 1651

Francis Wyndham led the royal party back to his home in Trent.
He made it clear that he was willing to host the king for as long as
necessary, but Charles was already concerned at the length of time
he had been spending in this one place. More and more people
were coming into contact with him, in a household that was the
fulcrum of local society. Also, he remained acutely aware that the
surrounding area had a large Parliamentary element in it.

The king was startled one day by the frantic ringing of the
nearby church's bells. Seeing a number of villagers buzzing excitedly in the churchyard, he asked one of Wyndham's housemaids to
go to find out the cause of the commotion. She reported back that
a Parliamentary soldier had arrived, proudly brandishing a buff
coat that he claimed to have stripped from the king's body after
having killed him. The crowd was clearly thrilled by the news.

Charles thought hard about other people nearby whose loyalty to the Crown could be relied upon to help him in his escape. That Wednesday night, Anne Wyndham's brother-in-law Edward Hyde (a cousin of Charles's adviser Sir Edward Hyde) was visiting Trent House from his home in West Hatch, halfway between Trent and Salisbury. At dinner he mentioned that he had recently seen Colonel Robert Phillips. Phillips was of solid Royalist stock; as a result he had been in custody while Charles's army moved south, but had been released after the battle of Worcester had neutered the Crown's cause, and allowed to return to his family, forty miles away in Salisbury.

Charles decided to send Lord Wilmot and Harry Peters to talk through plans with Phillips. While in Salisbury they would also sound out another trusty supporter, John Coventry, the son of the former Keeper of the Great Seal. Their task was to see if either man could help secure the elusive transport abroad. Wilmot and Peters met Coventry in the King's Arms inn, which was run by a Royalist called Henry Hewett. Coventry then asked Phillips to join them, 'who presently came; and after my Lord and he had saluted, they having been formerly acquainted in the army, Mr Coventry left them together, saying he would go into the next room and take a pipe of tobacco with Mr Hewett. Then my Lord asked the Colonel whether he could help a gentleman in distress out of the kingdom.'[1]

Phillips said he would certainly do so, since that was his duty as a gentleman, but Wilmot sensed that he was only going to assist half-heartedly unless he was let in on the great secret. 'Sir,' said Wilmot, 'I am commanded to be free with you, and to let you know that the King is at Colonel Wyndham's house at Trent, and his condition is such that he knows not how to dispose of himself. He is assured of your fidelity, and is told that no man is more capable to serve him in this exigent. He therefore commits himself to your care to provide for his safety.'[2]

Phillips was astonished by the news. His first words were pessimistic: knowing how powerful the enemy was, and how tightly they now seemed to control all of England, he said he thought it highly unlikely that they would get anywhere. However, he promised to do all he could to save the king, vowing to perish in the attempt if need be.

John Coventry rejoined Wilmot and Phillips with a cheery, 'Well, gentlemen, are you agreed?' Reassured that they were, and that the great adventure was on, he called for bottles of wine, over which Wilmot told the other two all that he had been through in the three weeks since the defeat at Worcester. The most remarkable aspect of the tale was the good luck that Wilmot had enjoyed throughout, especially given his aversion to disguise.

They eventually parted, with Wilmot setting off for Trent once again, while Coventry and Phillips walked along Salisbury Cathedral Close. Phillips, still incredulous at the secret he had been let into, told Coventry all that he and Wilmot had discussed. Coventry assured his friend that he could rely on him for any help, at any time, and wished him the best of luck in his efforts on the king's behalf.

Phillips set about his task with great energy. He headed off for Southampton to sound out a reliable merchant called Horne, who operated out of the port. Horne was not at home when Phillips called, but he was expected back the following day, so Phillips left a message that he would be staying nearby at a friend's house, and asked him to visit him there as soon as he could.

Horne appeared the next day, and Phillips asked him to accompany him on a walk outside. He told him that he needed to get some friends of his across to France without anyone knowing. Horne paused, then replied, 'There is such a man now at home, so honest a fellow that I would trust 10,000 lives, were I master of as many, in his hands; and I will make haste home and speak with him.'

He asked Phillips to meet him at three o'clock the next day, Sunday, 28 September, at Redbridge, a shipbuilding hamlet to the west of Southampton. Horne reported that he had brokered the negotiations between the master and Phillips for a boat lying on the shore, which could sail three days later. A fare of £40 would be charged, with half paid up-front, and the rest on the day of the voyage.

But again, it was not to be. With no warning, the vessel was seized by the Parliamentarians and pressed into service for their attack on Carteret's Royalists on Jersey. The only consolation was a return of part of the £20 down-payment.

Meanwhile, in London, the leaders of the Commonwealth were trying to make sense of their continued inability to hunt down Charles.

On 27 September the *Weekly Intelligencer* newsbook amplified earlier rumours of the king's death in battle as an explanation for his remaining unfound: 'It is confirmed by several personages of worth, that the Earl of Lauderdale hath reported, that at Worcester fight he saw one of our soldiers make a great blow at the Scots King, and that he fell down under the weight and violence thereof; It is conceived he is dead, and that being stripped of his clothes where he fell in the Royal Fort, he was taken the less notice of, his skin being of a sad complexion, and that undiscovered, he was buried with the multitude of the slain, to partake of the same numerical corruption, and to crumble with them into promiscuous dusts, never hereafter to be regretted.'[3]

Not entirely happy with this theory, the same publication decided the following week to summarise all that it had heard about Charles's possible fate in the three weeks since the battle of Worcester. 'The Reports of the Scots King are various,' it acknowledged:

*I made mention in my last that the Earl of Lauderdale reported, that he saw him fall under a violent blow which one of our Soldiers gave him. There are many others who affirm, that they beheld him in person with that Body of Horse which afterwards fled out of Worcester, and (in a speed full of tumult and distraction galloping from Beaudley [sic] to Wolverhampton) they heard him repeat these words, 'Shift for yourselves, Gentlemen, shift for yourselves!' By this it seems he perceived that the many Troops that were with him would serve rather to betray him than assist him, and that, in the conditions in which he was, his greatest safety was in the fewest numbers. There are others who for one night have lodged him in a Castle within four miles of Kendal, and they will tell you that he lay there one night at his entrance into Englance [sic]; but if you ask further of them they cannot tell you with whom on his return he came thither, or how he got away. Some are most confident that he is not amongst the living, and have been so precisely curious as to seek for him among the graves of dead. Others will tell you, that about four days after the great fight at Worcester, he was within three miles of London, and ferried over the River to Wandsworth, and (if you please to believe them) they will persuade you that on the next morning he came over the Bridge into the City with one man only in his company. Others will tell you, that Hind the famous robber whom they call his Scout-master General, did provide him with a Bark at Pensey in Suffolk; and they can tell you too that it cost threescore pound, in which bottom, say they, he was transported into France, although the last letters from thence make not the least mention of it. In this contrariety and contradiction of Reports we know not where to ground; but in this all wise men do agree, that the Parliament are happily rid of an Implacable Enemy; and that if he be not a dead man, yet wherever he is, he is but a lost man, and never any more able to be in the Head of an Army against them in the English Ground.*[4]

After finding that the ship at Redbridge that had been arranged for Charles's escape had been requisitioned for service against the Royalists on Jersey, Colonel Phillips headed back to Salisbury. There he consulted with John Coventry and Dr Humphrey Henchman, the canon and precentor of Salisbury Cathedral, who advised the king to look to the Sussex coast for his escape, since Southampton was so overrun by Parliamentarians.

The Royalist network sparked back into life. Henchman and Phillips recommended contacting Lawrence Hyde, who lived at Hinton Daubney, a hamlet in Hampshire near to Hambledon. Hyde was a committed Royalist, his late father having served Charles I as chief justice of the King's Bench.

If Hyde was unable to help, another possibility would be George Gunter, whose home was in Racton, four miles from Chichester, in West Sussex. In the end, Gunter proved the more convenient choice, but it was a matter of great good luck that he was on hand to help at all.

George Gunter had served as a colonel in Charles I's army, and was still being made to pay for that loyalty in the autumn of 1651. Because of Parliament's fear of the recent invasion from Scotland, Gunter had been one of many Royalists across the land who had been ordered not to stray more than five miles from his home. If he ventured further than that, he would be arrested.

Meanwhile, in the wake of Worcester, the huge expense of maintaining the army and of raising the militia for the defence of the new regime was more than the government could bear. Irregular units were paid off and disbanded as quickly as possible, but the New Model Army's continued vigilance still came at a high price. Cavaliers like Gunter were consequently punished for their allegiance to the Stuarts, and forced to pay enormous fines against their estates.

In late September 1651, three weeks after Worcester, Gunter received an order from the Committee for the Advance of Money for the Service of the Parliament. It had been established nine years earlier, under 'An Ordinance for the assessing of all such as have not contributed upon the Propositions of both Houses of Parliament for the raising of money, plate, horse and horsemen, etc.' Its tentacles originally spread everywhere, but since the end of the First Civil War in 1646 it had focused all its attention on Royalists, demanding forced payments.

The committee was at that time recovering from a scandal. Its previous chairman had been Lord Howard of Escrick, who had been ousted in disgrace after Major General Thomas Harrison exposed him in 1650 for taking bribes from Royalists. Lord Howard had been sent as a prisoner to the Tower of London.

The committee worked out of Haberdashers' Hall in the City of London, and it was to this address that Colonel Gunter was instructed to present himself immediately. With him he must bring payment of a £200 fine, which the committee calculated to be one twenty-fifth of his total worth. If he failed to obey, he was advised, all his assets would be seized by the committee.

Gunter told the messenger who delivered this sobering news that the order was impossible to obey. He pointed out that he could not possibly go to London, as he was not permitted to move more than five miles from home. The messenger 'told him it should be at his peril if he did not obey'.

The next day Gunter rode to Chichester, a predominantly Parliamentary city during the Civil Wars, to ask the enemy authorities there which of their two directives took precedence: the one confining him to his immediate neighbourhood, or the one ordering him to London. Unsurprisingly, they said that he must go to Haberdashers' Hall in time to avoid his property's complete confiscation. The happy result of this, given what was to transpire, was that Gunter, from this point until his financial dealings with the committee were finally concluded, was able to go where he wanted, without restriction.

Gunter travelled up to London, and argued hard that the fine was set at too high a rate. He made his case well, and managed to have his fine halved. The problem he now faced was how to raise the required £100 in cash against his estate, given the difficulty prominent Royalists were all experiencing in securing credit. Not only had their army been defeated, but it was increasingly believed that their king was most likely lost. On 7 October *A Perfect Account of the Daily Intelligence* reported from London that all Charles's friends 'have clad themselves in mourning'.[5] Everything seemed turned against any who supported the Crown. 'The current running [was] then so hard against the King, the royal party, and all good men,' Gunter recalled, 'that [I] could not borrow the money in all London.'

Aware that the date by which he had to make full payment of the reduced figure was fast approaching, Gunter raced back home to Racton. On 7 October he successfully secured the sum from a moneylender who already held the bond on his estate. He returned home between eight and nine o'clock that evening to find his wife Katharine waiting for him in the doorway. She told him that a gentleman called Barlow, from Devon, was waiting for him in the parlour to talk about an urgent matter 'which none besides yourself can decide'.[6]

Gunter followed his wife into the room, and saw two men sitting on either side of the fireplace: his cousin, Captain Thomas Gunter, and opposite him, in a ludicrously inadequate disguise, Lord Wilmot. The colonel immediately recognised Wilmot, and was amazed to realise that his cousin Thomas had failed to do so. This was especially surprising because the captain had served under Wilmot's command in the earlier wars.

Gunter had some food and a bottle of sack brought to the table – he would later remember how, to everyone present's astonishment, two hornets buzzed out of the bottle when it was unstopped. He noticed Wilmot's retainer, Swan, quietly warn his master to be careful of Captain Gunter's young servant, 'Ponie', who was outside. Ponie had previously served the Earl of Cleveland, and during that period of service he must have set eyes on Wilmot many times.

After supper Gunter insisted on showing his Devonian guest to his quarters himself, since his wife had given the household serv- ants the day off. He led the way upstairs, a candle in his hand, and then bade his wife and cousin to head for their bedrooms while he waited to check that 'Mr Barlow' had all he required.

The two men now being alone, Wilmot went straight to the point: 'The King of England, my master, your master, and the master of all good Englishmen, is near you, and in great distress. Can you help us to a boat?' Gunter's immediate concern was for the man, not the plan: 'Is he well? Is he safe?' Wilmot reassured him that he was. 'God be blessed,' Gunter replied. He went on to say that it would take him a little time to sort out a boat, and the king must be kept in safe hands in the meantime. Wilmot then qualified what he had said about the king's safety: he had not seen him for a short while, but believed he was being sheltered safely.

The task of securing a boat, though, was not as straightforward as Wilmot might have hoped. Gunter was candid about his lack of maritime knowledge or connections. As he would recall, 'for all he lived so near the sea, yet there was no man living so little acquainted with those kind of men. However, as he thought himself bound by all obligations, sacred and civil, to do his utmost to preserve his King, so he would faithfully promise with all possible care and alacrity, yea expedition (which he accounted to be the life of such a business), to acquit himself of his duty.'[7]

The relentless pressures of the prolonged escape attempt are easy to forget. Wilmot would have been put to death on capture, as certainly as the Earl of Derby had been. He had nearly been caught several times in the days immediately following Worcester. For five weeks he had been responsible for overseeing the safety of his master: he had been the constant, while others had dipped in and out of their life-or-death odyssey. Deeply affected by the sincerity and passion of Colonel Gunter's declaration of loyalty, he embraced the colonel, 'and kissed his cheek again and again'.

Gunter reassured Wilmot that he was sure everything would work out well for the king and for him, and then went to his own bedroom. His wife was waiting anxiously for him, and demanded to know who the strange Mr Barlow really was. She had tried to get the same information out of Thomas Gunter earlier in the evening, but he was adamant that the Devonian was none other than he claimed to be. But Mrs Gunter was insistent: her husband must share this man's true identity with her.

This was an age when husbands believed themselves to be superior to all others in the family hierarchy, be they wives, children or (if there were any) servants. It had been that way in England since Anglo-Saxon times: the husband governed the household as the monarch reigned over the nation. Just as a country benefited from a strong ruler, so a household was believed to blossom if the husband remained firmly in charge. Even in wealthy circles, such as the Gunters inhabited, a wife remained under the 'rod' of her husband from the moment her father handed over such power at her marriage until one of the couple died.

The colonel apologised to his wife, but said he could not talk to her about their guest, and that she must not worry herself about things that did not involve her. But Mrs Gunter was not to be silenced, believing that this matter did in fact involve her and the rest of her family. She suspected that, in an age when a man's condemnation for high crimes could also lead to the confiscation of all his possessions, her husband was embroiled in a project that could damn them all: him to death, and she and her family to eternal poverty. 'And in that,' she said, 'I am concerned.' She then burst into a loud sobbing fit, which the colonel was unable to stop.

Gunter took his candle and made as if to move to another room. But once he was out the door he went straight back to Wilmot's quarters, knocked on the door, and apologised for disturbing him. He then asked if it might be allowable to share all that the two of them had discussed earlier with his wife. Gunter stressed that he entirely trusted her to keep everything to herself, but assured Wilmot that if he preferred that he did not share the information, he would placate her as best he could. 'No, no,' Wilmot soothed, 'by all means acquaint her with it.'

Gunter returned to his wife and explained that 'Mr Barlow' was in fact Lord Wilmot. He also told her about the king's highly dangerous predicament, and how he had been asked to help find a boat to carry Charles and Wilmot overseas. He dabbed the tears from his wife's eyes, then was pleased to see that, now she understood the great secret, she was quickly cheering up. She declared herself fully supportive of her husband's mission, though she was sceptical about its likely success: 'Go on, and prosper. Yet I fear you will hardly do it.' The colonel himself was equally pessimistic: 'However, I must endeavor, and will do my best, leaving the success to God Almighty.'

Brought up to believe that women were, as the Bible termed them, 'the weaker vessel', Gunter congratulated himself on his luck in having a wife who deported herself 'during the whole carriage of the business, with so much discretion, courage, and fidelity, that (without vanity be it spoken) she seemed (her danger considered) to outgo her sex'.[8]

Gunter slept very little that night, thinking through all that he had to plan, aware of the consequences of failure to him and his family, and eager to come up with a scheme that gave the greatest chance of success to the king.

The next morning, Wednesday, 8 October, he agreed with Wilmot that he would go to make enquiries about a boat, and would return home as soon as he had news. He asked a retired servant, John Day, to accompany him as he rode the two miles or so south-west through Bourne (called Westbourne now) to the coastal village of Emsworth. On their short journey they crossed over from West Sussex into Hampshire.

While Gunter knew nobody in the local seafaring community, Day was connected to some of them by blood. They had hoped to find boats lying idle at Emsworth awaiting work, but there were none to be seen. The two men headed back, wondering what to do next. Gunter was surprised, when nearly home, to bump into Wilmot. With the possibility of escape so tantalisingly close, Wilmot had found it impossible to wait patiently for the colonel's return, and on the spur of the moment he had decided to find out for himself what was going on. But, prone to forgetfulness at the best of times, he found that he had left behind a black purse stuffed with gold coins that he usually kept on him.

Wilmot had checked everywhere, and by now accepted that he had somehow left Gunter's home without the money needed to finance the escape. He sent his manservant, Swan, back to see if it was in his bedroom. Fortunately Katharine Gunter, when she checked on her guest that morning, had seen the pouch lying on Wilmot's bed, and kept it safe before handing it over to Swan.

Meanwhile Colonel Gunter and Wilmot, undaunted by the setback at Emsworth, decided to try Langstone Harbour, three miles to the west. The harbour lay in an inlet between Hayling Island and Portsea Island, and was the site of a salt works, where sea water was boiled in a large lead pan before being added to the salt harvested naturally after each high tide. Langstone was also a busy fishing port, which was why the Royalists had chosen to scout it out. However, yet again, no boats were available for the king's use.

Wilmot and Gunter shared a plate of oysters at Langstone, and then went their separate ways. Wilmot returned to the safety of Lawrence Hyde's home at Hinton Daubney, where Gunter promised to come that evening with a fresh plan. Gunter then met up with his cousin Thomas Gunter, and let him in on the secret. The colonel appreciated the need to act fast, he trusted his cousin implicitly, and the captain's involvement would be useful in increasing the number of avenues that could be explored.

Colonel Gunter arrived at Hinton Daubney in time for supper. He proposed that they all meet again the following day in the larger port of Chichester, when he would let Wilmot know of any progress he and his cousin had made. Gunter then 'took his leave of the Lord [Wilmot], it being a very dismal night for wind and rain, which made the Lord very much to importune the Colonel to stay. But he refused, replying that delays were dangerous; and let the weather be what it would, he had a sure guide.'

Gunter set off home, which he reached in the early hours. Allowing himself a short sleep, he then headed for Chichester, where he joined forces with his cousin. Thomas Gunter reported that he and his friend William Rishton had already made numerous enquiries, but without success: not a single English merchantman was due to head out in the coming days.

Colonel Gunter now had the idea of turning things on their head: rather than searching for an English ship heading overseas, why not look for a French vessel heading home?

He checked which French merchants were then in Chichester harbour, and recognised the name of Francis Mançell. The colonel went to Mançell, plied him with French wine and Spanish tobacco, then changed the tone of the convivial meeting by admitting, 'I do not only come to visit you, but must request one favour of you.' Mançell said he would be happy to help in any way that he could. Gunter said he needed to hire a small ship, 'for I have two special friends of mine, that have been engaged in a duel; and there is mischief done, and I am obliged to get them off if I can'.

Mançell, thrillingly for Gunter, said he could see no problem with this, and suggested Brighton, thirty miles away, as the port of departure. Gunter was so excited at having at last found a possible avenue for escape, albeit at a slight distance, that he asked Mançell to set off with him immediately for Brighton. But Mançell pointed out that this would not be possible, because Chichester was hosting its traditional annual festival that day – the Sloe Fair was a holiday that attracted revellers from across all the surrounding area. Even people from Brighton would be there in large numbers, meaning it would be impossible to make any arrangements for a boat. But they could, he said, set out the next day.

Gunter set off home, again into a stormy night, this time on a horse borrowed from Lawrence Hyde – his own was exhausted by all the recent frequent journeys along the south coast of England looking for a way out for the king. He himself was also extremely tired, but once again he only had time for a couple of hours' sleep before he was back on the road to Chichester.

On Friday, 10 October the colonel met up with Mançell, and lent him a horse. At two o'clock that afternoon they rode into Brighton, whose population of 4,000 made it the largest town in Sussex. Its transformation from a small village with a few dozen boats in the previous century, to a significant town at this time, had arisen from its long history as a fishing centre, and its growing importance as a port. By the mid-seventeenth century it had a thriving business in wine, coal, salt and stone, yet it would still be small enough in the 1730s for the surrounding cornfields to draw admiration from visitors.

Brighton was a place of commerce, that chose not to be burdened by politics. It was happy to be a major centre of carriage for Parliament, and the previous year ships protecting the town's fishing fleet had captured a Royalist crew after being attacked. The people of Brighton were equally content to defy the authorities, taking part in clandestine, but lucrative, work for Royalists.

Mançell found that the man he usually dealt with in Brighton, Nicholas Tattersall, was out of town, having gone to Chichester's Sloe Fair. But he soon heard that Tattersall was only four miles away, in Shoreham. Mançell sent a message asking Tattersall to come and see him as soon as he could, because he had an interesting proposal to put to him.

The Royalists' luck seemed at last to have turned. Tattersall revealed that he had an active licence for his ship, the *Surprise*, allowing departure from Shoreham for Poole in Dorset with a cargo of coal. Gunter left it to Mançell to make the deal with the ship's captain. Tattersall insisted on knowing who the men were that he was to carry before he would agree to anything. Mançell repeated the tale that he believed to be true – that the stowaways were two friends of the colonel's who had been involved in a duel, and who needed to get away quickly and secretly before being held to account. This was acceptable to Tattersall, and by two o'clock in the afternoon of Saturday, 11 October his fee of £60, to be paid in advance, was agreed. For a further £50 he agreed to be ready to sail at an hour's notice, since Gunter and Mançell could not yet tell when the two duellists would make it to Shoreham.

Colonel Gunter, exhaustion battling with exhilaration, rode to tell Lord Wilmot that the plan was in place. Wilmot was with Lawrence Hyde, Colonel Phillips and Thomas Gunter at the house of Anthony Brown, a tenant of Hyde's, and a brother-in-law of Thomas. On hearing the news, Phillips told Colonel Gunter, 'Thou shalt be a saint in my almanac forever!' Gunter then went to where Wilmot was hiding, saluted his senior officer, and gave him a full account of everything that had occurred since their last meeting. Wilmot could not have been more delighted.

Gunter was then told he must sleep, while Phillips was entrusted with going the next day to inform the king that he must immediately come to Lord Wilmot and Colonel Gunter, in preparation for a voyage to France.

Meanwhile, in London that same day, the Council of State composed an urgent directive to be sent to the customs officers of all the ports in England:

*Council has informations inducing probabilities that Charles Stuart is still in England, as also the Duke of Buckingham, obscured and under disguise, expecting a fit time to pass into foreign parts. Have a special care of that which is otherwise your duty, and use your utmost diligence to make a strict search, and take due consideration of all such as attempt to pass beyond the seas from your port, or any creek, and suffer none to pass whom you may have cause to suspect to be Charles Stuart or the Duke of Buckingham, or any other such person of quality. We need not put you in mind that Parliament has appointed £1,000 to be given to him or them that shall apprehend the leader of the late invading army. For your better discovery of him, take notice of him to be a tall man, above two yards high, his hair a deep brown, near to black, and has been, as we hear, cut off since the destruction of his army at Worcester, so that it is not very long; expect him under disguise, and do not let any pass without a due and particular search, and look particularly to the bye creeks of embarkation in or belonging to your port.*

# Surprise Ending

*I need not tell you, that we were lately upon a fear, of
having oppression renewed upon us, and to have had
those to rule over us, whose little finger would have been
heavier than our former oppressor's loins. I need not tell
you of an enemy that came like an overflowing flood,
that would even have swallowed us up quick.*

From the sermon of Joseph Caryl at the service
of thanksgiving for the victory at Worcester,
2 October 1651

We must now go back a few days, to reconnect with the king's
progress during the period when Colonel Gunter was working so
hard with Wilmot to find a ship. On Monday, 6 October Charles
had set off from Trent House with Juliana Coningsby, Wyndham's
servant Harry Peters, and Colonel Phillips. They had ridden for
forty miles, over back roads, towards Heale House, the home of
Katherine Hyde, near Salisbury. En route they passed through
Wincanton, and lunched at the George inn at Mere. Charles was
quietly amused when the innkeeper, Christopher Philips, raised a
glass to toast the king.

Heale House, in Nether Woodford (as the village of Middle Woodford was then known), was a few miles north of Salisbury. The large and beautiful house had been built in the previous century by William Green, on a bank of the River Avon, above a stretch rich with trout. The Hyde family had suffered several recent losses: in 1641 there had been the death of Heale House's seventy-nine-year-old owner Sir Lawrence Hyde, a respected lawyer who had been attorney general to Charles's grandmother, Anne of Denmark; Sir Lawrence's heir, another Lawrence, had also died, and his widow Katherine now occupied Heale.

In 1650, Katherine's brother-in-law Sir Henry Hyde had paid for his loyalty to the Crown with his life. Sent to Turkey to try to gain support for Charles's cause, he had been intercepted, arrested and handed over to Parliament. Imprisoned in the Tower of London, he was condemned to execution. On the scaffold he kissed the blade of the axe that then beheaded him.

Katherine Hyde welcomed Charles as he arrived at Heale at dusk. He was introduced to her merely as Phillips's friend, but she was not fooled. Charles did not know it, but she had seen him several years earlier, near Salisbury, when he had been a prince riding in his father's Civil War army, and she had not forgotten him.

At Mrs Hyde's table that night sat the king, Phillips, Frederick Hyde – whose father-in-law had been hanged for helping a Royalist plot in 1643, but who seems not to have participated in the Civil Wars himself – and his widowed sister-in-law, and Dr Humphrey Henchman, who Charles had asked to meet him there.

During dinner, Charles was aware of Mrs Hyde and Frederick looking intently at him. After everyone had finished eating, he took Mrs Hyde aside and told her who he truly was. It came as no surprise to her. She assured him that she could keep him safe, but warned that she trusted nobody in the household except her sister. She advised him to leave the house temporarily the next day, because there was a fair in Salisbury then, which she could allow all her servants to go to. Charles and Colonel Phillips, and Juliana Coningsby and Harry Peters, should pack up their things, and appear to depart from Heale for good, before the staff left to enjoy their day off. The pair would then secretly return to the house while it was free of servants, and hide before their return.

Charles left with Phillips the following morning to spend the day riding on Salisbury Plain while Mrs Hyde saw her plan through. They made their way to view 'the great wonder of that country', Stonehenge. It was even more of a mystery then than it is now. Charles's grandfather, James I, a man with a keen intellect, had sent his Architect General, Inigo Jones, to study the stones, and establish what they were, and who had built them.

For more than 300 years, from the early twelfth century, the common belief was that the wizard Merlin had placed them there. From the fifteenth century, the mythical theory was replaced by one based on actual history, the assumption being that the ancient Britons were responsible for the monument.

Inigo Jones felt that the structure would have been too sophisticated for woad-daubed savages to have designed. He believed, rather, that the stones were the remains of a massive hexagonal building designed by the Romans during their occupation of Britain. Following that proposition through, and studying the designs listed by the Roman architect Vitruvius, he asserted that what visitors to Salisbury Plain witnessed were the remains of a Roman temple dedicated to Caelus, the sky god who was the equivalent of the Greek deity Uranus. Other seventeenth-century observers believed them to be the work of the Druids.

Charles, who had a keen scientific mind – this was a man who later chose to sleep with a dozen clocks in his bedroom because of his fascination with their inner workings – would remember that he 'stayed looking upon the stones for some time'. That time stayed with Colonel Phillips too. He noted that he and the king 'took a view of the wonder of that country, Stonehenge, where they found that the King's Arithmetic gave the lie to the fabulous tale that these stones cannot be told alike twice arising'.[1]

After their morning visiting Stonehenge, Charles and Phillips rode back towards Heale in the afternoon. Dr Henchman was waiting to greet the king in a nearby field, and escorted him to the house. After handing the king over to the priest's care, Colonel Phillips led Charles's horse away with him, so as to leave no clue of his return. When Charles reached the house, he found that Juliana Coningsby and Harry Peters had already returned to it.

Charles went into the priest hole at Heale for several days, hoping that luck might finally go his way. Mrs Hyde and her sister took it in turns to bring him food in his hiding place. Meanwhile, Colonel Phillips rode off to find out from Gunter what progress he had managed to make.

Gunter greeted him with the good news that Tattersall had contracted with Mançell to take the fugitives, and that they would be departing from Shoreham on Tuesday, 14 October. While Tattersall's vessel, the *Surprise*, had permission to sail for Poole with its shipment of coal, the plan was for the ship to divert to France before resuming its legitimate voyage. Gunter explained that Tattersall was unaware that one of the men he would be carrying was the king.

Colonel Phillips reached Salisbury on Sunday, 12 October, and transmitted the plan to Dr Henchman, who then brought the promising update to the king. Because the journey to Shoreham was eighty miles, Phillips insisted that the party set off as soon as possible. He arranged to be outside Heale, with the king's horse in hand, at three o'clock the following morning. But Charles's mount seems to have panicked on entering a meadow, snapping its bridle before charging off into the darkness. 'After some time, with no small trouble', the colonel caught it and knotted the leather together again.

While waiting for the king, Lord Wilmot, Colonel Gunter and Captain Gunter rode to visit Colonel Gunter's sister at Hambledon, which was halfway between Heale and Brighton. On reaching her house, they decided to keep themselves active before Charles's anticipated arrival. They borrowed two greyhounds from her, and went to join in the hare-coursing that was taking place that day on the Downs.

After the hunting, Colonel Gunter set off to join up with the king and Colonel Phillips. He came across them outside Warneford, near Winchester. In case anyone was watching, he rode past them without a second glance, and stopped to smoke his pipe and drink some beer in the George and Falcon inn. He then went back the way he had just come, and caught up with Charles and Phillips. He bowed to the king, then led the way, as he had already established the safest route for them to take.

When they got to Broad-Halfpenny Down, near Hambledon, Charles asked Colonel Gunter, 'Canst thou get me a lodging hereabout?' Gunter told him that he had arranged for his cousin, Lawrence Hyde, to take him in. 'Know you no other?' Charles asked. For some reason he preferred not to stay at Hyde's house, despite knowing it to be very safe. 'Yes,' replied Gunter. 'I know divers yeomanly men where for a night we may be welcome. And there is one who married my sister, whose house stands privately and out of the way.' 'Let us go there,' Charles said.

Colonel Gunter led the king, Wilmot and Phillips to his sister and brother-in-law's home by a back route, while Captain Gunter and Robert Swan scouted the neighbourhood for any possible hazards. Dismounting by the front door of the modest house, Charles told Phillips to walk before him, saying, 'Thou lookest the most like a gentleman, now.' They were welcomed in by Colonel

Gunter's sister, Mrs Symonds, who Phillips would remember as 'a most hearty loyal gentlewoman'. She was certainly a generous hostess. The fire was roaring, and as night closed in they sat and enjoyed wine, ale and biscuits together before dinner.

Thomas Symonds, the owner of the house, arrived home as the group sat down to eat. He had spent a long time in the nearby inn, and his manners were dulled by alcohol. He met the sudden infusion of uninvited guests with a distinct lack of charm. 'This is brave,' he said. 'A man can no sooner be out of the way, but his house must be taken up with I know not whom.' Before he could embarrass himself or his guests further, he suddenly recognised Colonel Gunter.

'Is it you?' he asked his brother-in-law. 'You are welcome; and, as [for] your friends, so they are all.' He now surveyed the visitors with delight, till his gaze fell on the tall, dowdily dressed man with the plain haircut who stood out so starkly from the group of Cavaliers. Symonds looked suspiciously at Charles, and challenged him with: 'Here's a Roundhead.' He then turned to Colonel Gunter and said, 'I never knew you [to] keep Roundheads' company before.'

The colonel reassured him that his pudding-bowled friend was no supporter of Cromwell: "Tis no matter; he is my friend and, I will assure you, no dangerous man.' Relieved, Symonds took Charles cheerily by the hand, and jokingly toasted him as 'Brother Roundhead'.

Charles decided that the best way to navigate the situation was to go along with it. He pretended to be a Puritan, and chided his host whenever he swore with little tellings-off, such as 'O dear brother, that is a 'scape: swear not, I beseech you.' Meanwhile, with the drunken Symonds pouring ever more generous measures of spirits and beer, Charles relied on his companions to whisk away his own cup, whenever their host was not looking, in order to spare him from an excess of alcohol. Colonel Gunter wrote later of how impressed all of those accompanying Charles were with his poise, good grace and fine acting during his ordeal by drunken host.

Knowing that the king was only halfway through his long journey to Shoreham, Gunter felt that he needed to extricate him from this awkward situation. He achieved this by appealing to his brother-in-law's debauchery. 'I wonder how thou shouldest judge so right: he is a Roundhead indeed, and if we could get him to bed, the house were our own, and we could be merry.' In this way, Charles was able to slip away to bed, with Colonel Phillips lying nearby to guard him. Wilmot, able to roister as well as any man, stayed downstairs with Symonds, happily matching him drink for drink.

The royal party left in the morning, Gunter bringing two ox tongues along for provisions. They had only got to Arundel Hill when they saw ahead of them the careering figure of Colonel Herbert Morley, who was, in Colonel Gunter's words, 'full-but, hunting'. He was so distracted by his pursuit that he did not take closer notice of the group of men passing nearby.

Morley came from a prominent, wealthy Sussex family whose home was at Glynde Place. He had been brought up by Puritan guardians from the age of sixteen, following the death of his father, and had subsequently sided with Parliament, commanding a cavalry regiment during the First Civil War. He had been appointed one of Charles I's judges twenty-one months earlier, but had refused to take part in the trial. He was now governor of Arundel Castle, which had been taken from the Royalists eight years earlier after a siege. Colonel and Captain Gunter had both served in the force that had surrendered the castle to Morley.

The king's party all dismounted and led their horses down a steep hill to avoid this influential enemy, whose duties included raising Parliamentary troops and confiscating Royalist estates in Sussex. 'The King being told who Morley was,' Colonel Gunter remembered, 'replied merrily: "I did not like his starched mouchats [handkerchief]."'

After this close shave, the party repaired to an inn at Houghton Bridge, where they ordered drinks and bread, with which they enjoyed the pair of ox tongues that Colonel Gunter now produced from his pockets.

Afterwards they came to Bramber, where they saw ahead of them a large number of enemy soldiers on both sides of the street. They realised that the rebels had seen them first, and Wilmot's immediate reaction was that they should turn back. But Colonel Gunter argued, 'If we do, we are undone. Let us go on boldly, and we shall not be suspected.' Charles nodded in agreement: 'He saith well.' Gunter led the party through the enemy troops, who, they overheard, were off duty after a night's guarding nearby Bramber Bridge.

The king and his companions had not gone far when they heard horse hooves pounding towards them: it was thirty or forty of the troops they had passed, galloping in their direction. The Royalists, realising that flight was impossible, dropped their pace, but the Roundheads pushed past them, and sped off into the distance, oblivious of the great prize they had twice let slip through their fingers in quick succession.

Colonel Gunter had arranged for Charles to be hidden in the home of a Mr Bagshall, in the small village of Beeding (now called Upper Beeding). But Wilmot, unsettled by the recent close brushes with the enemy, felt that this was no longer safe enough, and 'carried the King out of the road, I know not whither', Gunter remembered.[2] The colonel himself rode on to Brighton, to await a summons from Wilmot when he was required.

Wilmot continued to seek help from Royalists in the area. Thomas Henslow, of Boarhunt, near the Hampshire coast, was one who was approached at this time, and he appears to have passed on the news of the king's proximity to the Earl of Southampton.

Southampton was a Royalist grandee of the old school. A close political ally of Sir Edward Hyde's, he had been so trusted by Charles's late father that he had tried to negotiate for peace on the Crown's behalf in 1643 and 1645. He now got word to the king that he was happy to offer whatever assistance might be needed. But, trusting that Gunter's ship would prove to be the answer to all his hopes, Charles forbade his comrades from bringing Southampton in on the design. After so many near misses and dashed hopes, he was prepared to gamble everything on this plan to flit from Shoreham across the Channel.

Also daring to hope that successful escape was imminent, Wilmot dispatched Colonel Phillips to London, to meet a Royalist sympathiser who could arrange a speedy transfer of money to France. Wilmot told Phillips to ask for this credit to arrive as soon as possible in Rouen – a favourite French haunt of Royalists in exile (particularly those unable to afford Parisian court life), which Wilmot thought an excellent destination for the king.

Colonel Gunter arrived in Brighton and went to the George,* which he found empty. He booked the best bedroom for himself, ate his supper, and was enjoying a glass of wine when Charles and Wilmot also arrived in the inn. The landlord, Gaius Smith, said, 'More guests!' to Gunter, before going forward to greet them.

Gunter ignored the new arrivals, until he heard Charles toast Wilmot with: 'Here, Mr Barlow, I drink to thee!' Smith the landlord was next to Gunter at that moment, and the colonel said to him, 'I know that name – I pray enquire, and whether he was not a major in the King's army.' Smith went to ask the question, and returned to say that Gunter was quite correct. 'Mr Barlow' and the

---

\* Referred to in contemporary documents as 'the Oulde George'. There was another George in Middle Street, which has often been thought of as the inn in question, but it seems more likely that the fugitives would have avoided the centre of Brighton, and selected a rendezvous in a quiet neighbourhood that was on the Shoreham side of town.

supposed major then invited Gunter to join them for a drink, and they all moved to Gunter's room, because of its larger size.

Colonel Gunter would remember how 'At supper, the King was cheerful, not showing the least sign of fear or apprehension of any danger, neither then nor at any time during the whole course of this business. Which is no small wonder, considering that the very thought of his enemies, so great and so many, so diligent, and so much interested in his ruin, was enough, as long as he was within their reach and as it were in the midst of them, to have daunted the stoutest courage in the world.'[3]

Francis Mançell, the French merchant who had secured the ship, and the ship's captain, Nicholas Tattersall, joined the group for further supper at the George. Charles, as ever, was extremely conscious of when he was being looked at too intently. Over supper he felt Tattersall's eyes constantly on him.

After the five men had eaten, Tattersall called Mançell over to tell him that he was most upset that he had not told him who the 'man of quality' was, for, he said, 'He is the king, and I very well know him to be so.' Mançell assured Tattersall that he was wrong, but Tattersall was adamant: 'I know him very well, for he took my ship, together with other fishing vessels, at Bright-Hempson [Brighton] in the year 1648!' This was while Charles was in charge of the Royalist fleet during the Second Civil War, when the then Prince of Wales was denied battle by a sudden storm. His only successes had been picking off a few enemy ships, one of them Tattersall's.

Tattersall continued: 'But be not troubled at it, for I think I do God and my country good service in preserving the king, and by the grace of God I will venture my life and all for him, and set him safely on the shore (if I can) in France.'

Mançell reported every word back to the king, who realised he had no choice but to trust Tattersall. He took the precaution of keeping the merchant and the ship's captain with him, drinking and smoking, rather than allowing them to go home, where they might spread the thrilling (and highly valuable) information they now knew.

This was not the only unsettling moment for the king during that long night waiting at the George. While Charles 'stood [with] his back against the fire, leaning over a chair', the landlord, Gaius Smith, made a point of chatting to him. When the two were briefly alone, Smith bent over, took Charles's hand, which was resting on the back of a chair, and kissed it, before whispering, 'God bless you, wheresoever you go – I do not doubt before I die but to be a lord, and my wife a lady.' Another who was present heard Smith say, 'It shall not be said but I have kissed the best man's hand in England.'

Charles laughed nervously, and moved to another room. Colonel Gunter was amazed by his poise at such a moment of danger: 'It was admirable to see how the King (as though he had not been concerned in these words, which might have sounded in the ears of another man as the sentence of death) turned about in silence, without any alteration of countenance or taking notice of what had been said.'

Charles could only hope that the innkeeper would remain focused on possible future royal rewards, rather than opting for an immediate bounty by turning him in. After a while, Charles retreated to his bedroom, and Colonel Gunter followed to say how appalled he was at the landlord's outburst. 'Peace, peace, Colonel,' the king said. 'The fellow knows me, and I him. He was one that belonged to the back-stairs [staff] to my father. I hope he is an honest fellow.'

Tattersall, however, proved increasingly awkward. When pressed by Colonel Gunter about whether he was ready for the voyage, he announced that they would be going nowhere that night, given the state of the tide and the direction of the wind. He revealed that he had brought the *Surprise* into a creek, from which it would be impossible to move her in such conditions. It seemed that the great disappointment at Charmouth was about to be played out once more.

But Charles refused to give up this time. He waited outside, and it was he who noticed the wind suddenly change into a more helpful direction. Gunter offered a further £10 if the boat were made ready straight away. Tattersall, now that he was aware that one of his passengers was the king, held out for a better price all round, insisting that his boat be fully insured against the danger of the mission. The Royalists rounded on him for his opportunism, but Tattersall would not yield, forcing Colonel Gunter to agree to fully cover the *Surprise*'s supposed value of £200.

With the costs agreed, Tattersall next insisted that the debt be secured by a bond. Gunter was furious, and suggested they look for another vessel. But Charles realised there could be no further delays, and nobody else could possibly be brought into the plan at such a late stage. The king reassured Tattersall of Gunter's position, saying: 'He saith right – a gentleman's word, especially before witnesses, is as good as his bond.'

Now that all arrangements were finally in place, Colonel Gunter urged the king to get some rest. This he did, falling asleep fully dressed with Lord Wilmot nearby. Gunter woke them both at two o'clock, and they took a back road to the creek, where a boat was waiting to take them to the *Surprise*.

The king and Wilmot said farewell to their companions, and went with Tattersall, Colonel Gunter and Robert Swan to Shoreham. It turned out that their 'ship' was actually a small coal barge – the king estimated that she was not above sixty tons. She had a crew of just four men (we know one was named Thomas Tuppon, and that a Richard Carver was her master), and a boy. She was lying with her hull in the mud, because the tide was out.

Wilmot and Charles bid farewell to Colonel Gunter and to Swan, and scaled a ladder onto the ship, making for a small cabin which they stayed in while the tide began to rise. The king found a bunk there, and rested in it. Suddenly Tattersall entered the cabin, kissed Charles's hand, and professed his complete loyalty, as well as his determination to get him safely to France.

At seven there was enough water for the ship to pass out of Shoreham. She set off towards the Isle of Wight, as if on her approved route to Poole. Gunter waited on the shore with the horses in case anything went wrong. 'At eight o'clock I saw them on sail,' he would recall, 'and it was the afternoon before they were out of sight. The wind (O Providence!) held very good till next morning to ten o'clock.'

His job was done, but he did learn of one last drama: 'I was not gone out of the town two hours, but soldiers came thither to search for a tall black man, 6 foot and 2 inches high.' But the king was gone.

Early in the voyage, Tattersall again came to Charles's cabin, and asked him to talk the crew into taking him to France. Charles went to address them without Tattersall present, to make it look as though the captain was ignorant of the plan. This was to protect him from recriminations if the escape succeeded. Charles told the men that he and his companion unfortunately found themselves in debt, and they had to get away from England to avoid being punished for their temporary lack of funds. Debt was a serious issue: debtors' prisons did not recognise social class.

Charles said there was a solution to their problem: money owing to them in Rouen, which they urgently needed to collect, so they could return to England and pay off their creditors. He and his companion desperately needed to reach a port on the north French coast, so they could get to Rouen and achieve financial salvation. Charles gave them twenty shillings while they considered his plea.

The crew told Charles that they would do as he asked, provided he could persuade the captain of his plan. Tattersall was then fetched, and pretended to be taken aback at the request, making a great show of being concerned that such a diversion would delay his journey to Poole. But the crew joined Charles in pressing him, and he eventually agreed to the plan.

Ten hours after setting off from Shoreham, at five in the afternoon, the *Surprise* turned from within sight of the Isle of Wight towards France. The French coast could be seen as the sun rose the following morning. But the tide was against them, even as safety was within sight. The ship came to a halt two miles from shore, off the port of Fécamp.

As they waited at anchor for the tide to turn, a sleek vessel appeared in the distance. Charles, Wilmot and Tattersall took it to be a pirate ship. It looked as though the king, having evaded his many enemies in England, might now be taken prisoner by Spanish privateers, who were attacking French shipping as part of the ongoing Franco–Spanish War.

Charles persuaded Wilmot that the safest thing to do was to take the *Surprise*'s small boat, used for supplies, and row it ashore. He was worried that Tattersall, clearly scared by the suspected pirates, might put safety before his professed loyalty to the Crown, and sail as fast as he could back to England. In fact the 'Spanish pirate ship' proved to be a French sloop, and it left them alone.

Charles and Wilmot rowed for the French coast, and the *Surprise* headed for Poole, with a letter from Charles in Tattersall's pocket guaranteeing safe passage in case Carteret's Royalist vessels operating out of Jersey intercepted her. She had such a fair wind behind her that she reached her destination in perfect time. Nobody knew of the diversion to France, and the crew kept it secret.

In Fécamp, Charles and Wilmot spent some time arranging horses to take them the forty-five miles to Rouen. They checked into a fine inn near the town's fish market before setting off.

Their reception in Rouen was inhospitable, for the king and the lord were judged on their shabby clothes, and were suspected of being lowlifes. Charles later told a group including Samuel Pepys that 'At Rouen he looked so poorly, that the people went into the rooms before he went away to see whether he had not stole something or other.'[4]

Charles knew of an English merchant based in Rouen called John Sandburne, and he was brought to speak for the duo. Colonel Phillips had successfully sent the bill of exchange to Rouen, which the king was now able to cash in. Charles and Wilmot then spent a day cleaning themselves up, and fitting themselves out in finer clothes. Charles also sent a message to his mother in Paris, letting her know that he was safely on French soil.

The next day, after spending the night at the home of a Mr Scot, the two escapees hired a coach and set off for Paris. It was the final leg of a six-week journey that had seen the king work his way secretively through ten English counties, before finally crossing the Channel.

PART FOUR

# REACTION, REWARDS
# AND REDEMPTION

# 17

# Reaction

*Now I hear the King is in France; I said by October we
should hear where he was if alive, on this ground that a
king is too great a person to conceal long; some said he
was killed, some said he was here and there.*

The diary of the Reverend Ralph Josselin,
30 October 1651

Henrietta Maria and the Duke of York had been in a state of 'fearful amazement' since the defeat at Worcester, until 'they received
the comfortable news of his Majesty being safely landed at
Feschamp in Normandy, being attended only by the Lord Wilmot.
On the news of his arrival the Duke thought it his duty to go and
meet him.'[1] The two brothers met up in Magny-en-Vexin, forty
miles north-west of Paris. On reaching the capital, Charles was
reunited with his mother and 'all the persons of quality then in
Town, with all the demonstrations of joy which could possibly be
expected.'[2] The Duke of Orléans was among those prominent in 'a
most Splendid and Honourable Cavalcade at [the king's] Reception
and Entry into Paris', attended by 'the most eminent French nobility', who congratulated Charles on his deliverance.[3]

The Marquess of Ormonde, the senior Irish Royalist, wrote from France: 'The King being by an eminent and high providence escaped the bloody hands of the Rebels is arrived at Paris ... The several dangers he hath been in ... are said to be so many that the miracle of his coming off gives us strong hope that God hath reserved him to do great things by him and for him.'[4]

The Cardinal de Retz was among those to greet Charles. In his memoirs he recorded his shock at the state of the young king: 'His Majesty had not changed his shirt all the way from England; upon his arrival at Paris indeed, he had one lent him by my Lord Jermyn, but the Queen, his mother, had not money to buy him another for the next day.'[5]

The cardinal was equally appalled at the lack of generosity of the French royal family now that the brave but impoverished escapee was again its guest: 'The Duke of Orléans went to compliment his Majesty upon his Arrival; but it was not in my power to persuade his Royal Highness to give his nephew one penny; because, said he, a little would not be worth his acceptance, and a great deal would engage me to do as much hereafter.'[6] Ashamed at the duke's tight-fistedness, the cardinal borrowed 1,500 pistoles from a magistrate friend, and quietly handed them over to Lord Taaffe, a courtier of Charles's, for the king's use.

For Parliament in London, there was utter astonishment that the king had managed to escape. Embarrassed at the failure of their armies to catch one man, and worried that the figurehead of their enemies was free to lead Royalists against their regime in the future, their newsbooks tried to downplay the significance of an escape that was the talk of Europe.

'The news this week is as observable from the sea as from the land,' began a begrudging report of 18 October in the *Diary*, 'for the report is free enough, that the Scots King is at The Hague; he came disguised to Gravesend, his hair cut close to his head, and his canvas habilements (as if he were some seaman) did so take of all suspicion, that not any in the ship had the least distrust of him. To this his language which was altogether Dutch to whomsoever he spake, did add to their disregard, insomuch that it is said, no man took notice who or what he was, until such time as he landed, & when being there acknowledged, he had such honour given to him, as the subjection of servile spirits do prodigally attribute to sole supremacy, when they idolize it.'

The account continued to try to make sense of an escape whose details remained unknown. The author wrote with feigned authority, stating categorically that Charles had stayed at the Red Lion inn in Gravesend, while in disguise. It was asserted with equal certainty and inaccuracy that Charles had been smuggled overseas in a Dutch ship, and that the Dutch would suffer for such interference. As for any Englishmen involved in getting the king from the battlefield of Worcester to the Dutch ship, the warning was clear: 'Those who have so long entertained him, directly against the tenor of the Act of Parliament, will undoubtedly be sought after, and their punishment be made exemplary.'[7]

*Mercurius Politicus*, the main Parliamentary propaganda sheet, also peddled the line that the hated Dutch were to blame for the king's voyage to freedom. 'We have certain intelligence from Holland of the King of Scots' late arrival at Scheveling, a mile from The Hague in a Dutch man of war, being accompanied with the Duke of Buckingham, my Lord Wilmot, and one or two of the gang more, all accoutered in seamen's habits. No sooner was the news brought to the Princess Royal's Court, but presently they took horse and away to the said village, where the Princess had the first sight of him; much rejoicing there was at this safe arrival, after they had condoled his great loss which seemed to be much lessened, by having his person safe amongst them.'[8] It was a short report, sandwiched by longer tales of Parliamentary triumphs in Ireland, and of bravery against the arrogant Dutch at sea.

The *Weekly Intelligencer* was openly astounded at how the extremely tall and swarthy king had managed to evade detection. 'It is certain his habit was but mean when he landed,' it noted, 'but whether he had on a canvas suit (as some report) or whether he discoloured his hair with saffron, and added by art a more clear complexion to his cheeks, to deceive the beholders, as others would have it, or whether his hair was cut off as some affirm, I cannot determine.' It was equally short of other details, but still hazarded a guess: 'Neither is it possible for the present punctually to tell you what or where his companions, or in what port in England he took shipping for Holland, but it is believed in some place not far from London.'[9]

Word reached Jane Lane in mid-October that the Council of State had got wind of her involvement in the king's escape, having interrogated a prisoner who had named her as one of two guilty parties. Its officers had then written to one of its military commanders in Stafford: 'The enclosed examination being sent to us, we desire you to send for and examine the persons therein mentioned, as to concealing and carrying away Charles Stuart and the Duke of Buckingham, and secure such of them as you think fit, and transmit their examinations, as also a copy of the former examination sent to us, concerning those two persons that were taken, and afterwards allowed to pass, about [Stafford's governor, Captain Henry] Stone.'[10]

Jane showed her customary resourcefulness, slipping away from Bentley Hall before the Parliamentarians arrived to arrest her on charges of treason. Disguised as a peasant woman, she walked nearly 200 miles across England, to the port of Yarmouth in Norfolk. From there she crossed to France, joining the Royalist court in exile, where she was celebrated as the heroine of the magnificent escape story. On seeing her, Charles is supposed to have greeted her with the words, 'Welcome, my life.'

Major General Edward Massey had been so badly wounded before Worcester that he had been unable to keep up with the Royalist band fleeing with the king from the battlefield. When he had parted from the king near Droitwich, Charles had bade Massey farewell with tears in his eyes, not expecting him to survive. But Massey had ridden on to Broadgate in Leicestershire, home of the Earl of Stamford and his son Lord Grey of Groby, a leading regicide and Parliamentary general. Massey had served with Stamford earlier in the Civil Wars, but any hope he may have had that the family's loyalty was greater to him than to the Parliamentary cause was quickly dashed. Massey was sent as a prisoner to Warwick Castle as soon as he could be moved, a month after the defeat at Worcester.

He was still 'in a very weak condition', but remained proud, an eyewitness noting that he rode from Leicester to imprisonment in Warwick 'as if he not much cared for Life, nor feared Death'. Massey had, however, not given up hope of freedom, and galloped away from his guards, but his horse was not fast enough. He was transferred to the tighter security of the Tower of London. Within a year he managed to escape from there, after clambering up the inside of a chimney. He then joined Charles in the Netherlands.

Another of the king's great helpers on his escape took rather less time to arrive on the Continent. Major William Careless had left Charles's side as the king set off with the Penderel brothers and the second Francis Yates from Boscobel House to Moseley Hall. Careless had eventually managed to get to safety overseas, arriving in the Netherlands after several weeks of trying, not long after Charles had arrived at Fécamp. In late October 1651 he made it to Paris, where he had audiences with Charles and with Louis XIV, and his role in the great escapade was celebrated to the full.

Charles's Knight of the Garter sash and jewellery also joined him in France. Colonel Thomas Blague, who had taken them from the king for safekeeping at Whiteladies early in the escape, never made it out of Staffordshire. Soon after leaving Charles, he was pinned down by the enemy in Blore Pipe House, near Eccleshall. Knowing that capture was inevitable, he just had time to bury the medal 'under a pile of chips and dust' before he was taken prisoner.

Blague had a friend secretly retrieve the garter, and this man smuggled it to him in the Tower of London. Blague, meanwhile, managed to convince his captors that he was a low-risk prisoner, the *Calendar of State Papers* for 30 December 1651 noting that he should be allowed to 'have the Liberty of the Tower', rather than being kept under constant guard. This comparative freedom gave him the chance to escape. After crossing the Channel in disguise, he handed the insignia back to the delighted king in person, fully justifying Charles's choice of him as the right man to protect his most prized possession.

In an age when God's hand was seen in every event, some Parliamentarians asked what sort of message the Lord was sending, in letting the chief malignant evade their righteous clutches. They had celebrated Worcester as the latest proof that God was on their side, but he had deprived them of the ultimate prize. The startling news of the escape of the erstwhile King of Scotland challenged the notion that divine favour rested solely on Parliament's side.

It was particularly galling to read the gloating taunts coming from the Royalists' printing presses. On 17 October the Council of State recorded that Colonel William Purefoy, one of Charles I's regicides, had 'moved the House that the Act for suppressing scandalous pamphlets may be revived'. Four days later the attorney general ordered the prosecution of the author, printer and publishers of the book *Lingua Testium: wherein Monarchy is Proved*, and other works celebrating royalty. Two years earlier the Levellers had urged that England's printing presses be free from censorship. But the

Commonwealth, despite its astonishing victory on the battlefield, realised that it still needed to keep the enemy's words under control.

To counter what was being written by Parliament's foes, and to set down forever its account of the truth, the Council of State ordered five of its most prominent citizens, including Oliver Cromwell and Major General Harrison, 'to be a committee to consider of some fit person to write the history of these times, and to take care and oversight thereof, and to consider likewise of a fit encouragement for the person or persons so employed, and how it may be raised and paid'.[11]

Meanwhile Parliament took its propaganda battle beyond the confines of England. A thousand copies of the official narrative of the battle of Worcester were sent by the attorney general, via post express, to the governor of Edinburgh Castle and the commissioners at Dublin, with a further 100 copies earmarked for New England.

The Royalists celebrated the deliverance of their champion long and hard. John Evelyn recorded in his diary for 12 November 1651 – the first Sunday that Charles attended chapel after his escape – how the priest, Dr Clare, took as his text, from the book of Genesis: 'And Jacob vowed a vow, saying, "If God will be with me, and will keep me in this way that I go, and will give me bread to eat, and raiment to put on, so that I come again to my father's house in peace, then shall the Lord be my God: And this stone, which I have set for a pillar, shall be God's house: and of all that thou shalt give me I will surely give the tenth [part] unto thee."'[12]

Evelyn also noted how, on Christmas Day, Wilmot was the first nobleman to follow Charles and the Duke of York into church. He was the great hero of the piece. This was difficult for Sir Edward Hyde, who disliked Wilmot because of his debauchery and his generally bad influence on Charles. Hyde scoffed at how Wilmot, 'in making his journeys … departed very unwillingly from all places where there was good eating and drinking'.[13] It was true. Apart from on his first, hair-raising, day on the run, Wilmot had steered a zigzag course from one substantial house to another. Somehow his luck had held.

One account of the king's escape marvelled at the miracle of it all. That Charles should have got away from his pursuers was such a highly unlikely ending to the tale that the writer could only conclude, in awe: 'Let it therefore suffice and content us, that it pleased the Divine Wisdom and Goodness to protect and defend our most gracious Sovereign in all dangers and places and conditions whatsoever, in that his encumbered passage through his own rightful dominions, and without the least umbrage of his suspicion, to convey him out of the hands of his bloodthirsty traitorous enemies, who thought themselves sure of him, *That so killing the Heir, the Inheritance might be theirs*.'[14] Two years later the Earl of Loudon wrote that 'it pleased God to preserve the King, and so miraculously to give him a way of escape to France'.[15]

But, despite Charles's astonishing escape, Worcester and its aftermath seemed still to guarantee the Crown's enemies a successfully established republic. Colonel John Jones, one of those who had sent the late king to the scaffold, wrote: 'The total overthrow of [the] Scots Pretender and all his forces, not in a blow (which might be ascribed to chance by those that have no other God to attribute to) but in a series of successes that his purpose might be seen (who disposeth of all powers) [seem certain] to make this the time of finishing our troubles, in England and Scotland.'[16]

This belief, that the God of Battles had spoken, spread from Parliament to parish. In Essex, the Reverend Ralph Josselin, who saw God's hand in all earthly matters (he had partly attributed the death of his baby son in 1647 to his own sin of 'unseasonable playing at chess'), wrote in his diary for 24 January 1652: 'All the threats of our enemies ended in the ruin of the Scotch design at Worcester, and the flight of the King into France.'[17]

Sir Edward Hyde, who had advised the king so firmly against his Scottish adventure, was in Antwerp when he received news of Charles's and Wilmot's arrival in Paris, and wrote to the king congratulating him on his escape.[18] Meanwhile he noted: 'God, by subjecting the King to these dangers, has instructed him in much knowledge which could not have been purchased, but at that price; his own fate, and that of his three kingdoms, depends now on his own virtue.'

As Charles's bravery and ingenuity were celebrated, he seemed the model of the perfect prince. Hyde wrote to Sir Edward Nicholas: 'If the King be improved as much as is reported, all will have comfort in following him; if not, he is yet ripe for deliverance.'[19]

Suffering terribly from gout, Hyde set off to serve the king, who, he hoped, would no longer be deaf to his sound advice, and would be prepared to wait for the right moment to secure his throne, should that opportunity ever arise. Never again could he seek to gain the English throne with the help of foreign invaders. Hyde reached Paris at the very end of 1651, and was delighted to find that he seemed to have the young king's complete trust. He joined a select royal council of four, which also included Wilmot.

Meanwhile Henrietta Maria lost influence as a result of the fiasco at Worcester. Charles had been encouraged by his mother and her Louvre group to undertake a risky venture, assisted by allies that his father had rejected out of hand. He had subsequently been humiliated by the Scots, trounced by Parliament, and forced to flee for his life from a victorious enemy. Having acted on his mother's bad advice, it was easier to blame her than to accept that his impulsive and reckless advance south into England had set the seal on his fate.

At the end of 1651, Charles's escape was the single bright spot in the gloomy Royalist firmament. Robert Jordan, governor of Richmond Island in New England, received from a friend in Plymouth, England, a pithy summary of the situation: 'There is little news. The Scots are totally routed. Ireland almost subdued. Scilly, the Isle of Man, Jersey, all reduced except one castle in Jersey. The Scots' King [is] in France, but little hopes to recover.'[20]

Two years later, in September 1653, the Earl of Loudon would look back and recall: 'After the defeat at Worcester there was such a general despondence of spirit and faintness of heart seized on most of men, as there was no hope of doing any good for the King or Country from people in such a distemper.'[21]

When Charles returned to the court in exile, Lucy Walter hoped to re-establish her relationship with him. During his absence, not knowing if she would ever see him again, she had continued her reliance on wealthy lovers. These had included Henry Bennet, the future Earl of Arlington, and Theobald Taaffe, an Irish lord. One of these two, probably Taaffe, had fathered Lucy's daughter Mary, who was born during Charles's time away.

James II's biographer recorded of Lucy that 'she lived so loosely, that when [Charles] returned from his Escape at Worcester into France, and she also coming thither in hopes of continuing in her former post, his Majesty would have no further commerce with her, though she made use of all her little arts, with the help of friends, to reingratiate herself'.[22] On 30 October he informed her that their relationship was over.

Lucy found this impossible to accept, and for the next four years she would be a loud embarrassment to the king in exile, claiming that she and Charles had married. But she weakened her credibility by being kept by other notable admirers, including Sir Henry de Vic, whom she considered marrying, and Thomas Howard, brother of the Earl of Suffolk.

In 1656 Charles tried to buy his way out of the problem, agreeing to pay Lucy a pension, and to give her a pearl necklace, on condition that she and her two children went to live in England. She agreed, and with one of her brothers and Thomas Howard, found lodgings in London. But her position became desperate when Howard left her, and Charles failed to pay her the promised pension.

At first, Parliament was suspicious of Lucy's presence in London. Apart from her known association with Charles, she came from a Royalist background: Roch Castle, her Welsh birthplace, had stood against Parliament until its capture in 1644. Lucy was arrested, the lawyer Bulstrode Whitelocke recording that 'The officers found a grant, when she was apprehended, signed Charles R., by which she had an annuity, or yearly pension, of 5,000 livres, granted to her for life, with an assurance to better the same, when it should please God to restore him to his kingdoms.'[23] She was kept in the Tower, and interrogated. But her captors were soon satisfied that she was neither a spy, nor any threat to the new regime at all. Her greatest use, it became clear, was as a continuing embarrassment to Charles. Cromwell had her dropped back across the North Sea, in Flanders.

Lucy returned to her protests, using Charles's fathering of her son James as a bargaining chip. The king tried to abduct James in December 1657, but the attempt was botched. Three months later one of Charles's spymasters succeeded in kidnapping the boy, allowing Charles to negotiate from this position of strength for custody of his son. In March 1658 the nine-year-old James was given as a tutor William Crofts, one of Charles's favourites, and was moved to Paris. That was where Lucy – the beautiful courtesan, used by a succession of powerful men – died, in the autumn or winter of that same year. She was twenty-eight years old, destitute, and ravaged by venereal disease.

Before she died, Lucy gave a confession of her life to Dean John Cosin, a leading churchman who was chaplain to some of the royal family in exile. She claimed that she and Charles had indeed married, and that she had the proof. This was supposedly contained in a black box entrusted to Cosin, and passed to his son-in-law Sir

Gilbert Gerard on Cosin's death. If it ever existed, it has never come to light.

Sir Edward Hyde watched a series of false dawns come and go during the mid-1650s. In early 1656 Charles obtained a promise of support from Spain, provided English Royalists secured a port through which men and arms could be funnelled. The lessons of five years earlier were not lost on Hyde, who wrote: 'If the King were to land tomorrow in England with as good an army as can be hoped for, he would be overpowered as he was at Worcester while men sit still and wait for the effect of the first battle.'[24]

It was the unexpected death of Oliver Cromwell, on 3 September 1658 (the seventh anniversary of the battle of Worcester), that kicked away the cornerstone of the Commonwealth. Eighteen months of increasing instability brought about what Hyde had always hoped for: the need of the English people to seek the return of a king, to settle the nation. But the decision to revert to royalty was uncertain for much of that time. In March 1660 a vote in Parliament rejected a return to Stuart rule in favour of a continuation of Commonwealth government.

Just two months later, though, matters had spun decisively in favour of restoration. In May 1660 Charles returned to England in triumph, his reception as tumultuous as any in the nation's history. The last time he had been on English soil he had skulked in the shadows, desperate for any opportunity to flee to safety overseas. Now he was fêted as the great hope of a people who had become heartily disillusioned with their eleven-year experiment with a republic.

# 18

# Rewards

Oct. 1651. *The 14th day of this moneth King Charles the Second went from our towne out of Mr. Smiths house and was taken abroad by Nics: Tetersoale [&] carreyed by him to Fraunce, etc. And retorned [h]ome & landed at Dover againe the 29th of May 1660.*

Adam Cartwright, town clerk, writing in the
parish register of Brighton

The Cavalier Parliament met for the first time in May 1661, and sat for nearly three-quarters of Charles II's twenty-five-year reign. It became known as 'the Pensioner Parliament' because of the number of awards granted by the king to those who had supported him during his time waiting for the throne. As Colonel Gunter commented, when comparing the dire days of the autumn of 1651 with the subsequent prospects of rich prizes: 'So few friends then had his Sacred Majesty in his distresses, now so numerous in expectation of reward.'[1]

Those who had any claim at all to compensation for their services or their loyalty to the Crown came forward. Among them were the truly worthy, such as Mary Graves, who had helped to supply the king's army in Worcester during the run-up to the battle, and had also sent Charles two fine horses for his own use, and ten mounted fighting men for his army. After supporting a failed Royalist uprising in 1659 she had suffered the confiscation of all her property. She now sought £30,000 from the king.

George Paterick had served both Charles I and II in the army and the navy for sixteen years, and had consequently been imprisoned on several occasions by Parliament. A former waterman who ferried passengers across the Thames for a fee, he now asked for the honour of a place as an oarsman on the royal barge.

Katherine de Luke had suffered repeatedly and terribly for the Crown. She lost her husband to battlefield wounds, and a son to indentured slavery. After being caught smuggling secret letters she was sentenced to imprisonment, with the added punishment of a whipping every other day. She was tortured on various occasions, with lit matches applied to her body to try to get her to betray fellow Royalists.

Some other claims were, it has to be said, more tenuous. One man hoped for remuneration for having been in charge of Charles's tennis shoes and ankle socks as a young man. A Robert Thomas expected reward for being the son of Charles's childhood seamstress, even though she was dead. Another petitioner, Robert Chamberlain, trusted that the king would see fit to reward him because he was, he claimed, 110 years old. He seems to have confused the quality of loyalty with the luck of longevity.

Elizabeth Elliot hoped for special treatment. She was the daughter of Christabella Wyndham, who had served as wet-nurse to Charles as a baby, and been his first lover when he was fourteen. Relying on her mother's earlier role in the king's life, Elizabeth referred to herself in her petition as 'His Majesty's foster sister', and assured Charles that it was 'the greatest happiness that could befall her, to suck the same breast with so great a monarch'.[2] This was not to prove a strong enough bond for her to secure a rich reward.

All those who were known to have helped the king on his famous escape were celebrated for their involvement in it. The new monarch wanted everyone to know about the adventure, and even planned to found an exalted new chivalric fellowship based on the most celebrated episode during his time as a fugitive: the Order of the Oak Tree. Meanwhile, 29 May, the day of Charles's restoration, became Oak Apple Day, a public holiday that would serve as an annual celebration of the miraculous escape. With this desire to luxuriate in the tale came a necessity to reward its key players.

Lord Wilmot did not live to see the Restoration. At the end of 1652 Charles had granted 'his faithful and watchful attendant', as Colonel Gunter would call him, the first peerage of his reign, making him the 1st Earl of Rochester.

The new earl was sent on an embassy to the diet of the Holy Roman Empire at Regensburg, in Bavaria. Against the expectations of the demoralised court in exile, he managed to secure the promise of £68,000. When payment was delayed he circulated Germany, overseeing its collection with determination and charm. The money eventually raised by Rochester would pay Charles and his attendants' expenses for three years.

Less successful was a return to England in 1655, to instigate and oversee the northern part of a general Royalist rebellion, led by Colonel John Penruddock, whose other focus was in Salisbury. Cromwell's spies were aware of Rochester's presence from the moment he landed, but the Lord Protector chose to follow his progress closely, rather than seize the Royalist hero. This time Rochester did resort to disguises, one of them as a Frenchman with a blond wig. Another, which must have been more challenging for this caricature of a high-living Cavalier to carry off, had him dressing as a peasant farmer.

Rochester spread the word of the impending uprising amongst Royalist sympathisers, meeting groups of them in bogus hunting parties. They were to meet at Marston Moor, scene of their crushing defeat eleven years earlier, and then march on York. Based on promises that had been made to him, Rochester counted on the support of 4,000 men, but only a tiny fraction of that number materialised at the appointed time and place, many having become confused about key details, including the date on which they were meant to muster.

The result was, in a way, a repeat of Worcester, with cautious Englishmen remaining at home to see the outcome of the first encounter before venturing their lives in the king's cause. When Rochester saw how few men had actually rallied, he decided to abandon the endeavour, and ordered everyone to stand down.

On his way south afterwards he showed his customary disregard for his own safety, staying in a succession of inns rather than keeping off the beaten track, and even making a detour to inspect some of his wife's property. His luck ran out when he was detained in Aylesbury, but he bribed his captor and got away to London. There he was on the point of being recaptured, but he was alerted to the danger by the regicide Colonel Hutchinson, and managed to ride on to Sussex, where he once again called on the assistance of Colonel George Gunter. This time Gunter and his old servant John Day were able to secure a small boat at Emsworth in Hampshire that took Rochester across the Channel to safety. He eventually reached Charles in Cologne.

In 1656 Rochester led the English regiment that Charles had placed in Spanish service to fight the French, after France had allied with Cromwell's England. Rochester was thus the first colonel of the Grenadier Guards, the senior infantry regiment of the British Army to this day.

During the winter of 1657–58, conditions in camp were terrible. Rochester became ill, dying at Sluys in Flanders on 19 February 1658, at the age of forty-five, and was buried in Bruges. After the Restoration his body was moved to the family tombs in Spelsbury church, in Oxfordshire.

His son John, 2nd Earl of Rochester, was born on 10 April 1647.* Addicted to women and wine, and famous for his lewdness and wit, young Lord Rochester became one of the more outrageous figures in Charles II's hedonistic court. His verses included blatant digs at his partner in excess, Charles II. One reads:

*Here lies our sovereign Lord the King*
*Whose word no man relies on.*
*Who never said a foolish thing*
*Nor ever did a wise one.*

Many of the other participants in the escape were still alive at Charles's restoration, nine years after the escape from Worcester.

Before the king left for Bristol disguised as Jane Lane's servant, he promised to look after Father John Huddleston if he was ever restored to the throne. Some time after this Huddleston joined the Catholic order of the Benedictines of the Spanish Congregation. After the Restoration in 1660 he was invited to live at Somerset House in London, under the protection of Queen Henrietta Maria.

In 1661 the General Chapter of the English Benedictines, held at Douai, elected Huddleston to the titular dignity of cathedral prior of Worcester, in recognition of his services to the Crown a decade earlier. After Henrietta Maria's death in 1669 he was appointed chaplain to Queen Catherine, Charles II's wife, with a salary of £100 a year and a pension of a further £100. On the accession of James II in 1685 Huddleston continued to stay with Queen Catherine at Somerset House. He died at the age of ninety, after a period of dementia.

---

* John's childhood tutor was a member of the Giffard family, which had provided Whiteladies and Boscobel House as hiding places during Charles's flight.

Charles had made a similar personal promise to the Penderels to reward them should he ever return to the throne. This was given when he thanked four of the brothers after they had safely delivered him to Lord Wilmot at Moseley Hall. It was immediately honoured. On 13 June 1660, when Charles had only been back in England two weeks, the five brothers and their mother Jane were summoned to come to see the king at Westminster. During this audience the family took great pleasure in reminding Charles of Humphrey's line when leading his slow horse through the night from Boscobel House to Moseley Hall: 'My liege, can you blame the horse to go heavily, when he has the weight of three kingdoms on his back?'

'Trusty Richard' received £200, to which a pension was later added, for him and his heirs in perpetuity. Richard died of a fever in February 1672, while visiting London. He was buried at St Giles-in-the-Fields, a church then on the outskirts of the capital, which had strong connections with Charles I and the Royalists.

Elizabeth, the Penderel sister who was the widow of the Francis Yates who guided Charles II to Whiteladies, and who was later hanged at Oxford without revealing the king's whereabouts, was given an annual pension of £50 'for her and her heirs forever'.

Margaret, the Penderel sister who fed the king in Spring Coppice while the enemy was all around, was married to the Francis Yates who lent Charles ten shillings and helped to take him from Boscobel to Moseley. This Francis Yates knew immediately after the Restoration that he was dying, and it was noted 'that the said Francis had lately died of grief, that he could not present himself to his Majesty'.[3]

Another of the women from the family, Joan, the wife of William Penderel, had to wait for her reward for a key moment in the escape. The *Calendar of State Papers* records that on 10 July 1663 there was a warrant 'for £100 for Joan Pendrel, the person who gathered sticks and diverted the horseman from the oak His Majesty was in'.

Humphrey, the fourth Penderel brother – the miller – lived till 1710. In 1673 he claimed that the pension he had been awarded was only being paid in part, and that he was consequently in debt. Seven years after that, Samuel Pepys noted that Humphrey was 'still' serving Queen Catherine as a footman in Somerset House.

Major William Careless, having joined Charles in France after his own escape, returned to serve him in Flanders in 1656, fighting alongside other Royalist exiles, including Wilmot, in the English force that Charles put forward to fight the French. In May 1658 Charles marked Careless out for unique distinction, having the major change his name to 'Carlos', the Spanish version of the king's Christian name. He also granted Carlos a coat of arms that would forever recall their most celebrated day together. The Letters Patent describe it as being 'upon an oak proper, in a field or, a foss gules, charged with three royal crowns of the second, by the name of Carlos. And for his crest a civic crown, or oak garland, with a sword and sceptre crossed through it saltier-wise'. This was a suitable honour for a man who, the king would inform the College of Arms, possessed 'singular fidelity' and 'an ever generous heart'.

After the Restoration Carlos was made the beneficiary of various petty taxes levied around London, involving horse feed and shipping supplies, and he received a pension as well. He was one of those who would have become a Knight of the Royal Oak, had that order come into being. He was buried near Boscobel House on Oak Apple Day, 1689.

Once the story of Charles's flight from Worcester became well known, the Boscobel oak became the most celebrated tree in England. It was a point of pilgrimage after 1660, with souvenir hunters pulling bits off it as relics of what was seen as a tale of divine intervention. Snuffboxes were made from it, and walking sticks carved from it. In 1680 a wall had to be built to protect it, but it could not be fully shielded, and by 1712 the oak was all but destroyed. Its acorns were harvested, and a descendant of the original tree thrived in much the same spot until it was badly damaged in a storm in 2000.

Charles had got on very well with Anne, the widowed mother of Thomas Whitgreave, during his stay at Moseley Hall. On the Restoration he made sure she received the confiscated estate and house back in her name, something repeatedly denied to her during the years of Cromwell and the Commonwealth because of her family's Royalism and Roman Catholicism.

Francis Reynolds, one of the three boys tutored by Father Huddleston who had acted as lookouts at Moseley, was rewarded for having been 'very serviceable in holding the king's horses' before he rode from Moseley to Bentley. Huddleston noted that Reynolds 'received considerable kindness from the King since, by an office' in the Royal Household,[4] but he lost it during the enormous political instability in England in 1678, in the wake of the Popish Plot.

This 'plot' was a fabrication put about by the Anglican priest Titus Oates, claiming that Roman Catholics were conspiring to kill Charles II. While this provoked a backlash against Catholics, Parliament voted that Major Carlos, Father Huddleston, Thomas Whitgreave, the Penderel family, and all the main Catholics involved in the king's escape should 'for their said service live as freely as any of the King's Protestant subjects, without being liable to the penalties of any of the laws relating to Popish recusants'.

Jane Lane had been a popular member of the court in exile since her arrival there at the end of 1651. John Evelyn would record proudly in his diary how he had met her: 'Came to visit my wife Mrs Lane, the Lady who conveyed the King at his escape from Worcester to the seaside.'[5] The dowager queen Henrietta Maria and Charles himself greatly enjoyed her lively company.

In 1652, as Charles settled reluctantly back into a life of waiting – hoping – for a chance to reclaim his throne, he had found Jane a position in his sister Mary of Orange's household in the Netherlands. That summer Jane wrote to Charles, saying that he had probably already forgotten her, while informing him that her elderly father, whose supposed grave illness had been so crucial during their travels, and her brother, Colonel John Lane, had been imprisoned by Parliament. Charles replied with playful affection, gratitude, and some concern:

> *Mrs Lane,*
>     *I did not think I should ever have begun a letter to you in chiding, but you give me so just cause by telling me your fear you are wearing out of my memory that I cannot choose but tell you I take it very unkindly that after all the obligations I have to you, 'tis possible for you to suspect I can ever be so wanting to myself as not to remember them on all occasions to your advantage, which I assure you, I shall and hope before long I shall have it in my power to give you testimonies of my kindness to you which I desire. I am very sorry to hear that your father and brother are in prison, but I hope it is of no other score than the general clapping of all persons who wish me well and I am the more sorry for it. Now it hath hindered you from coming along with my sister that I might have assured you myself how truly I am*
>     *Your Most affectionate friend, For Mrs Lane,*
>     *Charles R.*

Charles made good his promise eight years later. On his restoration to the throne he granted Jane £1,000 per year for life, and gave her a portrait of himself, as well as a gold watch and a lock of his hair. He also rewarded the Lane family as a whole, allowing them to incorporate the three lions of England into their coat of arms. Included in the design was the strawberry roan horse on which

Charles had ridden to Bristol with Jane. It is seen carrying a crown, and the motto 'Garde Le Roy' – 'Protect the king'. In the general celebration of Royalism that marked the return of the king to England, Parliament voted Jane a further £1,000, with which to buy a memento of her part in Charles's escape.

In December 1663 she married Sir Clement Fisher, who had hidden Lord Wilmot in his Warwickshire mansion when Wilmot had been on his way to join Jane and the king at Abbots Leigh. Sir Clement had other Royalist credentials, having been fined heavily for his service to the Crown. This loyal couple's marriage was officiated by the Archbishop of Canterbury. There would be no children. Jane lived an extravagant life, perhaps relying on the timely payment of her pension when it was, in reality, often delayed owing to hiccoughs in the royal finances. At her death in 1689 she left just £10.

George Norton, Jane's cousin, in whose home, Abbots Leigh, Charles had hidden till Ellen Norton's miscarriage, was given a knighthood and a pension.

Henry Lascelles, the cornet who accompanied Charles and Jane, died in or before 1662. On the back of her late brother's service, his sister sought a place as laundress to the queen.

The other woman to help Charles on his way on horseback, Juliana Coningsby, petitioned in 1665 for a pension that had been promised to her, and was eventually awarded £200 a year.

Father Humphrey Henchman, so helpful in the final leg of the escape, was made the Bishop of Salisbury.

Colonel George Gunter had died, in his late sixties, a year before the Restoration.

His cousin, Captain Thomas Gunter, was made Clerk of the Crown for North Wales in 1661. He also received a bounty of £200 for his help in getting Charles away from Shoreham.

Colonel Robert Phillips was arrested and committed to the Tower of London in 1653. He escaped and joined Charles in

France. After the Restoration he was granted a pension of £500. A lawyer, he became an MP and the Chancellor of the Duchy of Lancaster.

Colonel Francis Wyndham, of Trent in Somerset, had been imprisoned as a suspected rebel after Penruddock's unsuccessful rising of 1655. At the Restoration the military ability of the brave defender of Dunster Castle was recognised when he was made a major in the Royal Horse Guards. His important part in the king's escape was also acknowledged on 17 December 1660, when the speaker of the Commons thanked him on behalf of the House for 'great and eminent service, whereby it pleased God to make you instrumental in the safeguard and preservation of his Majesty's sacred person'. Wyndham was voted an annual pension of £1,000. He was also given a reward of £10,000 in 1670, and was created a baronet. As an MP he took particular interest in suppressing high-waymen. In 1675, when very ill indeed, he wrote from Bath: 'I fear I shall not hereafter be capable to do His Majesty any further service than by my prayers for the long continuance of his prosperity and happiness.' He died the following year, aged sixty-six, and was buried at Trent.

Anne Wyndham, the colonel's wife, was given a pension for life of £400, but its payment was delayed, and she only received it from 1667 onwards.

Thomas Symonds, Charles's well-oiled host at dinner in Hambledon, who had goaded the king for being a Roundhead, was rewarded at the Restoration with the fitting gift of a drinking cup.

Francis Mançell, the French merchant, had been declared an outlaw by the Commonwealth and left penniless. After the Restoration he was granted a pension of £200. In 1667 he petitioned to have it honoured, since he had not received the money for four years.

At the Restoration, the *Surprise* became a fifth-rate vessel in Charles II's navy, and was renamed the *Royal Escape*. Her captain,

Nicholas Tattersall, was given a pension of £100, a miniature of the king, and the rank of captain in the navy. This promotion was not a success, and he was subsequently dismissed. He died in the summer of 1674. On his tombstone was a fourteen-line verse that included a very full celebration of his part in the story:

> ... *In this cold clay he hath now taken up his station*
> *At once preserved ye church, ye Crown and Nation*
> *When Charles ye Great was nothing to a breath*
> *This valiant soul stepped between him and death ...*
> *Which glorious act of his for Church and State*
> *Eight princes in one day did congratulate ...*[6]

Lieutenant General David Leslie, Charles's deputy in the Scottish invasion of England, who had held back his men from engaging at Worcester, and had then ridden north in the hope of escape, had spent the intervening eight and a half years in the Tower of London, where he took to drink.

Soon after arriving there, Leslie was allowed to have the liberty of the Tower and to have his servant with him. In contrast to other prisoners who were suffering appalling treatment within the same walls, he was permitted to receive friends bringing clothes and other supplies, 'provided they only speak to him in the presence of the Lieutenant [of the Tower], or such as he shall appoint'. The Scottish general's lenient treatment had long been anticipated, an eyewitness who had seen him in Newcastle nine days after the defeat at Worcester writing: 'I believe old Leslie may find the more civil usage, in regard he was formerly a General for the Parliamentarians in England.'[7]

Many of those closest to Charles remained convinced that Leslie had acted treacherously. Thomas Wall wrote to his brother John at the end of 1651: 'All intelligent people conclude that [the king] was betrayed by David Leslie.'[8] But the king saw fit to free him, and even reward him, giving him the title of 1st Baron Newark for his services to the Royalist cause. This was seen as a slap in the face to many Cavaliers who had suffered more harshly for true loyalty.

Leslie's fellow Scottish lieutenant general, John Middleton, also prospered. He had been taken prisoner by Parliamentary troops at the battle of Preston in 1648, and had been released on condition that he never fight against them again. When he had been wounded at, and quickly captured after, Worcester, it seemed all but certain that he would be charged with treason for breaking his word, and sentenced to death. Awaiting trial, he managed to escape from the Tower of London by changing clothes with his wife during one of her visits. He joined Charles in exile in Paris, and returned to Scotland in 1654 to lead an unsuccessful rising, before returning to the king's side. His reward at the Restoration was being created Earl of Middleton, and receiving various high offices. Having been humiliated by the Scottish Presbyterians a decade earlier, when they forced him to wear sackcloth and ashes in public penance, he now focused on cutting back their power, and restoring the bishops.

There were losers as well as winners.

One of Charles's reasons for allying with the Scots had been to have their assistance in bringing his father's murderers to justice. More than twenty of the eighty regicides had died in the eleven years between Charles I's execution and the Restoration, but the rest were now held to account for their crime.

The first to be sentenced was Major General Thomas Harrison, who was connected so closely in people's consciousness with Charles I's final journey to trial and execution. He was also remembered clearly by Charles II, as the man put in charge of his capture after the battle of Worcester. Harrison refused to flee at the return of the Stuart regime. He was arrested at home, and brought to London. He readily admitted to his actions in court, and was condemned to die by hanging, drawing and quartering. Harrison was magnificently brave on the day of his execution, firm in his belief that whatever suffering he had to undergo, it was for his God. After being hanged half to death, then mutilated terribly by the executioner with knives and other tools, he still managed to swing a punch that sent his slaughterer flying. Samuel Pepys witnessed the major general's death, recording how 'his head and heart [were] shown to the people, at which there was great shouts of joy'.

In vengeance for the death of the Marquess of Montrose, his great enemies were executed. The Marquess of Argyll went to London on the Restoration to pay his respects to the new king, but Charles refused to see him, and had him arrested. Argyll was taken north, and sentenced to death. The watching crowd expected to see a cowardly display on the scaffold, but he died with dignity. Montrose's rotted head was removed from the spike on Tolbooth prison, and replaced by Argyll's.

Sir Archibald Johnston, Lord Wariston, fled abroad at the Restoration, but was captured in Rouen in early 1663. His wife petitioned Charles for mercy, stating that she 'and her 12 children were reduced to a poor and desolate condition,'[9] but it was no good. He was sent on a procession through Edinburgh, similar to that endured by Montrose, watched over by Charles's life guards 'with their carbines and naked swords' at the ready, kettle drums and trumpets sounding, and a regiment of Edinburgh's soldiers displaying their colours. He ended his life on 'gallows of extraordinary height' at Mercat Cross.

Montrose's limbs were retrieved from Aberdeen, Glasgow, Perth and Stirling, and his trunk and bowels were brought from Burgh Moor. The parts were placed together in a coffin, and interred with fitting ceremony in the High Kirk of St Giles in Edinburgh.

The Covenanters received payment for the humiliation they had heaped on Charles a decade earlier, when he had chosen to sacrifice his and his father's principles in his ill-fated bid for the English throne. Now he renounced the Covenants that he said had been forced out of him by the Scots. In 1662 they were rendered unlawful oaths, which nobody in public office could subscribe to. In a final vindication of his father's stand, bishops were brought back to oversee the Scottish Church.

A long way further down the religious pecking order, the Reverend Benjamin Westley, the Puritan parson of Charmouth who had raised the alarm over the king's presence nearby, was deprived of his parish. He continued his ministry as an itinerant preacher. The following century his great-grandsons, John and Charles Wesley, would found Methodism.

Sir Edward Hyde had a key hand in brokering the generous terms on which the king returned, and became his most important and trusted adviser. Charles was happy to dump the hard work and subtle requirements of government on Hyde's shoulders, while he buried himself in pleasure.

The ecstasy that had greeted Charles's return soon turned to disappointment, as his extravagance became out of control. Further goodwill was eroded early in his reign when in 1662 he sold the French port of Dunkirk to Louis XIV for five million livres. There were also disasters that Charles was not responsible for: in 1665–66, the bubonic plague claimed the lives of 200,000 of his subjects, while in 1666 the Great Fire of London consumed more than 13,000 houses in the city. There was national humiliation in 1667, when the Dutch fleet sailed up the River Medway and destroyed thirteen ships while capturing the *Royal Charles*. It was this last that proved disastrous for Hyde.

Just as Charles had turned away from Hyde when he had advised playing a waiting game, and not allying with enemies of England

and its established Church, so he chose to listen to Hyde's enemies in court and Parliament. They were jealous of his influence, which had increased in 1660 when the Duke of York married Hyde's daughter Anne, whom he had made pregnant. Hyde was given the title of Earl of Clarendon, and £20,000 to support that position, the following year. In 1663 he became one of the eight Lords Proprietor of a huge tract of land in America that became the colony of Carolina.*

Clarendon disapproved of much of Charles's behaviour, and never shirked from telling him so. A particular bone of contention was the king's pleasure-seeking, which Clarendon resented because it kept him from the business of kingship. Clarendon would make the fatal mistake of meddling in matters involving the king's mistresses.

In 1663 Charles became infatuated with Frances Stuart, a fifteen-year-old member of his wife's court. She was the daughter of another court beauty, famous for her dancing skills, and of a doctor. Samuel Pepys reckoned Frances the most beautiful woman he had ever seen. The Comte de Gramont qualified this assessment: 'It would be difficult to imagine less brain combined with more beauty.' Her favourite pastimes certainly tended to the childish: 'blindman's buff, hunt the slipper, and card-building'.[10] Her nickname at court was 'La Belle Stuart'.

Charles's lust reached new heights when Frances seemed unobtainable, refusing to become his mistress. When his queen was seriously ill, he contemplated taking Frances as his wife as soon as he became a widower. At other times he was so distracted by sexual

---

* A fellow Lord Proprietor was Sir George Carteret, who had held the island of Jersey for the Crown, and had twice provided a safe haven there for Charles in the five years before Worcester. Carteret was also given joint ownership of a large tract of land between the Delaware River and the Hudson River. This was named 'New Jersey'.

longing that he thought of divorce, to free himself for Frances's hand in marriage.

The king was therefore furious when, in the spring of 1667, he learnt that his cousin the Duke of Richmond, whose second wife had recently died, had secretly married Frances. The Earl of Lauderdale, who had endured nine years of imprisonment by Parliament after the battle of Worcester, and who was now Charles II's favourite, wrote that he had never seen the king 'more offended than he is at the duke, and all concerned'.[11] Clarendon was viewed as having had a hand in the furtive marriage. His enemies said he wanted to keep Charles married to a queen who could not have children, rather than jeopardise the inheritance of his own granddaughters, who stood second and third in line to the throne.

Clarendon also managed to cross swords with Barbara Castlemaine, the king's favourite mistress throughout the 1660s. Charles wanted Barbara on hand in the court, even after the arrival of his wife Catherine of Braganza in 1662. The queen implored Clarendon to spare her from this humiliation, but when Clarendon asked the king to reconsider Castlemaine's court position, Charles bared his teeth: 'If you desire to have the continuance of my friendship, meddle no more with this business ... whosoever I find to be my Lady Castlemaine's enemy in this matter, I do promise, upon my word, to be his enemy as long as I live.'[12] Castlemaine worked with Clarendon's rivals to unseat him. There were plenty of enemies to help in this, because of his famed arrogance and short temper, as well as jealousy at his power and influence.

Charles, bored with Clarendon's moralising and resentful of his executive power, agreed to his dismissal in disgrace. In 1667 Clarendon was made the scapegoat for the Dutch naval triumph in the Medway. Having originally hoped that he could ride out his master's displeasure, Clarendon took Charles's heavy hints and removed himself to France, hoping that this would eventually lead to forgiveness and accommodation. There he finished writing his great history of the Civil Wars before dying suddenly of a stroke, at the age of sixty-five, in 1674. Two of his granddaughters, Mary and Anne, became queens of England.

Charles's health was becoming troublesome after decades of hard living. His close confidants noted his obvious drop in energy. There had been seizures in 1679 that had caused serious concern for his life until, an attendant noted, he 'exchanged water-gruels and potions for mutton and partridges, on which he feeds frequently and heartily'. A return of his famed gluttony was a good sign.

Since the middle of 1684 he had been forced by gout, and a painful heel, to forgo the two vigorous daily walks that had kept him lean. He liked to take his dozen spaniels with him, and feed the ducks in St James's Park. The loss of this favourite exercise left him feeling low.

But on 1 February 1685 Charles found a way of passing his day that fitted his tastes and his reduced mobility. It was a Sunday, and after being taken by carriage for dinner with courtiers, where he filled his stomach with a variety of delicacies including a pair of goose eggs, he went to the sumptuous Whitehall quarters of Louise de Kérouaille, Duchess of Portsmouth, the intoxicating mistress sent by Louis XIV both to pleasure the king and to spy on him. By this time Charles's entertainment needed to be highly spiced to register on his jaded palate, and John Evelyn remembered that evening's raucous offerings with shock: 'I can never forget the inexpressible luxury and profaneness, gaming and all manner of dissoluteness, and as it were total forgetfulness of God (it being Sunday evening) which this day se'nnight [a week before] I was witness of, the King sitting and toying with his concubines, Portsmouth, Cleveland, and Mazarin, etc., a French boy singing love songs, in that glorious gallery, whilst about 20 of the great courtiers and other dissolute persons were at Basset round a large table, a bank of at least 2,000 in gold before them.'

Charles was in fine spirits, typically charming and relaxed. Those present recalled that they had not seen him so happy and well for some time.

As he was escorted back to his rooms, his groom's large candle suddenly went out. On reaching his bedroom, Charles went to the lavatory as usual, accompanied by the Earl of Ailesbury, providing light, and by Charles Killigrew, standing ready with paper.

The two senior courtiers then changed into their night clothes, locked the door, and lay down to sleep near their master's bed. It was a far from peaceful bedroom, with spaniels roaming, the fire crackling, and Charles's large collection of clocks ticking and whirring. But Ailesbury remembered an added disturbance that night: the sound of the king frequently tossing and turning. This was unusual for him.

In the morning, as staff were let in to feed the fire, Charles returned to the lavatory. A servant he passed on the way was shocked to see how pale and ill he looked.

There was mounting concern among the waiting courtiers, as well as the doctors who had come to inspect Charles's ankle, when the king eventually reappeared from the lavatory, helped by Mr Chiffins, a courtier whose titles included that of Keeper of the Closet. Charles was unsteady on his feet, his colour was terrible, and he was unable to take part in the customary morning exchanges. He was silent and distracted. When he could speak, he would lose the thread and stop in mid-sentence.

Charles liked to be shaved by his bedroom window, and this daily ritual started at eight o'clock that Monday morning. The barber was halfway through tucking in the towel around the king's neck when Charles suddenly lurched backwards, seized by violent convulsions. The Earl of Ailesbury caught him, and two royal physicians rushed forward.

Sir Edmund King, a well-respected surgeon and a keen chemist, insisted that Charles be bled, otherwise he would certainly die. This was a daring assessment, as the procedure was considered an act of treason unless approved by the king's senior councillors, but

Sir Edmund said he would take full responsibility.* As Charles slumped in the barber's chair, sixteen ounces of blood were taken from his right arm. A muzzle was put in his mouth to stop him from biting off his tongue as the terrible convulsions continued. This was the start of the king's torment, as he was subjected to ordeal by medical ignorance, inflicted on him by what one of their number believed to be 'physicians of the greatest loyalty and skill'.[1] Their loyalty cannot be questioned.

The royal doctors agreed that Charles's system needed extreme stimulation, to stop him drifting into sleep. They burnt his shoulders with three scorching cupping-glasses, and then removed another eight ounces of his blood through superficial incisions.

The next objective was a complete purge of the king's system. An emetic was poured into his mouth, made from 'half an ounce of Orange Infusion of the metals, made in white wine', but only half of it went down. They added a shot of zinc sulphate in peony water, to further induce nausea. These attacks on the contents of Charles's stomach and intestines were further reinforced by laxatives and an enema.

His hair was clipped away, so that his scalp could be covered with plasters doused in a blistering agent. The convulsions continued while other parts of Charles's body were cauterised. He was given another enema, then hellebore root was rubbed into his nostrils to burn the membrane, while his scalp was given fresh caustic plasters.

The queen now appeared, but, a delicate and gentle lady, she was so upset at the sight of her husband in his terrible suffering that she had to return to her rooms, distraught. James, Duke of York – Charles's heir – arrived in such haste that he had a shoe on one foot

---

* Parliament voted Sir Edmund King a reward of £1,000 for his bold decision to bleed Charles, though it was never paid.

and a slipper on the other. He would remain with his brother throughout nearly every moment of his illness.

Charles was moved to his bed, and had a slight resurgence. He was able to talk, and explained how he had felt ill while in bed the previous night, so he had gone to his bathroom to take some 'King's Drops', an expensive concoction made of alcohol with powder from ground-up human skulls (often provided by Irish gravediggers). The King's Drops had failed to improve his condition. But now, after the initial bloodletting and the other remedies, he said he felt a little better. The physicians pronounced him out of danger.

That evening, feeling the king was in need of further medical help to prevent a recurrence of his terrible fits, the doctors reverted to their rich repertoire of quackery. They put pungent plasters containing pigeon droppings on his feet, and applied poultices elsewhere, made of cowslips mixed with hydrochloric acid and ammonium. Charles was encouraged to drink an emulsion at frequent intervals, to reduce the burning in his urine caused by all the blistering agents he had been forced to endure. This contained a blend of barley, licorice and almonds, sweetened with sugar. He was to alternate this with a thin broth, while at night he was allowed as much 'light ale made without hops' as his doctors thought he needed.

On the Tuesday a dozen doctors assembled by Charles's bed, to find their patient apparently much improved. He was given a gargle of elm bark and barley water for his sore throat, and was then encouraged to drink black cherry water, in which the cherries were mixed with lilies of the valley, flowers of lime, peony, lavender, sugar and crushed pearls. It was believed that this would reduce the likelihood of further convulsions. Another ten ounces of blood were extracted, this time from his jugular veins.

The Wednesday morning started with the doctors hopeful once more, but there were soon more convulsions, followed by more bleeding, and a laxative of white tartar, senna leaf, gentian root, chamomile flowers, white wine and nutmeg. As the day drew on, it became clear that the king was gravely ill. His skin was clammy, and the convulsions returned. He was given forty drops of 'Spirit of human Skull'.

Convinced that he was showing symptoms of a fever that was currently doing the rounds in parts of London, and which also seemed to get worse as the day turned into night, the doctors decided to administer him with Peruvian Bark – quinine, diluted at first with 'Antidotal milk water' and syrup of cloves (later in the illness this was sweetened with Rhine wine). There seemed to be another brief upturn in Charles's health, before it collapsed.

The Archbishop of Canterbury, supported by the bishops of London, Durham, Ely and of Bath and Wells, now turned to the business of preparing their king for his death. Charles showed little interest in the words of the archbishop, or of the Bishop of London. Senior courtiers encouraged Thomas Ken, the newly consecrated Bishop of Bath and Wells, to oversee the end. Ken had a sweetness of voice and manner that his colleagues could not match.

When Bishop Ken asked the king if he confessed his sins, he thoughtfully added that there was no need for him to attempt to list them, merely to be sorry for them. Charles confirmed that he was, but when pushed to take the sacrament, he said there was still time to think about that.

The French envoy, Jean-Paul de Barillon, was now taken aside by Louise de Kérouaille, who told him, 'Mr Ambassador, I am going to tell you the greatest secret in the world, and if it were known I should lose my head. At the bottom of his heart the King is Catholic, but he is surrounded by Protestant bishops.' She begged Barillon to talk to the Duke of York, and persuade him to help save his brother's soul.

The queen had ventured back to the side of Charles's deathbed whenever she felt strong enough to confront the awfulness of the situation. When Barillon re-entered the room, she had just fainted, after which the royal physicians had immediately bled her. She had now been removed, and Barillon seized the moment to pass on de Kérouaille's message. James agreed that his brother's soul was the priority, and that time was running out. He announced to the twenty or so bishops, doctors and courtiers in his brother's bedroom that he needed to talk to the king. Everyone left, assuming that the heir needed to discuss matters of state with the dying incumbent. The brothers were together in quiet conversation for a quarter of an hour. Those outside in the anteroom heard Charles say from time to time, 'Yes, with all my heart!'

James then left his brother's side, and told Barillon that Charles indeed wanted a Roman Catholic priest by his side. It would be impossible to bring in one of the queen's Portuguese chaplains, or the Duchess of York's Italian ones, since the Anglican bishops present would recognise them. Equally problematic was the fact that none of them spoke English.

It was now that the Count of Castelmelhor, one of the queen's courtiers, remembered Father John Huddleston. Huddleston's celebrated role in Charles's escape after the defeat at Worcester had resulted in his being excused, by name, from the severe attacks on Roman Catholic priests that had followed plots against the Crown during the previous decade. Castelmelhor realised that Huddleston alone could meet the dying king's urgent need. He was Catholic, and he spoke English. Also, despite the king's weakness, he would surely be recognised and trusted by the man whose life he had helped to save.

This time it was Huddleston who had to hide his true identity and conceal himself. His disguise involved a wig and a cassock, and his hiding place was behind a side door that led to Charles's bedroom. While waiting there, he realised that he had left behind the Holy Sacrament of the Altar. Fortunately Father Bento de Lemoz, one of the queen's Portuguese chaplains, now passed by, and Huddleston tasked him with finding the Sacrament as quickly as he could.

Charles's servant Chiffins waited with Huddleston until they heard James order the king's bedroom cleared of everyone except two of his and Charles's closest confidants, the Earl of Bath and the Earl of Feversham. Both were Protestant, which helped the subterfuge to succeed.

So it was that, a little before eight o'clock on the evening of 5 February 1685, James brought Huddleston to his brother's bedside. Charles greeted the kindly country priest with the welcome, 'You, that saved my body, is now come to save my soul.'

Huddleston led Charles through a declaration confirming that he wished to die in the faith and communion of the Holy Roman Catholic Church. He then heard the king's confession, and gave him absolution. Charles took the other sacraments offered, before Father Bento de Lemoz eventually arrived with the Sacrament, which he had most likely borrowed from Somerset House.

Charles tried to raise himself, saying, 'Let me meet my heavenly father in a better posture than lying on my bed.' Huddleston told him to lie comfortably, as it was the contents of the king's heart that mattered, not the posture of his body.

Charles received the Act of Contrition a second and third time. Huddleston said, 'Your Majesty hath now received the comfort and benefit of all the sacraments that a good Christian, ready to depart our world, can have or desire.' He then lifted a crucifix up for Charles to behold, while encouraging him to think hard about Christ's sacrifice.

Huddleston's prayers with the king lasted three quarters of an hour, after which he slipped away. The king seemed briefly to recuperate, but the fourteen doctors in attendance realised that he was too near to death to escape it now. Because they thought it could do no further harm, they gave him Raleigh's Antidote, a blend of many herbs and animal parts, given extra grit through the addition of ground coral and pearls. This was followed by a dose of powdered Goa stone, extracted from a goat's intestine, which was thought to offset the effect of poisons.

Perhaps it was because of the lift that Huddleston had given his spirits, but Charles defied the physicians' expectations, and survived the night. With his customary politeness, he apologised to those attending him for the long time he was taking to die.

James was in real anguish, kneeling by Charles's bed, kissing his hand. One of the physicians present, Dr Charles Scarburgh, wrote of James that he was 'so anxious for his recovery, that he scarcely ever had the heart to leave the prostrate King's bedside, at times completely overwhelmed with grief, at times himself watching attentively the following out of the physicians' instructions, at other times imploring Heaven's Arch-Healer for help and succor with most earnest prayers and vows and with repeated lamentations'.[2] Charles thanked James for having always been such a fine brother to him, and wished him a successful reign.

The queen came again, and fainted again, later sending a message to her husband begging that he would forgive her faults. Charles, thinking of his constant infidelity to her, replied, 'Alas! Poor woman! She begs my pardon. I beg hers, with all my heart.'

He then asked his brother to look after two of his favourite mistresses, Louise de Kérouaille and Nell Gwynne, once he was gone, and to be good to all but one of his natural children. The exception was the Duke of Monmouth, his eldest son with Lucy Walter, who was skulking on the Continent. He had had a difficult relationship with his father and uncle for some years, after Charles discovered that he had known of an assassination plot against him and his brother at Newmarket races, yet had not revealed it. But the king's other five illegitimate sons were there at the end, and he blessed them, before also blessing all others who were in the room.

The next morning, at six o'clock, he asked for the curtains to be opened so he could see the sun rise for the last time. He was having great difficulty breathing, and slipped into a coma four hours later, dying shortly after noon on Friday, 6 February 1685. This was thirty-six years and one day after the Scots had proclaimed him their king, in the week after his father's beheading.

At his autopsy, it was noted that the arteries and veins in his brain were 'unduly full', and that his liver 'was inclined to be livid in colour, perhaps because of the abundance of blood in it, with which the kidneys and spleen were also engorged'.[3]

A third of a century earlier the English had stood on two distinct sides, as Charles had run for his life in what was to be the adventure of that life: half had wanted him captured, while half had prayed that he might, somehow, escape. Now, despite the controversies of his reign, and the inadequacies of key aspects of his languid kingship, his personal charm was remembered: the mourning was almost universal.

# *Acknowledgements*

I would like to thank Nigel Fortnam, of Lyme Regis, who wrote to suggest the subject of this book to me after reading my 2014 effort *Killers of the King*. I had no idea how rich the subject would be.

I will forever be grateful to Gillon Aitken, my late literary agent, who was a truly great man, combining the very best attributes of gentleman and scholar. Gillon was a passionate believer in my telling this tale, at a time when I was reluctant to write for a while. I am grateful to Clare Alexander for keeping everything on an even keel after Gillon's death.

Arabella Pike has proved to be the cleverest of editors. Her constructive comments after the first draft have been truly invaluable to structure and tone. It has been the easiest of working relationships, which is really all a writer wants. I would also like to thank her colleagues at HarperCollins, including Robert Lacey who copy-edited the final manuscript with a quiet finesse.

Relevant facts have been kindly shared with me by John Giffard, descendant of Charles II's first supporters on his escape attempt, and by Dr David Bartle, company archivist of the Haberdashers' Company.

My wife, Karen, deserves the greatest credit, helping me to juggle our diary-defying lives so that I have had time to write.

Meanwhile, her ear for prose, and her editor's instincts, have been invaluable. To her go my endless thanks.

# Notes

## Introduction
1. *Charles II's Escape from Worcester*, Colonel Gounter's Report, p.147
2 'S. Pepys to the Duke of York' – Rawl. MSS. A.194, f.253

## 1: Civil Warrior
1. From John Aubrey's *Brief Lives*
2. Quoted in Samuel Elliott Hoskins, *Charles the Second in the Channel Islands*, Vol. II, p.85
3. Quoted in *DNB*, 'Edward Hyde', by Paul Seaward
4. Diary of Samuel Pepys, 3 December 1665
5. Clarendon, *History of the Rebellion*, Vol. IV, pp.22–3
6. Quoted in Hoskins, Vol. I, p.85
7. Quoted in *DNB*, 'Edward Hyde', by Paul Seaward
8. *The Memoirs of Ann, Lady Fanshawe*, p.41
9. Quoted in Hoskins, Vol. I, p.98
10. Mary Anne E. Green (ed.), *Letters of Queen Henrietta Maria*, pp.314–15, Richard Bentley, London, 1857
11. *The Memoirs of Ann, Lady Fanshawe*, pp.41–2
12. Clarendon, *History of the Rebellion*, Vol. IV, p.202

13. Original MS of Carte's *Life of James, Duke of Ormonde*, Vol. III, *1647–63*, p.181
14. Quoted in Hoskins, Vol. II, p.86
15. Quoted in ibid., p.43
16. John Evelyn's diary, 15 July 1685
17. E.S. de Beer (ed.), *The Diary of John Evelyn*, Vol. II, pp.561–2, Clarendon Press, Oxford, 1955
18. MacPherson, 1.76
19. John Evelyn's diary, 15 July 1685
20. BL Add. MS 32690/9–10
21. Marie Catherine, Baronne d'Aulnay, *Memoirs of the Court of England in 1675*, quoted in Lord George Scott, *Lucy Walter: Wife or Mistress*, George Harrap & Co., London, 1947, pp.43–4
22. David Laing (ed.), *The Letters and Journals of Robert Baillie*, 3 vols, Edinburgh, 1842, Vol. III, p.88
23. Sir Robert Long, *State Papers*, Vol. II, p.416, The Hague, 24 September 1648
24. Clarendon, *History of the Rebellion*, Vol. III, p.388
25. *Clarendon's State Papers*, Vol. II, p.237

**2: Royal Prey**

1. *The Letters and Journals of Robert Baillie*, Vol. II, p.213
2. Serault, *Oraison Funèbre de Henriette Marie*, Paris, 1670, quoted in *Letters of Queen Henrietta Maria*, p.7
3. Henrietta Maria to Charles I, Harl. MS 7379, folio 35, 3/13 September 1643
4. *Letters of Queen Henrietta Maria*, p.294
5. Ibid., p.357
6. Agnes Strickland, *Lives of the Queens of England*, Vol. IV, p.126, James Miller, New York, 1843
7. Clarendon, quoted in Julia Cartwright, *Sacharissa*, p.116, Seeley & Co. Ltd, London, 1901
8. Clarendon, *History of the Rebellion*, Vol. III, p.495

9. Turner, p.15
10. Quoted in *DNB*, 'Princess Elizabeth', by Gordon Goodwin, revised by Sean Kelsey
11. 'The Autobiography of Anne Murray, Lady Halkett', p.20, Gettysburg College, 2006 (online)
12. Ibid., p.21
13. Ibid., p.22

## 3: A Question of Conscience

1. Noble (ed.), *Lives of the English Regicides*, p.xxxiii
2. *CSP dom. 1650*, p.174
3. Joseph Frank, *The Beginnings of the English Newspaper, 1620–1660*, Harvard University Press, Cambridge MA, 1961
4. *Letters of Queen Henrietta Maria*, p.358
5. John Bruce (ed.), *Charles I in 1646: Letters of King Charles the First to Queen Henrietta Maria*, Camden Society, 1856
6. Charles I to Prince Charles, 17 May 1646
7. Charles I to Henrietta Maria, February 1645, *King's Cabinet Opened*, p.7
8. Henrietta Maria to the Marquess of Newcastle, Harl. MS 7379, folio 152, Holograph
9. Henrietta Maria to Charles II, *Letters of Queen Henrietta Maria*, p.352
10. Henrietta Maria to the Duke of Orléans, 1 January 1646, *Archive des Affaires Étrangères*
11. *Letters of Queen Henrietta Maria*, pp.353–6
12. Charles I to Henrietta Maria, 7 November 1646
13. *The Letters and Journals of Robert Baillie*, Vol. III, p.53
14. Burnet, Vol. I, p.50
15. Charles I to Henrietta Maria, from Oxford, 3 March 1646
16. Ibid.
17. Original MS of Carte's *Life of James, Duke of Ormonde*, Vol. III, *1647–63*, p.75

## 4: The Crown, Without Glory

1. Edward J. Cowan, *Montrose: For Covenant and King*, 1977, quoted in Antonia Fraser, *King Charles II*, p.87, Weidenfeld & Nicolson, London, 1979

2. George F. Warner (ed.), *The Nicholas Papers*, Vol. I, p.160, Camden Society, 1886

3. John Byron to Ormonde, from Beauvais, 11 March 1650, MS Carte 213.2

4. Henry Seymour to Ormonde, from Beauvais, 16 March 1650, MS Carte 213.14

5. *Diary of Alexander Jaffray, Provost of Aberdeen*, p.32, Harvey & Darton, London, 1833

6. Thomason Tracts, E 601 {5}, *The Man in the Moon*, Issue 50, 10–26 April 1650, p.385

7. Richard Cavendish, 'The Execution of Montrose', *History Today*, Vol. 50, Issue 5, May 2000

8. A. Macdonald and J. Dennistoun (eds), *Miscellany of the Maitland Club*, Vol. II, Part 2, p.488, Edinburgh, 1840

9. Quoted in S.R. Gardiner, *Charles II and Scotland*, p.138

10. Scott, *Exile*, quoted in *DNB*, 'Charles II'

11. Sir George Downing, *A True Relation of the Progress of the Parliaments Forces in Scotland: Together with the King's Wholly Abandoning Scotland*, Thomason collection: printed by William Du-Gard, by the appointment of the Council of State, 1651

12. Bodleian Library, Tanner MSS, fol. 138

## 5: A Foreign Invasion

1. Downing, *A True Relation of the Progress of the Parliaments Forces in Scotland*

2. *Old Parliamentary History of England*, Vol. XIX, pp.68, 177, quoted in Blair Worden, *God's Instruments*, p.51, Oxford, 2012

3. Thomason Tracts, E 643 {10}, *The Diary*, Issue 3, 6–13 October 1651, pp.18–19, published by Bernard Alsop

4. Thomason Tracts, E 640 {25}, *True Informer*, 20–28 August 1651, pp.4–5

5. E. Hockliffe (ed.), *The Diary of the Rev. Ralph Josselin: 1616–1683*, p.90, Camden Society, London, 1908

6. 2 September, from Whitehall, l.96, in *Calendar of State Papers, Domestic: Interregnum, 1651*, p.490, London, 1877

7. Council of State to Lieut.-Col. Salmon, 4 September, Whitehall, in ibid.

8. 12 September, Senato, Secreta Dispacci, Francia. Venetian Archives: 'Venice: September 1651', in Allen B. Hinds (ed.), *Calendar of State Papers Relating to English Affairs in the Archives of Venice*, Vol. XXVIII, *1647–1652*, p.197, London, 1927

9. 15 September, Collegio, Secreta. Espozsizioni, Principi, in ibid.

10. *The Nicholas Papers*, Vol. 1, p.264

11. Ra. Parker to —, 8 September 1651, from Bruges, *Calendar of State Papers, Domestic: Interregnum, 1651*

12. Matthew Sylvester (ed.), *The Life of the Reverend Mr Richard Baxter*, Part 1, p.68, London, 1696

13. Thomason Tracts, E 640 {25}, *True Informer*, 20–28 August 1651, p.5

14. Ibid.

15. Vol. XVI, September 1651, in *Calendar of State Papers, Domestic: Interregnum, 1651*

16. John Milton, *Eikonoklastes*, in *Complete Prose Works*, Vol. III, p.568

17. Thomason Tracts, E 641 {2}, *Weekly Intelligencer*, Issue 35, 26 August–2 September 1651, p.268

18. Thomason Tracts, E 643 {9}, John Hall (ed.), *Mercurius Politicus*, Issue 70, 2–9 October 1651, p.1115

19. C.H. Simpkinson, *Thomas Harrison, Regicide and Major-General*, p.286, J.M. Dent, London, 1905

20. Downing, *A True Relation of the Progress of the Parliaments Forces in Scotland*
21. Ibid.
22. Thomason Tracts, E 640 {25}, *True Informer*, 20–28 August 1651, pp.7–8

## 6: The Battle of Worcester

1. *Boscobel*, from J. Hughes (ed.), *The Boscobel Tracts*, p.197
2. *Relation of the Defeat of the King*, 3 September, endorsed by Secretary Nicholas
3. Thomason Tracts, E 640 {25}, *True Informer*, 20–28 August 1651, p.7
4. Council of State to Colonels Duckenfield and Birch, 2 September, Whitehall, l.96, in *Calendar of State Papers, Domestic: Interregnum, 1651*, p.480
5. Thomason Tracts, E 641 {20}, John Hall (ed.), *Mercurius Politicus*, Issue 67, 11–18 September 1651, p.1072
6. *Relation of the Defeat of the King*, 3 September, endorsed by Secretary Nicholas
7. Council of State to the Militia Commissioners for Co. York, 2 September, Whitehall, in *Calendar of State Papers, Domestic: Interregnum*, Vol. XVI, *1651*
8. Council of State to Lieut. Gen. Monk [sic], 2 September 1651, in ibid.
9. Council of State to the Militia Commissioners of Co. Lancashire, 4 September, Whitehall, in ibid.
10. *Relation of the Defeat of the King*, 3 September, endorsed by Secretary Nicholas
11. *General Massey's Bartholomew Fairings for Colonel Poyntz and the London Reformadoes*
12. 'The Worcestershire Miscellany' – supplement – *The Boscobel Tracts*, p.7

13. Thomas Carlyle (ed.), *Oliver Cromwell's Letters and Speeches*, Vol. II, first edition, Letter 123
14. *Relation of the Defeat of the King*, 3 September, endorsed by Secretary Nicholas
15. Ibid.
16. 'The Account of Mr Hughes', from 'The Worcestershire Miscellany', *The Boscobel Tracts*, p.8

## 7: The Hunt Begins

1. *Letters of Queen Henrietta Maria*, p.373
2. *The Nicholas Papers*, Vol. I, p.274
3. Rev. J. Stanier Clarke, *The Life of James the Second, King of England*, Vol. I, p.52
4. Thomason Tracts, E 641{20}, John Hall (ed.), *Mercurius Politicus*, Issue 67, 11–18 September 1651, p.1067
5. Thomason Tracts, E 643 {9}, John Hall (ed.), *Mercurius Politicus*, Issue 70, 2–9 October 1651, pp.1114–15
6. *The Nicholas Papers*, Vol. I, p.267
7. 3 October, Senato, Secreta. Dispacci, Francia. Venetian Archives. 'Venice: October 1651', in *Calendar of State Papers Relating to English Affairs in the Archives of Venice*, Vol. XXVIII, *1647–1652*, p.200
8. W.C. Abbott (ed.), *Oliver Cromwell, Writings and Speeches*, Vol. II, p.463
9. Ibid., p.335
10. Council of State to Lieut. Gen. Monk, Cols. Fitch, Fenwick, and Salmon, Sir Arthur Hesilrigge, the Lord Mayor, and Militia Commissioners of London, and the Militia Commissioners of Westminster, the Hamlets, Southwark, York, Derby, Notts, Leicester, and Herts, 4 September, Whitehall, l.96, p.503, Vol. XVI, September 1651, in *Calendar of State Papers, Domestic: Interregnum, 1651*

11. Council of State to the Lord General, 4 September, from Whitehall, ibid., p.502
12. Thomason Tracts, E 641 {27}, Richard Collings (ed.), *Weekly Intelligencer*, 23–30 September 1651, p.306
13. C.H. Simpkinson, *Thomas Harrison, Regicide and Major-General*, p.101
14. Ibid., p.45
15. *An Exact and Perfect Relation of Every Particular of the fight at Worcester and ordering the battle on both sides of the river of Severn*, 5 September 1651, printed by Francis Leach, Worcester

## 8: Whiteladies

1. Thomason Tracts, E 641 {15}, *The Declaration of Major General Massey upon his death bed at Leicester*, p.3, printed in London, for George Wharton
2. Thomason Tracts, E 643 {6}, Richard Collings (ed.), *Weekly Intelligencer*, Issue 40, 30 September–7 October 1651, p.307, printed by F. Neile, in Aldergate-Street, London
3. Quoted in *Los Angeles Herald*, 9 July 1899
4. *Boscobel, The Boscobel Tracts*, p.213
5. *Charles II's Escape from Worcester*, p.88
6. Geoffrey Smith, *Royalist Agents, Conspirators and Spies*, Farnham, Ashgate, 2011
7. *Charles II's Escape from Worcester*, Colonel Gounter's Report, p.160
8. *Charles II's Escape from Worcester*, p.90

## 9: The London Road

1. *Charles II's Escape from Worcester*, Father Huddleston's account, p.102
2. Ibid., pp.102–3
3. Quoted in *Los Angeles Herald*, 9 July 1899

4. 'Nicholas Owen', in Charles Herbermann (ed.), *Catholic Encyclopedia*, Robert Appleton Company, New York, 1913
5. John Gerard, *The Autobiography of an Elizabethan*, 1951
6. BL, Stowe MS 168, fol. 364r, quoted in *DNB*, 'Nicholas Owen'

## 10: Near Misses
1. Report of the Irish and Scottish Committee, 9 September, l. 22, in *Calendar of State Papers, Domestic: Interregnum, 1651*, pp.37–8
2. Thomason Tracts, E 641 {15}, *The Declaration of Major General Massey upon his death bed at Leicester*, p.5
3. C.H. Simpkinson, *Thomas Harrison, Regicide and Major-General*, pp.132–3
4. *Charles II's Escape from Worcester*, Father Huddleston's account, p.105

## 11: Reunion
1. *Charles II's Escape from Worcester*, Father Huddleston's account, pp.112–13
2. Ibid., p.107
3. *Charles II's Escape from Worcester*, Thomas Whitgreave, p.120
4. *Boscobel, The Boscobel Tracts*, p.239
5. *Charles II's Escape from Worcester*, Father Huddleston's account, pp.109–10
6. Ibid., p.112

## 12: Heading for the Coast
1. Thomason Tracts, E 641 {11}, *Weekly Intelligencer*, Issue 36, 2–9 September 1651, p.280
2. Ibid.
3. Thomason Tracts, E 641 {20}, John Hall (ed.), *Mercurius Politicus*, Issue 67, 11–18 September 1651, p.1064

4. *Boscobel, The Boscobel Tracts*, p.262
5. Laurence Echard, *The History of England: From the Restoration of Charles the Second, to the Conclusion of the Reign of James the Second, and Establishment of King William and Queen Mary*, Vol. III, p.18, Jacob Tonson, London, 1718
6. Quoted in *Highways and Byways in Dorset*, p.268, Macmillan & Co., 1935
7. *Charles II's Escape from Worcester*, The Alford Depositions, p.124

## 13: Processing the Prisoners

1. Council of State to Lord Chief Baron Wylde, 16 September, from Whitehall, l.96, in *Calendar of State Papers, Domestic: Interregnum, 1651*, p.533
2. Thomason Tracts, E 641 {20}, John Hall (ed.), *Mercurius Politicus*, Issue 67, 11–18 September, p.1076
3. John Aubrey, *Three Prose Works*, p.349
4. *The Memoirs of Ann, Lady Fanshawe*, pp.78–81
5. Peter Draper, *The House of Stanley*, pp.203, 205, published by T. Hutton, Ormskirk, 1864
6. Thomason Tracts, E 641 {18}, Anon., 'The Charges and Articles of High Treason against the Earl of Derby', p.1, printed for George Horton, 1651
7. Thomason Tracts, E 643 {9}, John Hall (ed.), *Mercurius Politicus*, Issue 70, 2–9 October 1651, p.1115
8. Ibid.
9. Thomason Tracts, E 641 {15}, *The Declaration of Major General Massey upon his death bed at Leicester*, p.4
10. *Relation of the Defeat of the King*, 3 September, endorsed by Secretary Nicholas
11. Ibid.

12. *An Exact and Perfect Relation of Every Particular of the fight at Worcester and ordering the battle on both sides of the river of Severn*, p.5, printed by Francis Leach, 5 September 1651, from Worcester

13. Thomason Tracts, E 640 {20}, John Hall (ed.), *Mercurius Politicus*, Issue 67, p.1070

14. Thomason Tracts, E 641 {14}, Anon., *Another Victory in Lancashire obtained against the Scots*, pp.3–4, London

15. C.H. Simpkinson, *Thomas Harrison, Regicide and Major-General*, pp.128–31

16. Thomason Tracts, E 643 {5}, *Diary*, Issue 2, Monday, 29 September 1651, p.11, published by Bernard Alsop

17. Thomason Tracts, E 641 {17}, *The Declaration of Duke Hamilton*, pp.4–5, printed by Robert Wood, London, 1651

18. Thomason Tracts, E 643 {6}, p.309

19. Council of State to Sir Arthur Hesilrigge and the Militia Commissioners for the four Northern Counties, 16 September, Whitehall, l.96, in *Calendar of State Papers, Domestic: Interregnum, 1651*, p.535

20. Council of State to Luke Robinson, Col. Lascelles, and George Eure, 16 September, from Whitehall, l.96, ibid.

21. Thomason Tracts, E 641 {14}, Anon., *Another Victory in Lancashire obtained against the Scots*, pp.1–3

## 14: Touching Distance

1. *Charles II's Escape from Worcester*, The Alford Depositions, pp.135–6

2. Ibid., pp.125–6

3. Ibid., pp.128–9

4. Ibid., p.130

5. Treves, *Highways and Byways in Dorset*

## 15: Still Searching for a Ship

1. *Charles II's Escape from Worcester*, Original Notes from Colonel Phillips, p.139
2. Ibid., pp.139–40
3. Thomason Tracts, E 641 {27}, Richard Collings (ed.), *Weekly Intelligencer*, 23–30 September 1651, pp.304–5
4. Ibid., pp.307–8
5. Thomason Tracts, E 643 {8}, *A Perfect Account of the Daily Intelligence*, Issue 39, 1–8 October 1651, p.312, published by Bernard Alsop
6. *Charles II's Escape from Worcester*, Colonel Gounter's Report, p.149
7. Ibid., p.150
8. Ibid., p.151

## 16: Surprise Ending

1. *Charles II's Escape from Worcester*, Colonel Gounter's Report, p.142
2. Ibid., p.159
3. Ibid, pp.159–60
4. Pepys's diary, 23 May 1660

## 17: Reaction

1. Clarke, *The Life of James the Second*, Vol. I, p.52
2. Ibid.
3. *Charles II's Escape from Worcester*, p.97
4. *The Nicholas Papers*, Vol. 1, p.279
5. *Memoirs of the Cardinal de Retz*, p.234, London, 1723, printed for J. Brotherton at the Bible, in Cornhill
6. Ibid.
7. Thomason Tracts, E 643 {20}, *Diary*, Issue 4, p.32, published by Bernard Alsop – article of Saturday, 18 October, in 13–20 October 1651 edition

8. Thomason Tracts, E 643 {24}, John Hall (ed.), *Mercurius Politicus*, Issue 72, 16–23 October 1651, p.1148

9. Thomason Tracts, E 643 {21}, *Weekly Intelligencer*, Issue 41, 14–21 October 1651, p.322

10. Council of State to Colonel Danvers, Governor of Stafford, l.96, in *Calendar of State Papers, Domestic: Interregnum, 1651*, p.580

11. Council of State's Proceedings, 27 October 1651

12. Genesis 25: 20–22

13. Richard Ollard, *The Escape of Charles II After the Battle of Worcester*, p.31, Dorset Press, 1966

14. *Charles II's Escape from Worcester*, p.97

15. C.H. Firth (ed.), *Scotland and the Commonwealth*, p.206, University Press, Edinburgh, 1895

16. Joseph Mayer (ed.), *Inedited Letters of Cromwell, Colonel Jones, Bradshaw and other regicides*, p.12, T. Brakell, Liverpool, 1861

17. *The Diary of the Rev. Ralph Josselin: 1616–1683*, p.96

18. Hyde to Charles II, 10 November [31 October?] 1651, Bodleian, 583

19. Hyde to Nicholas, 21 November [11 November?] 1651, Bodleian, 590

20. William Hingston to Robert Jordan, 16 December 1651, *The Manuscripts of His Grace the Duke of Portland Preserved at Welbeck Abbey*, Vol. II, p.31, London, HM Stationery Office, London, 1893

21. Letter from the Earl of Loudon to Charles II, received 19 September 1653, quoted in Firth (ed.), *Scotland and the Commonwealth*, p.206

22. Clarke, *The Life of James the Second*, Vol. I, p.492

23. Bulstrode Whitelocke, *Memorials*, Vol. II, p.649, 1732

24. Clarendon State Papers, 3.359, quoted in *DNB*, 'Edward Hyde'

## 18: Rewards

1. *Charles II's Escape from Worcester*, Colonel Gounter's Report
2. Quoted in Geoffrey Smith, *The Cavaliers in Exile: 1640–1660*, p.107, Palgrave Macmillan, 2003
3. *Calendar of State Papers, Domestic*, 5 September 1660
4. *Charles II's Escape from Worcester*, Father Huddleston's account, p.112
5. John Evelyn's diary, 21 December 1651
6. Quoted in F.E. Sawyer, 'Captain Nicholas Tettersell and the Escape of Charles II', *Sussex Archeological Collections*, Vol. XXXII, p.104
7. Thomason Tracts, E 641{20}, John Hall (ed.), *Mercurius Politicus*, Issue 67, 11–18 September 1651, p.1075
8. William Hingston to Robert Jordan, 16 December 1651, *The Manuscripts of His Grace the Duke of Portland Preserved at Welbeck Abbey*, Vol. II, p.30
9. Diary of Sir Archibald Johnston, Lord Wariston, 1663, p.8
10. *DNB*, 'Frances Stuart', by Stuart Handley
11. Quoted in ibid.
12. T.H. Lister, *The Life and Administration of Edward, Earl of Clarendon*, 3 vols, 1837–38, Vol. III, pp.202–3, quoted in *DNB*, 'Edward Hyde', by Paul Seaward

## 19: Redemption

1. Quoted in Raymond Crawfurd, *The Last Days of Charles II*, p.80, Clarendon Press, Oxford, 1909
2. Ibid.
3. Quoted in ibid., p.81

# Bibliography

**Manuscript and Archive Sources**

*Another Victory in Lancashire obtained against the Scots*, Anon.,
Thomason Tracts, E 641 {14}

*The Black Almanack, or predictions foreshewing what will happen to
the King of Scots this present year*, Thomason Tracts, E 1301 {4}

*Bloudy Newse from the North, and the ranting Adamites
declaration concerning the King of Scotland*, Thomason Tracts,
E 622 {1}

*A briefe relation of some affaires and transactions, civill and
military, both forraigne and domestique*, published by Edward
Husband, Issue no. 39, 21 May 1650

*British History Online*, Vol. 16: May 1651; September 1651; October
1651

*British History Online*, Venice: October 1651

*The Charge and Articles of high treason exhibited against the Earl
of Derby*, Anon., printed for George Horton, 1651

*The Declaration of Duke Hamilton*, printed by Robert Wood,
London, 1651

*A Declaration of his Imperial Majestie, Alexea, Emperor of Russia
– detestation of the murder of Charles the First*, Thomason
Tracts, E 623 {17}

*The Declaration of Major General Massey upon his death bed at Leicester*, printed in London for George Wharton, Thomason Tracts, E 641 {15}

*The Diary*, published by Bernard Alsop, Issue 1, 29 September 1651; Issue 2, 6 October 1651; Issue 3, 13 October 1651; and Issue 4, 20 October 1651

*Exceeding true and joyfull newes from Worchester*, James Blake, 1642

*The Fair Brother*, December 1650, Thomason Tracts, E 620 {13}

*The Forme and Order of the Coronation of Charles the Second … at Scone Castle*, Aberdeen, 1651, Thomason Tracts, E 793 {2}

*The last discourse of the Right Honble the Lord Warestonne, as he delivered it upon the scafford* [sic] *at the Mercat-Cross of Edinburgh, July 22 1663*, by a Favourer of the Covenant and work of reformation, 1663

*The Last Newes from the King of Scots*, printed in London for G. Wharton, September 1651

*A letter from the Lord General Cromwell*, 4 September 1651, Thomason Tracts, E 641 {6}

*A Letter of the Surrender of Sterling Castle*, printed by Francis Leach, London, 28 August 1651

*The Man in the Moon*, by John Crouch, Issue 51, 26 April 1650

*Manuscripts of His Grace the Duke of Portland*, Vol. II, 13th Report, London, HM Stationery Office, 1893

*Mercurius Britannicus*

*Mercurius Elenticus*, Number 5, 20 May 1650

*Mercurius Politicus*, ed. by John Hall, Issue 64, 28 August 1651; Issue 67, 18 September 1651; Issue 69, 2 October 1651; Issue 70, 9 October 1651; Issue 72, 23 October 1651

*Mercurius Pragmaticus*, by John Cleveland, Issue 53, 14 May 1650

*Mercurius Scoticus*, 23 September 1651

*The Modern Intelligencer*, printed by I. Clowes, 3 September 1651

*The None-Such Charles his Character*, 6 January 1650, Thomason
 Tracts, E 1345 {2}

*The Oppressor Destroyed*, Joseph Caryl, Thomason Tracts, E 643
 {4}

*A Perfect Account of the Daily Intelligence from the armies in
 England, Scotland and Ireland*, published by Bernard Alsop,
 Issue 39, 8 October 1651

*A Relation of the Execution of James Graham, late Marquesse of
 Montrose*, printed by E. Griffin, London, 1650

*Remarkable Observations of God's mercies towards England*,
 Anon., Thomason Tracts, E 641 {26}

*A strange and wonderful Prophesie of Mr Douglas, a Scotchman,
 sent to their young King*, Thomason Tracts, E 622 {6}

*The True Informer*, 28 August 1651, Thomason Tracts, E 640 {25}

*The True Manner of the Crowning of Charles the Second, King of
 Scotland*, Thomason Tracts, 669.f.15 (8L)

*The Weekly Intelligencer*, Issue 35, 2 September 1651; Issue 36, 9
 September 1651; Issue 39, 30 September 1651; Issue 40, 7
 October 1651; Issue 41, 21 October 1651

*Wonderful News from the North ... apparitions seen in ... Chester*,
 11 April 1650

*A Word of Advertisement to the Godly Party in Scotland, by a
 Scotch Man*, Thomason Tracts, E 623 {8}

**Printed Primary Sources**

Baillie, R., *The Letters and Journals of Robert Baillie*, ed. David
 Laing, 3 vols, Bannatyne Club, Edinburgh, 1841–42

Barclay, J. (ed.), *The Diary of Alexander Jaffray*, Aberdeen, 1856

Baxter, R., *Reliquiae Baxterianae*, ed. M. Sylvester, Parkhurst,
 London, 1696

Blount, Thomas, *Boscobel*, 1660

Bruce, John (ed.), *Letters of King Charles the First to Queen
 Henrietta Maria*, Camden Society, London, 1856

Bulstrode, R., *Memoirs*, Charles Rivington, London, 1721

Burnet, *Burnet's History of my own time*, 2 vols, Oxford, 1897 and 1900

*Calendar of State Papers, Venetian*

Carte, Thomas, *Life of James, Duke of Ormonde*, 3 vols, 1735–36

Carte, Thomas, *A Collection of Original Letters and Papers*, 2 vols, 1739

Charles II, *An Account of the Preservation of King Charles II, after the Battle of Worcester, Drawn up by Himself to which are added His Letters to Several Persons*, Glasgow, 1766

Cheruel, A. (ed.), *Mémoires de Mademoiselle de Montpensier*, 4 vols, Paris, 1892

*Clarendon's State Papers*, Vol. II

Cobbett, William (ed.), *The Parliamentary History of England*, Vol. V

Cromwell, Oliver, *Writings and Speeches*, ed. W.C. Abbott, 4 vols, Harvard University Press, Cambridge MA, 1937–47

Evelyn, John, *The Diary of John Evelyn*, ed. E.S. de Beer, 6 vols, Clarendon Press, Oxford, 1955

Fanshawe, H.C. (ed.), *The Memoirs of Ann, Lady Fanshawe*, John Lane, London, 1907

Firth, C.H. (ed.), *The Memoirs of Edmund Ludlow*, Vol. II (of 2 vols), Clarendon Press, Oxford, 1894

Green, Mary Anne Everett (ed.), *Letters of Queen Henrietta Maria*, Richard Bentley, London, 1857

Halkett, Anne, *The Autobiography of Anne Murray, Lady Halkett*, Gettysburg College, Pennsylvania, online

Hamilton, W.D. (ed.), *Calendar of State Papers, Domestic Series*, 1649–50, 1651–52

Huddleston, John, *A Brief Account of Particulars occurring at the happy death of our late Sovereign Lord King Charles II*, 1688

Hughes, J. (ed.), *The Boscobel Tracts: Relating to the Escape of Charles the Second after Worcester*, Edinburgh and London, 1830

Hutchinson, Lucy, *Memoirs of Colonel Hutchinson*, ed. N.H. Keeble, Phoenix, London, 1856

Hyde, Edward, *History of the Rebellion*, Oxford University Press, Oxford, 1967

Hyde, Edward, *Selections From 'The History of the Rebellion' and 'The Life by Himself'*, Oxford University Press, Oxford, 1978

Jaffray, Alexander, *Diary of Alexander Jaffray, Provost of Aberdeen*, Harvey & Darton, London, 1833

Josselin, Ralph, *The Diary of the Rev. Ralph Josselin: 1616–1683*, ed. E. Hockliffe, Camden Society, London, 1908

Ludlow, Edmund, *The Memoirs of Edmund Ludlow*, ed. C.H. Firth, 2 vols, Clarendon Press, Oxford, 1894

Matthews, William (ed.), *Charles II's Escape from Worcester: A Collection of Narratives Assembled by Samuel Pepys*, Berkeley and Los Angeles, 1966

Mayer, Joseph (ed.), *Inedited Letters of Cromwell, Colonel Jones, Bradshaw and other regicides*, Liverpool, 1861

Pepys, Samuel, *King Charles preserved: An Account of his Escape after the Battle of Worcester dictated by the King himself to Samuel Pepys*, Rodale Press, 1956

Rushworth, J., *Historical Collections*, 8 vols, London, 1722

van Beneden, Ben, and de Poorter, Nora (eds), *Royalist Refugees*, Rubenshuis & Rubenianum, Antwerp, 2006

Warner, Sir G.F. (ed.), *The Nicholas Papers: Correspondence of Sir Edward Nicholas*, Camden Society, Vol. I (of 4 vols), 1886

Warwick, Sir Philip, *Memoires of the Reign of King Charles I, with A Continuation to the Happy Restoration of Charles II*, London, 1701

Whitelocke, Bulstrode, ed. R. Spalding, *The Diary of Bulstrode Whitelocke*, Oxford University Press, Oxford, 1990

Wormsley, K.R. (trans.), *Memoirs of Madame de Motteville on Anne of Austria and her Court*, 3 vols, 1902

**Published Sources**

Adamson, John, *The Noble Revolt*, Weidenfeld & Nicolson, London, 2007

Adamson, John, *The English Civil War: Conflict and Contexts, 1640–49*, Palgrave Macmillan, Basingstoke, 2009

Ashley, Maurice, *Charles II: The Man and the Statesman*, London and New York, 1971

Ashley, Maurice, *Oliver Cromwell and His World*, Thames & Hudson, London, 1972

Ashley, Maurice, *The English Civil War*, London, 1974

Atkin, Malcolm, *Worcestershire Under Arms*, Pen & Sword, Barnsley, 2004

Atkin, Malcolm, *Worcester 1651*, Pen & Sword, Barnsley, 2008

Aubrey, John, *Brief Lives*, Clarendon Press, Oxford, 1898

Balleine, G.R., *All for the King: The Life Story of Sir George Carteret*, Société Jersiaise, St Helier, 1976

Bryant, Arthur (ed.), *The Letters, Speeches and Declarations of King Charles II*, 1935

Cartwright, Julia, *Sacharissa*, Seeley & Co. Ltd, London, 1901

Cavendish, Richard, 'The Execution of Montrose', *History Today*, Vol. 50, Issue 5, May 2000

Clifton, Robin, 'Lucy Walter', *New DNB*

Coffey, John, 'Sir Archibald Johnston, Lord Wariston', *New DNB*

Coward, Barry, *The Stuart Age*, Longman, London and New York, 1980

Farr, David, *Major-General Thomas Harrison*, Ashgate, Farnham, 2014

Fea, Allan, *After Worcester Fight*, 1904

Firth, C.H., *Scotland and the Commonwealth*, Edinburgh University Press, Edinburgh, 1895

Frank, J., *The Beginnings of the English Newspaper, 1620–1660*, Cambridge MA, 1961

Fraser, Antonia, *King Charles II*, Weidenfeld & Nicolson, London, 1979

Gardiner, S.R., *Letters and Papers Illustrating the Relations between Charles II and Scotland in 1650*, Edinburgh, 1894

Gardiner, S.R., *The Commonwealth and Protectorate*, 4 vols, 1903

Gaunt, Peter, *The British Wars, 1637–1651*, Routledge, London, 1997

Goodwin, Gordon, rev. Sean Kelsey, 'Princess Elizabeth', *New DNB*

Handley, Stuart, 'Frances Teresa Stuart', *New DNB*

Henderson, T.F., 'David Leslie, first Lord Newark', *New DNB*

Hill, Christopher, *God's Englishman*, Weidenfeld & Nicolson, London, 1970

Hill, Christopher, *The World Turned Upside Down*, Temple Smith, London, 1972

Hobbes, Thomas, *Leviathan*, Penguin, London, 1984

Hodgetts, Michael, 'Nicholas Owen', *New DNB*

Holmes, R., and Young, P., *The English Civil War*, Wordsworth edition, Ware, 2000

Hoskins, Samuel Elliott, *Charles the Second in the Channel Islands*, 2 vols, Richard Bentley, London, 1854

Hughes, J. (ed.), *The Boscobel Tracts*, William Blackwood & Sons, Edinburgh and London, 1857

Hunt, Tristram, *The English Civil War*, Phoenix, London, 2003

Hutton, Ronald, 'Henry Wilmot, first Earl of Rochester', *New DNB*

Jordan, Don, and Walsh, Michael, *The King's Bed*, Abacus, London, 2016

Keay, Anna, *The Last Royal Rebel*, Bloomsbury, London, 2016

Kelsey, Sean, and Goodwin, Gordon, 'Princess Elizabeth', *New DNB*

Kenyon, J.P., *The Stuart Constitution, 1603–1688*, Cambridge, 1966

Kingston, H.P., *The Wanderings of Charles II in Staffordshire and Shropshire after the Worcester Fight*, Birmingham, 1933

Kitson, Frank, *Old Ironsides*, Weidenfeld & Nicolson, London, 2004

Maguire, Nancy Klein, *Regicide and Restoration: English Tragicomedy, 1660–1671*, Cambridge University Press, 1992

Marshall, Alan, 'Joseph Bampfield', *New DNB*

Molesworth, William (ed.), *The English Works of Thomas Hobbes*, 11 vols, London, 1839–45

Morris, J. (ed.), *The Condition of Catholics Under James I: Father Gerard's narrative of the Gunpowder Plot*, Longmans, London, 1872

Murray, Anne, *The Autobiography of Anne Murray, Lady Halkett*, Gettysburg College, online, 2006

Oakeshott, Michael, *Hobbes on Civil Association*, Basil Blackwell, Oxford, 1975

Ollard, Richard, *The Escape of Charles II After the Battle of Worcester*, Dorset Press, 1966

Ollard, Richard, *This War Without an Enemy*, Hodder & Stoughton, London, 1976

Peters, Eleanor Bradley, *Hugh Peter*, New York, privately printed, 1902

Plowden, Alison, *Henrietta Maria*, Sutton Publishing, Stroud, 2001

Porter, Linda, *Royal Renegades*, Macmillan, London, 2016

Scott, Eva, *The King in Exile: The Wanderings of Charles II from June 1646 to July 1654*, London, 1904

Scott, Lord George, *Lucy Walter: Wife or Mistress*, George G. Harrap & Co., London, 1947

Scott, Jonathan, *England's Troubles*, Cambridge University Press, 2000

Seaward, Paul, 'Edward Hyde, Earl of Clarendon', *New DNB*

Seel, Graham E., *Regicide and Republic*, Cambridge University Press, 2001

Simpkinson, C.H., *Thomas Harrison, Regicide and Major-General*, J.M. Dent, London, 1905

Smith, Geoffrey, *The Cavaliers in Exile: 1640–1660*, Palgrave Macmillan, Basingstoke, 2003

Smith, Geoffrey, *Royalist Agents, Conspirators and Spies*, Ashgate, Farnham, 2011

Stevenson, David, 'James Graham, Marquess of Montrose', *New DNB*

Strickland, Agnes, *Lives of the Last Four Princesses of the Royal House of Stuart*, Bell & Daldy, London, 1872

Stubbs, John, *Reprobates*, Viking, London, 2011

Sutton, John, 'William Carlos', *New DNB*

Turner, Francis James, *James II*, Eyre & Spottiswoode, London, 1950

Wanklyn, M., *Decisive Battles of the English Civil War*, Pen & Sword, Barnsley, 2006

Willcock, John, *The Great Marquess: Life and Times of Archibald 8th Earl and 1st (and only) Marquess of Argyll*, Edinburgh and London, 1903

Woolrych, A., *Battles of the English Civil War*, Pimlico, London, 1991

Worden, Blair, *The English Civil Wars, 1640–1660*, Weidenfeld & Nicolson, London, 2009

Worden, Blair, *God's Instruments*, Oxford University Press, Oxford, 2012

Wormald, Jenny, *Court, Kirk, and Community*, Edinburgh University Press, 1981

Wynne, S.M., 'Barbara Villiers, Duchess of Cleveland', *New DNB*

Young, Peter, and Holmes, Richard, *The English Civil War*, Eyre Methuen, London, 1974

## Collections of Edited Documents

Firth, C.H., and Rait, R.S. (eds), *Acts and Ordinances of the Interregnum, 1642–1660*, 3 vols, HMSO, London, 1911

Haller, W., and Davies, G. (eds), *The Leveller Tracts*, Columbia University Press, New York, 1964

Raymond, J., *Making the News: An Anthology of the Newsbooks of Revolutionary England, 1641–1660*, Windrush, Moreton-in-Marsh, 1993

# Index